Framing Places
Second Edition

Framing Places is an account of the nexus between place and power, investigating how the built forms of architecture and urban design act as mediators of social practices of power. Explored through a range of theories and case studies, this account shows how our lives are 'framed' within the clusters of rooms, buildings, streets and cities we inhabit. These silent framings of everyday life also mediate practices of coercion, seduction and authorization as architects and urban designers engage with the articulation of dreams, imagining and constructing a 'better' future in someone's interest.

This second edition is thoroughly revised with one new chapter. Updates include a look at the recent Grollo Tower development in Melbourne and a critique on Euralille, a new quarter development in Northern France. The book draws from a broad range of methodology, including the analysis of spatial structure, discourse analysis and phenomenology. These approaches are woven together through a series of narratives on specific cities (Berlin, Beijing, Bangkok) and global building types (the corporate tower, shopping mall, domestic house and enclave).

Kim Dovey is Professor of Architecture and Urban Design at the University of Melbourne. He has published and broadcast widely on issues of place and ideology including the book *Fluid City* (Routledge 2005).

THE ARCHI*TEXT* SERIES

Edited by Thomas A. Markus and Anthony D. King

Architectural discourse has traditionally represented buildings as art objects or technical objects. Yet buildings are also social objects in that they are invested with social meaning and shape social relations. Recognizing these assumptions, the Archi*text* series aims to bring together recent debates in social and cultural theory and the study and practice of architecture and urban design. Critical, comparative and interdisciplinary, the books in the series, by theorizing architecture, bring the space of the built environment centrally into the social sciences and humanities, as well as bringing the theoretical insights of the latter into the discourses of architecture and urban design. Particular attention is paid to issues of gender, race, sexuality and the body, to questions of identity and place, to the cultural politics of representation and language, and to the global and postcolonial contexts in which these are addressed.

Kim Dovey

Framing Places

Mediating power in built form

Second Edition

Routledge
Taylor & Francis Group

LONDON AND NEW YORK

First published 1999
by Routledge
Second edition first published 2008 by Routledge
2 Park Square, Milton Park, Abingdon, Oxon OX14 4RN

Simultaneously published in the USA and Canada
by Routledge
270 Madison Ave, New York, NY10016

Routledge is an imprint of the Taylor & Francis Group, an informa business

Typeset in Frutiger by Wearset Ltd, Boldon, Tyne and Wear
Printed and bound in Great Britain by TJ International Ltd, Padstow, Cornwall

British Library Cataloguing in Publication Data
A catalogue record for this book is available from the British Library

Library of Congress Cataloging in Publication Data
Dovey, Kim.
Framing places : mediating power in built form / Kim Dovey. — 2nd ed.
p. cm. — (The architext series)
Includes bibliographical references and index.
ISBN 978-0-415-41634-4 (hbk : alk. paper) — ISBN 978-0-415-41635-1 (pbk : alk. paper)
1. Architecture and society. 2. Space (Architecture) I. Title.
NA2543.S6D69 2007
720.1'03—dc22
2007023668

ISBN10: 0-415-41634-5 (hbk)
ISBN10: 0-415-41635-3 (pbk)
ISBN13: 978-0-415-41634-4 (hbk)
ISBN13: 978-0-415-41635-1 (pbk)

FOR SANDY

Contents

Figures

Preface

I have long been fascinated by the meanings and mysteries of places – rooms, buildings, streets and cities; typical and exceptional; wonderful and awful. This book is driven by a belief in the potency of places to touch our lives – in the best and the worst of ways. Such an interest does not fit neatly into the discipline of architecture, which is my background, nor of urban design, urban planning or landscape architecture. Instead it entails a slippage between categories, a crossing of boundaries as regularly as we do in everyday life. I write from a context of teaching architecture and urban design in a university and therefore with a view to the task of designing places. It has always seemed to me that this task is, in a small way, to literally 'change the world'. But whose interests prevail in this practice of 'changing the world'? What do justice, democracy or liberation mean with regard to built form? What does 'change' mean in a world that is transforming in a bewildering range of ways that often seem both destructive and inevitable? The task of changing the world requires more than a capacity to climb on, or submit to, the Juggernaut.

Architecture and urban design are the most contradictory of practices – torn between a radically optimistic belief in the creation of the new, and a conservative acceptance of the prevailing order. Architects and urban designers engage with the articulation of dreams – imagining and constructing a 'better' future in someone's interest. This optimistic sense of creative innovation largely defines the design professions which are all identified with constant change. Yet architecture is also the most conservative of practices. This conservatism stems from the fundamental inertia of built form as it 'fixes' and 'stabilizes' the world – space is deployed to stabilize time. It is this antinomous quality – coupling imaginative innovation with a stabilizing conservatism – that makes the interpretation of place so interesting yet problematic.

This book also arises from a certain tension between academic and public discourse. Social theory has turned its attention towards spatial issues in a major way since the 1980s and scholars such as Foucault, Derrida, Eagleton, Giddens, Lefebvre, Habermas, Bourdieu and Harvey are widely cited in architectural discourse. Yet these theorists rarely write about the specifics of built form and the ways in which their work is applied to design practice, and public debate is generally superficial. Theory can be used as a form of insulation from the world as easily as a tool of engagement. How does such theory help us to engage in the invention of the future? How does one articulate the 'public interest' or decode the meaning of the latest grand project for a public audience? What, if anything, is wrong with another shopping mall, suburban enclave, theme park or corporate tower? The bridge between theory and built forms, between academic dialect and public debate, is crucial to the task of changing the world.

I shall focus primarily on issues of coercion, seduction and authority in built form, addressing only indirectly issues of empowerment and liberation. This negative focus, however, is not an exercise in pessimism. It is infused with an optimistic desire to see the potency and exhilaration of place experience deployed in the public interest. The impulse towards such a role for architecture and urban design is quite rightly strong among design students. Many of the movements and 'isms' of design can be seen in light of the attempt to bypass or resist the appropriations of the market and political power. 'Rationalism', 'arche-typalism', 'critical regionalism', 'community design', deconstruction and the various retreats into 'gallery architecture' or cyberspace can all be so construed. As will become apparent, I reserve both respect and scepticism for most of these movements. However, I have a primary aim to disturb any illusion of autonomy from the mediations of power. The world of architecture and urban design is sat-urated with struggles over the meaning and use of places. I suggest there is no way around such issues, only ways into them. As human interests are more clearly articulated so are the possibilities for new forms of design and discourse. What follows is a critique born of the desire to clear a space for the realization of dreams; and for a more rigorous debate over whose dreams get realized.

PREFACE TO THE 2ND EDITION

This is a book about the ways in which place stabilizes power, yet my views about the ways in which this happens are not stable and this is a field that has developed a great deal in almost a decade since the first edition of this book was written. Two of the case study chapters have been replaced with new work and the remainder of the book has been updated and rewritten. A chapter on representations of democracy in Australia has been replaced by one on the strug-gles for democracy in public space in Bangkok. Another chapter on Melbourne entitled 'On the Move' has since been subsumed by a full book on the topic ('Fluid City', Routledge, 2005) and is replaced here by a critique of the Euralille project in France which brings together some of the material on shopping malls and corporate towers as global types. My general shift in thinking about these issues in recent years is reflected in an update of the theory chapters that com-prise Part I of the book. Theories of 'place' are particularly unstable. Another change has been the incorporation of Deleuzian thinking and concepts into the various theories and critiques.

Acknowledgements

Partners are usually left until last but Sandy Gifford has been an astute, tolerant and loving critic whose contribution to this work has been fundamental. Tony King and Tom Markus generously agreed to launch the Archi*text* series with this book and have been incisive and challenging with their comments. Ross King and Quentin Stevens supplied highly useful critiques of the first edition. A large number of other colleagues and Ph.D. students have supplied encouragement, references, debates and responses; foremost among them are Clare Cooper Marcus, Stephen Cairns, Kess Dovey, Karen Franck, Ruth Fincher, Philip Goad, Greg Missingham, Bob Mugerauer, David O'Brien, Sitthiporn Piromruen, Kasama Polakit, Darko Radovic, Julia Robinson, Leonie Sandercock, Steven Whitford, Ian Woodcock, Stephen Wood, Larry Vale and Zhu Jian Fei. Caroline Mallinder has been a supportive and effective editor at Routledge. Andrew Simpson and Craig Tan have assisted with illustrations.

Some of these chapters have appeared in earlier versions: Chapter 2 appeared in *Evolving Environmental Ideals* (M. Gray (ed.) (1997) Stockholm: IAPS 14 Proceedings); portions of Chapters 8 and 10 appeared respectively in *Environment and Planning B* (19, 1992: 173–188) and *Beasts of Suburbia* (S. Ferber, C. Healy and C. McAuliffe (eds) (1994) Melbourne: Melbourne University Press); Chapter 12 appeared in an earlier form in *Meanjin* (52 (2) 1993: 277–290). The reworking of Chapter 4 in the second edition is largely based on 'Dialectics of Place: Authenticity, Identity, Difference' (in S. Akkach (ed.) *De-Placing Difference*, Conference Proceedings, University of Adelaide, 2002, pp. 45–52) and in a keynote lecture for the Environmental Design Research Association in 2003 at the University of Minnesota. An early version of Chapter 11 appeared as: 'Memory, Democracy and Urban Space' (*Journal of Urban Design*, 6 (3), 2001, pp. 265–282).

ILLUSTRATION CREDITS

Cover images: Kim Dovey
All photographs and drawings not otherwise credited are by Kim Dovey.

5.1   Drawing by Craig Tan from sources in Krier (1985b) and Helmer (1985)
5.2   Drawing by Andrew Simpson from sources in Goodsell (1988) and O'Donnell (1979)
5.4, 5.5, 5.6 Archives d'Architecture Moderne/Speer Archive (from Krier 1985b)
6.1   Drawing by Craig Tan based on plans in Weng (1982) and Yu (1984)
6.4   Photograph: Ng Mau-Sang, from Yu (1984)
6.5   Drawing by Craig Tan
7.5   Wandee Feature Magazine
7.7   Wandee Feature Magazine
7.8   Photograph: David O'Brien
8.1   Jones Lang Wootton, Melbourne (advertising material)
8.2   101 Collins Street Pty Ltd (advertising material)
8.3   Becton/Baillieu Knight Frank, Melbourne (advertising material)
8.4   Raine and Horne/Jones Lang Wootton, Melbourne (advertising material)
8.5   Tower Life Australia Limited (advertising material)
8.6   Melbourne Docklands Authority (advertising material)
9.2   Photograph: Antony Sihombing
10.2 Warmington Homes, northern California (advertising material)
10.4 Perceptions Homebuilders, Western Australia (advertising material)
10.7 Pacific Cornerstone Group, California (advertising material)
11.7 Photograph: Francois-Olivier Hoizey
12.1 Drawing by Craig Tan based on Ferguson (1986). R.J. Ferguson and Associates, West Perth
12.2 Battye Library, Perth, 354B/18

While the author and publisher have made every effort to contact copyright holders of material used in this volume, they would be grateful to hear from any they were unable to contact.

My thanks to Kasama Polakit (for translations) and to Sitthiporn Piromruen, Kamthorn Kulachol, David O'Brien, Rujiroj Anambutr, Marc Askew and Michael Connors. Figures 4 and 6 courtesy *Wandee Feature* magazine and Figure 7 by Kamthorn Kulachol and David O'Brien.

Introduction

The most successful ideological effects are those that have no words, and ask no more than complicitous silence.

Bourdieu (1977: 188)

Architecture and urban design 'frames' space, both literally and discursively. In the literal sense everyday life 'takes place' within the clusters of rooms, buildings, streets and cities we inhabit. Action is structured and shaped by streets, walls, doors and windows; it is framed by the decisions of designers. As a form of discourse, built form constructs and frames meanings. Places tell us stories; we read them as spatial text. The idea of 'framing' contains this ambiguity. Used as a verb, to 'frame' means to 'shape' things, and also to 'enclose' them in a border – like a mirror or picture. As a noun, a 'frame' is an established 'order' and a 'border'. 'Framing' implies both the construction of a world and of a way of seeing ourselves in it – at once picture and mirror. In each of these senses, the design of built form is the practice of 'framing' the places of everyday life. A frame is also a 'context' that we relegate to the taken-for-granted. Built form can 'frame' its subjects in a place where not all is as it seems – as in a 'frame-up'. Through both these literal and discursive framings, the built environment mediates, constructs and reproduces power relations. The ambiguities of 'framing' reflect those of the nexus between place and practices of power. This difficult nexus is the subject of this book.

This nexus of built form with power is, at one level, a tautological truth – place creation is determined by those in control of resources for better and for worse. Places are programmed and designed in accord with certain interests – primarily the pursuit of amenity, profit, status and political power. The built environment reflects the identities, differences and struggles of gender, class, race, culture and age. It shows the interests of people in empowerment and freedom, the interests of the State in social order, and the private corporate interest in stimulating consumption. Because architecture and urban design involve transformations in the ways we frame life, because design is the imagination and production of the future, the field cannot claim autonomy from the politics of social change. Such a rejection of autonomy entails no suggestion of determinism; the relations of architecture to social behaviour are complex and culturally embedded interactions. Like the frame of a painting or the binding of a book, architecture is often cast as necessary yet neutral to the life within. Most people, most of the time, take the built environment for granted. As the quote from Bourdieu above suggests, this relegation of built form to the unquestioned frame is the key to its relations to power. The more that the structures and representations of power can be embedded in the framework of everyday life, the less questionable they become and the more effectively they can work. This is what lends built form a prime role as ideology. It is the 'complicitous silence' of place as a framework to life that is the source of its deepest associations with power.

A study of the framings of 'place' at a range of scales entails engagement with a range of audiences and paradigms of knowledge. The practices of architecture and urban planning have taken divergent routes and adopted different paradigms of knowledge over the past 40 years. Despite its flirtations with the social sciences, architecture remains decisively wedded to a formal aesthetic paradigm where the impact of the architecture is found in its image. Urban planning, which began in physical planning, has progressively retreated from spatial design to build a base in social theory and urban studies where power is located primarily in process and programme. Yet this has never been a complete nor satisfactory separation and has led to a revitalization of urban design as the bridge between paradigms. If I slip rather easily between references to 'architecture', 'urban design' and 'built form', it is because the boundaries between them are slippery, and because we all slip easily between them in everyday life.

Any study of 'place' also entails a bridging of interest across different academic paradigms, particularly the fields and sub-fields of cultural studies (based in post-structuralist critique) and human-environment studies (with a humanist and empirical base). There is no singular methodological position or school of thought on which this book is based. This is a key starting point which deserves some comment. One of the important and liberating lessons of the postmodern movement has been the recognition of difference; the end of singular and privileged 'metanarratives' (Lyotard 1984). The proliferation of paradigms of knowledge seems to reflect such a condition. Yet a cursory observation of the internecine battles within these fields and sub-fields would indicate that this lesson has not gone too far. A radical acceptance of difference entails exploring the relations between incommensurable methodologies and interpretations. While rigorous critique and refutation is necessary for the development of theory, in studies of place the deployment of different and even incommensurable paradigms of knowledge is both necessary and enlightening. This does not entail collapsing them into newly totalizing metanarratives. Rather, it is a recognition that different knowledges, soundly based within their own paradigms, may be useful to a multiplicitous understanding of built form.

It is the very nature of the mediations of power in place that make this pluralism necessary. There are three primary intellectual paradigms which I will draw upon: spatial syntax analysis, discourse analysis and phenomenology. These paradigms are reflected in the titles of the three theory chapters – program, representation and place. There is no suggestion that these critiques, of spatial structure, narrative and everyday experience respectively, are discrete or unified forms of enquiry. Indeed the intersections between them are often most interesting and the cutting edge of thinking is often to be found between such fields where program, text and place intersect.

I realize that such pluralism leaves many kinds of readers uncomfortable – phenomenologists, cultural studies and spatial syntax folk alike. It is an aim to disturb these categories a little, to undermine singular viewpoints. In the later chapters I will slide between methodologies, seamlessly at times, with a view to revealing the tensions between them and the opportunities for multiplicitous interpretation. The aim is to show that the practices of power as mediated in built form are multi-dimensional; they cannot be simply addressed as forms of spatial structure, representation or lifeworld experience – rather places are constructed, experienced, practised and understood within the tension between these paradigms.

The book begins with theory and proceeds to interpretations of specific places and project types. The first part, 'Frames of Theorization', will briefly outline some theoretical frameworks and deals first with the use (and misuse) of the concept of 'power'. It defines some terms and lays the ground for a more specific understanding of practices of 'force', 'coercion', 'authority', 'seduction', 'manipulation' and 'legitimation'. These concepts are linked to a set of oppositional dimensions, along which it is argued such practices are mediated in space. Chapter 2 explores the spatial programming of buildings based on the social theories of Giddens, Bourdieu, Foucault and Deleuze coupled with methods of spatial analysis. Giddens' structuration theory suggests that spatialized practices of power can be modelled as enabling and constraining relations between 'structure' and 'agency'. Bourdieu's theory of the *habitus* suggests that the built environment constructs the real as spatial ideology – a congruence between the 'division' of space and our 'vision' of the world. Foucault's work suggests that modern power is a dispersed set of micropractices, many of which operate through the normalizing gaze of surveillance regimes. Spatial practices construct subjects employing architecture as disciplinary technology. Deleuzian theory suggests ways of re-thinking spatial programs as forms of striation and as congealed desires. As a means of analysing mediations of power through spatial segmentation I have adapted methods of spatial syntax analysis of building plans developed by Hillier and Hanson. Such analysis maps the 'social logic' of architecture to reveal ideology embedded in architectural genotypes.

Chapter 3 explores the theoretical bases for interpreting architecture and urban design in terms of representation. Much of this work stems from the discursive turn in social theory which seeks to problematize the relation of language to reality. The human 'agent' is in this sense replaced by the 'subject' who is enmeshed and constructed in discourse. Forms of discourse and representation can construct desires, joys, fears and identities; oppositions between the normal and the deviant. Truth-effects are produced in representation as reality is socially constructed. Important here is the early work of Barthes in the construction of mythology – the manner in which arbitrary meanings are naturalized and the discourse of power is rendered benign. The chapter includes a critique of post-structuralism, deconstruction and Bourdieu's account of aesthetic taste and symbolic capital.

Chapter 4 proceeds to an account of theories of 'place'. These begin in phenomenology, the lived-space of the body and the ontology of dwelling stemming from the work of Merleau-Ponty and Heidegger. It explores ways in which built form mediates the spatial dialectics of vertical/horizontal, inside/outside and local/global – tensions between the primacy of the lived and its ideological framings. The ideas of Lefebvre, de Certeau, Harvey and Massey are introduced in the quest to frame place as a conjunction of practice, representation and experience.

Part II on 'Centres of Power' involves interpretation of three narratives of power in urban space in Berlin, Beijing and Bangkok. Chapter 5, 'Take your Breath Away', explores the Nazi use of architecture and urban design, well known for its use of monumental neo-classical imagery. This narrative suggests that such spatial propaganda was marked more by instrumental eclecticism than by style, deploying the combined effects of a range of themes with echoes to follow in other chapters. Chapter 6, 'Hidden Power', is an account of the Forbidden City and Tienanmen Square in Beijing. Constructed as the antithesis of the Forbidden City, Tiananmen Square is the largest open space in urban history, a signifier of 'liberty' and a representation of the 'people'. Its meanings and global visibility were then mobilized for purposes of resistance in 1989. Tienanmen shows the possibilities of semantic inversion and the inseparability of spatial practices and representations; meanings and uses are never guaranteed. Chapter 7, 'Paths to Democracy', is an account of the use of particular public spaces by the democracy movement in Bangkok and the ways that practices and meanings have intersected. The Democracy Monument, produced by a fascist regime, becomes the focus of a struggle for democracy that veers from joyful to bloody. This is also a struggle over memory and over whose meanings are to be represented in public space.

Part III, 'Global Types', explores the framing of places in everyday life, using examples of global development types including the corporate office tower, shopping mall, suburban house and gated community. Chapter 8, 'Tall Storeys', explores the meanings and contradictions of the corporate tower through the lens of its advertising. The successful corporate tower offers corporate identity, authenticity and authority. It embodies metaphors of strength, stature and strategy, of physical dominance translating into financial domination. The symbolic capital of the skyscraper is not so much created as it is moved around from one temporary landmark to another. In the global quest for height, the tower is converted into an anti-urban building type. Chapter 9, 'Inverted City', is an interpretation of the suburban shopping mall as a form of urban inversion. As a collective dream world of mass culture, the mall at once captures and inverts the urban. It is a realm of relative shelter, safety, order and predictability which is semantically and structurally severed from the city. The mall constructs a permanent festivity within an illusion of urban civic life, carnival minus community. In its quest for size, community and authenticity the mall evolves into mega-malls, skyways, lifestyle malls and dead malls.

Chapter 10, 'Domestic Desires', explores the meaning of the suburban dream house and gated community. Model houses display an ideal world as a mirror in which a suburban subject is constructed and in which we can read the suburban condition and its cultural values. The house plans reveal genotypes which reflect and reproduce ideologies of family life – the mediation of age, gender and class relations. The nostalgic linking of the ideal home to an unchanging past reflects both a desire for escape and for ontological security in an uncertain world. Many of these structures and meanings are writ large in the gated enclave – a retreat in both space and time to a purified 'community'.

Part IV, 'Localities', proceeds to critiques of two specific places. Chapter 11, 'A Sign for the 21st Century', is an account of the innovative urban design project of Euralille in northern France. This is a vision for a twenty-first century generic city, geared to new sensibilities of globalization, time–space compression and virtual space under the urban design direction of Rem Koolhaas. Euralille seeks the redemption of over-determined, banal and manipulative building types such as the mall, tower and plaza, but is interpreted here as a future locked in a past and as place reduced to text. Chapter 12, 'Rust and Irony', is a more personal narrative which explores the dual nature of place/power relations as both liberation and oppression. Rottnest Island was a prison that became a holiday camp and then a luxury enclave; where military space enabled liberation; where the vicissitudes of history opened spaces for the imagination. This is a story of the contingencies and ironies of place experience; of the mutability of meaning and the perils of determinism.

In the afterword I open up the question of a liberating design practice – the dream which has long prevailed as a guiding narrative in architecture and urban design. This issue is explored through the interpretation of several places, each driven by such imperatives yet caught in the complicities of power. Such complicity is the condition of environmental design. As the invention of the future, practices of placemaking are inherently political. Architecture and urban design are highly social arts wherein the task is to link aesthetic imagination to the public interest. 'Community architecture' is, in a sense, a tautology. Is there any architecture which exists outside the 'common' interest? The academic task is to make clear whose interests are served. This may produce a certain pessimism in those whose passion it is to avoid engagement with the 'meaning market' or the instrumentalizing functions of the program. I can only suggest that this is a temporary condition born of the collapse of illusion. Beyond lie more interesting and diverse forms of both theory and practice.

This text cannot stand outside the power relations and theories that it addresses. Languages of representation are primary tools in the practices of power. Like built form, language is a structure which both reproduces and frames our experience. As Heidegger (1962) put it, language is the 'house of Being'. Language is slippery, subject always to shifting social constructions, to Derrida's (1974) play of *differance*. While I accept Derrida's arguments, I am also compelled by Habermas' (1971) view that systematically distorted communication is a primary tool of power. In writing this material I have felt persistently torn between the enlightenment desire to uncover and clarify power/place relations in general (to generalize) and the post-structuralist desire to unpack, to deconstruct. I write from within this problematic. This is no easy task because each of these tendencies creates the space for new and destructive practices of power. To generalize and universalize is to totalize and repress difference. Yet the rug-pulling, neologisms and paren(theses) of post-structuralist critique can be equally complicit with new currents of power and can embody new forms of closure. The retreat into private dialects that characterizes much academic discourse often says more about the struggles between fields of discourse than it does about the subject in question. It divides its readership into those who are willing and able to follow in such an intellectual retreat and those who are not; it immunizes theory against attack from those who are left behind. I find much of this move towards private dialects unnecessary and disempowering and I will avoid it where possible. To the extent that theories of power in architecture and urban design become intellectual enclaves, they also become ineffective in public debate. This is a particular problem for a book that attempts to reach a broad audience and to weave together a range of methodologies, each of which has its dialect. While there is a good deal of what I would call necessary jargon, my goal is to use the simplest possible language consistent with rigor. I am inspired in this matter by the work of Berger who writes:

> One does not look through writing onto reality – as through a clean or dirty window-pane. Words are never transparent. They create their own space, the space of experience, not that of existence . . . Clarity, in my view, is the gift of the way space, created by words in a given text, is arranged. The task of arranging this space is not unlike that of furnishing and arranging a home. The aim is similar: to accommodate with ease what belongs there and to welcome those who enter. There are hospitable and inhospitable writings. Hospitality and clarity go together.
>
> (Berger 1992: 241–242)

My aim is to be hospitable to a broad range of critiques and audiences, to let theoretical differences coexist. Indeed I believe that it is in the friction between paradigms that a good many insights are to be discovered.

The book has a critical tone, focusing on the most problematic mediations of power in place. However, there is no intended implication either that there is anything wrong per se with the nexus of place with power, or that there is some ideal form of placemaking that operates outside such framing processes. The design of built form is intrinsically hinged to issues of power precisely because it is the imagination and negotiation of future worlds. The invention of the future will always be contentious and places will always mediate power relations. I have no firm prescription for how designers should practise, except that they should not do so with heads inserted in sand. The hope is that a greater transparency of the practices of power can lead to more imaginative, liberating and empowering placemaking practices.

Part I

Frames of Theorization

Chapter 1: Power

Power is one of the splendours of man that is eminently prone to evil.

Ricoeur (1965: 255)

DEFINING POWER

The term 'power' is widely used, and misused, in a rather global manner to refer to a variety of different capacities and effects. The danger is that 'power' can mean anything and therefore nothing. I want to try to avoid this through a short analysis of 'power' as a concept. The term derives from the Latin *potere*: 'to be able' – the capacity to achieve some end. Yet power in human affairs generally involves control 'over' others. This distinction between 'power to' and 'power over', between power as capacity and as a relationship between people, is fundamental to all that follows (Isaac 1992: 47; Pred 1981). Yet the former of these has a certain primacy. According to Rorty (1992: 2) 'Power is the ability . . . to define and control circumstances and events so that one can influence things to go in the direction of one's interests'. The 'capacity' to imagine, construct and inhabit a better built environment is what we mostly mean by empowerment here. The capacity to appropriate a room, choose a house, walk to a beach or criticize an urban design scheme are all forms of empowerment. When we say that someone is empowered, we mean their capacity to act is increased. Empowerment is linked with 'autonomy' and 'freedom', both of which imply a 'liberation' from arbitrary forms of 'power over' us. The primacy of power as capacity stems from the fact that power over others has a parasitic relation with power as capacity (Isaac 1992: 41). Power over others is largely driven by the desire to harness the capacities of others to one's own empowerment. These two forms of power, as capacity and relationship, are reciprocal. Yet power as capacity is both the source and the end of this relation.

In everyday life we tend to notice power *over* while power *to* is taken for granted. This creates the illusion that power *over* is somehow primary –

an illusion which suggests an opposition between power and emancipation. Yet emancipation is precisely a form of empowerment, of enhanced capacity. Oppression and liberation are the two sides of the power coin. While the power *to* is the primary form of power, linked to empowerment, one person's empowerment can be another's oppression. And power *over* others can be used to increase empowerment. To define power primarily in terms of power *over* others is a category mistake which constructs a zero-sum game wherein every loss in power is another's gain. There is a fundamentally important materialist sense in which the struggle for resources is a zero-sum game; space is a finite resource and design is often a cake-slicing operation. Yet the exercise of power *over* can diminish or increase the total power *to* as resource. In this important sense the practice of power is not a zero-sum game. Power is both positive and negative; it liberates and oppresses. While my attention will focus on the contentious forms of power *over*, power *to* remains the primary form. It is this positive and primary notion of power as the human capacity to imagine and create a better built environment that drives the arguments of this book.

FORMS OF POWER 'OVER'

'Power over' is the power of one agent (or group) over another, the power to ensure the compliance of the other with one's will. There are many concepts which are partially synonymous with power in this regard, and the distinctions between them are important. For my purposes I want to consider some distinctions between force, coercion, manipulation, seduction and authority.[1]

'Force' is the overt exercise of power which strips the subject of any choice of non-compliance. Typical examples in built form include all kinds of enforced spatial confinement (prisons and institutions of incarceration) and of enforced spatial exclusion (the medieval fortress; the housing enclave; locks, bars and walls). The use of force in built form is common since all walls, doors, fences and security devices which prevent access enforce spatial practice in this rather obvious manner. While force is the most common mediation of power in built form, it is also limited since it can prevent action more easily than it can create it.

'Coercion' can be defined as the threat of force to secure compliance and may be construed as a latent kind of force. Coercion is more effective than overt force because it operates under the cover of voluntarism. It gains its power from implied sanctions, which often prevent the subject from ever forming any intention of resistance. When the subject anticipates the exercise of force and acts accordingly, power remains latent. Coercion operates through built form in at least three main ways. The first of these may be termed 'domination or 'intimidation' where the forms of architecture, urban design and spatial behaviour can signify a threat of force. Guards of 'honour', military parades and 'armed response' signs are overt signifiers of latent force. Public monuments often use the memory of a past use of force by the State to signify such future possibility. Spatial domination through exaggerated scale or dominant location can belittle the human subject as it signifies the power necessary to its production.

Yet there are far more subtle forms of spatial coercion linked to the Latin root *coercere*, 'to surround'. For Weinstein organizational control of space is a form of coercion:

> Coercion consists in transforming private, communal, group or cultural spaces into organizational spaces in which people perform actions directed towards the fulfilment of another's plan, or refrain from performing actions subversive of the realization of another's plan.
>
> (Weinstein 1972: 69)

The built environment frames everyday life by offering certain spaces for programmed action, while closing other possibilities. In a myriad of ways every day we avoid those behaviours and boundaries that we believe will be met with force. Most forms of spatial surveillance and control are coercive in this sense, but to label these forms of spatial control 'coercion' is not to imply sinister motives. While spatial coercion may be clear in intentional terms, in practice there is no clear line between necessary and problematic forms of spatial order. 'Manipulation' is a form of coercion which operates primarily by keeping the subject ignorant. The exercise of power is made invisible to its subject and the possibility of resistance is thereby removed (Wrong 1979). The subject is 'framed' in a situation that may resemble free choice, but there is a concealment of intent. A common example from architecture and urban design occurs when representations of design projects are distorted to produce a form of 'manipulated consent' by ignorant participants.

Barnes argues that coercion is a conjunction of knowledge and ignorance wherein the subjects are 'well aware of the direct connection between their behaviour and possible sanctions, but unaware of the longer range indirect connections by which their (compliant) behaviour . . . helps to constitute and sustain the feedback of coercion and sanctioning that controls them' (Barnes 1988: 101). The organization of space and time to mediate social interaction – particularly the visibility and invisibility of others – becomes crucial to effective practices of coercion. A fragmented experience of space and time with the loss of a sense of orientation and community can be conducive to coercive control. The ideal subjects of coercive power 'should live as atoms, wholly in the public realm, under surveillance, but as far as possible without social relationships' (Barnes 1988: 101).

'Seduction' is a practice which manipulates the interests and desires of the subject. This is a sophisticated form of 'power over', hinged to constructions of desire and self-identity, with significant implications for the built environment. As Lukes writes:

> Is it not the supreme and most insidious exercise of power to prevent people, to whatever degree, from having grievances by shaping their *perceptions*, *cognitions* and

> preferences in such a way that they accept their role in the *existing order* of things,
> either because they can see or *imagine no alternative* to it, or because they see it as
> *natural* and *unchangeable*, or because they value it as *divinely* ordained and beneficial?
>
> (Lukes 1974: 24, my emphasis)

My emphases here are intended to link with the manner in which built form shapes perception and cognition. It structures the taken-for-granted spatial order in a manner that we often see as natural and unchangeable. There is nothing necessarily sinister about this – all architecture both constructs and meets certain desires. All architectural representation constructs images of nature and order, shapes imagined futures. Seduction carries the implication that desire has been manipulated and that we indulge such desire against our real interest. Thus the concept of seduction rests upon a distinction between 'real' and 'perceived' interests. This is a highly problematic distinction since it implies that the subject cannot judge their own interests. From what position can one suggest that another's pleasure is not in their real interest? It is the condition of architecture and urban form to play upon our desires; the task is to understand rather than to eradicate these seductive capacities.

'Authority' is a form of 'power over' which is integrated with the institutional structures of society such as the state, church, private corporation, school and family. Authority is marked by the absence of argument; it relies on an unquestioned recognition and compliance. When we are stopped by the police for speeding we may argue about the speed, but if the trappings of authority are evident (the police car and uniform) we do not argue the right to enforce it. In a likewise manner we may dispute government regulations but we often do so across a counter framed by the architecture of a State authority. Based on socially acknowledged rights and obligations, authority is the most pervasive, reliable, productive and stable form of power. It embodies the power to circumvent argument and to frame the terms of reference of any discussion. Yet authority rests upon a base of 'legitimation' (Arendt 1986: 65). We recognize authority as legitimate because it is seen to serve a larger interest; in the case of the State this is the public interest.

The perception of legitimacy is fragile; it often needs both the trappings of authority and the coercive threat of force – if the 'right' of authority doesn't work then it is backed by the 'might' of force. Conversely, legitimation is one of the means by which *might* is transformed into *right* (Wrong 1979); the inefficient exercise of force is transformed into unquestioned authority. The key linkage to built form here is that authority becomes stabilized and legitimated through its symbols. These trappings of authority are important forms of legitimation that become crucial to the exercise of authority (Olsen 1993: 33). The symbols of authority are institutionally embedded from the family house to the corporate tower and the public buildings or urban designs of the State. Rituals, ceremonies and symbolic displays are often a means by which State authority is reproduced under the cover of diplomacy. Such ritual displays have a contradictory capacity to affirm violence and wealth as the base of power at the same time as they affirm friendship and solidarity (Barnes 1988). Buildings and urban designs are often integrated with such rituals and ceremonies. For the State, as Kertzer (1988) suggests, symbolic ritual is much more than window dressing since the nation-state is invisible and its authority would evaporate without the imagery of legitimation. Symbolic ritual enables the collapsing of disparate meanings into a form of political solidarity in the absence of consensus. Rituals of legitimation are powerful because one can't argue with them – they are the way things are done, the way the 'real' is constructed. Geertz puts it well:

> No matter how democratically the members of the elite are chosen . . . they justify their existence and order their actions in terms of a collection of stories, ceremonies, insignia, formalities and appurtenances . . . that mark the center as center and give what goes on there its aura of being not merely important but in some odd fashion connected with the way the world is built.
>
> (Geertz 1985: 15)

While it is important to distinguish between these different forms of power, such practices rarely appear in isolation. The most problematic buildings and urban designs are often a complex mix of seduction, authority and coercion. And the exercise of power can slide from one form to another, thereby masking itself. It is generally in the interest of those in power to hide conflict, and in the interest of the subject to expose it. A large part of the struggle over power is the struggle to make its operations visible, to bring it into a domain where its legitimacy can be tested. As Foucault (1980: 86) argues: 'power is tolerable only on condition that it masks a substantial part of itself. Its success is proportional to its ability to hide its own mechanisms'. The struggle to make power visible has to deal with the fact that the exercise of power is slippery and ever-changing. Power naturalizes and camouflages itself, chameleon-like, within its context. In this regard built form often operates as metaphor, wherein it simultaneously represents and masks its associations with power. A metaphor is a figure of discourse where one thing is represented as if it is, and yet simultaneously is not, another. And the power of metaphor is linked to its subtlety; it is most powerful when least literal (Ball 1992). A building form may suggest a metaphoric 'mountain' yet to spell this out can undercut the metaphoric power. Metaphor has the capacity to seduce and legitimate simultaneously while masking these very practices.

Imagination plays a key role in the discourse of power since empowerment implies a capacity to perceive one's real interests and connect them reliably to an imagined future. As Rorty (1992: 13) argues, 'Imagination is the key to power . . . it determines the direction of desires'. If we cannot imagine a better world we cannot support it; as Machiavelli put it, the public 'do not truly believe in anything new until they have actual experience of it' (quoted in Wrong 1979: 121). This hints at a crucial role for architects and urban designers as imaginative agents. The capacity to stimulate desire and to enlarge the public imagination can be crucial to the discourses of power. There are also hints here about the role of critique; while there can be no simple decoding of the meanings of built form, critical thinking can enable new interpretations of urban and architectural images. Awareness of the ways power is mediated by built form enables us to change the way it is practised.

The discussion above tends to presume that the exercise of 'power over' is largely transparent to its agents. Yet for Nietzsche much of what we call civilized life is really a cover for an all-consuming 'will to power' (Nietzsche 1968). From this view, which is also rather Machiavellian (Ng 1980), all forms of legitimation are masks for the individual 'will'. Because the naked 'will to power' cannot be legitimized as an end in itself, either self-deceit or hypocrisy is necessary to the effective pursuit of power (Wrong 1979). Self-deceit is easily the most efficient of the two, generally taking the form of a belief that one's pursuit of power is really a form of public service. Such self-deceit is what Orwell (1954: 171) called 'doublethink'. A key secret to the success of the Party in *1984* was the capacity to hold contradictory beliefs, to deliberately service one agenda while justifying it with another. From a psychological viewpoint Greenwald (1980) argues that the ego operates rather like a totalitarian information control strategy, servicing itself with propaganda in order to maintain control.

The issue of self-deceit has considerable importance for aesthetic discourse. The Nietzschean view is that the aesthetic impulse is founded in the repression of the will to power; art fills the void left by such repression (Eagleton 1990: 238). From this view aesthetic experience may be understood as a tension between the hedonistic urge towards the intoxications of power (the Dionysian) and the need to dress such experience in a civilizing façade of purity and order (the Apollonian). Freud posits a similar tension between the 'pleasure principle' and the 'reality principle'; the pleasure-seeking 'id' is in secret collusion with the forces of social order in the 'superego' (Eagleton 1990: 263).

The nexus between self-aggrandizement and the public interest is particularly complex in public buildings and urban schemes which can serve at once to legitimize authority, reinforce a sense of community, gratify the political or architectural will, turn a profit and reinforce self-deceit. Many interests intersect in the production of built form and they are difficult to unravel. When confronted with arguments about damage to the public interest, architects are often genuinely offended and deny the importance of political, commercial or personal imperatives.

Self-deceit is a necessary condition to a large range of practices of power and it also afflicts the subjects of oppression. Subjection to unjust authority is inherently distasteful and there is some comfort in the belief that such authority is legitimate (Wrong 1979: 121). For the powerless to resist authority means the exposure of conflict, raising the risk of further marginalization and repression (Airaksinen 1992: 117). To remain docile and invisible is a safer choice but it is also a form of co-operation which is nourished by self-deceit. This issue is exemplified by the relative invisibility of impoverished 'informal' settlements that house the underclass in so many cities. The visibility of such settlements operates as a counter-image to the state's claims to legitimacy, democracy and social order. The exposure of such radical inequality exposes residents to the potential loss of home and community. And there can be comfort in the belief in leadership – images of corrupt and tyrannical leaders can take pride of place on the walls of slum dwellings.

Those with and without power both have a need for legitimation, but such needs are in a curious inverse relation. The need for legitimation increases as power becomes totalizing; as Wrong (1979: 111) puts it, the 'more absolute the power, the greater the need to believe that the power holder observes self-imposed restraints'. Institutional authority with high levels of legitimation and security has less need for the trappings of power. Thus authority relies on legitimating symbols in proportion to the vulnerability of that authority. This is precisely why monarchies, dictatorships and military states are so full of monuments, parades and ritual strutting – the demand for legitimation exceeds that in a democracy. And these forms of legitimation service the self-deceit of powerful and powerless alike.

There is a complex dialectic whereby overt expressions of power in space tend to be commensurate with the vulnerability of that power. This is evident in the nouveau riche phenomenon of the grand house produced in the attempt to turn new money into social status. It is often new corporations that attempt the same thing in office towers. Milne (1981) argues that the Parthenon was in part a legitimizing gesture linked to the threat to the Athenian state from the Peloponnesian War. Likewise the construction of New Delhi coincided with the decline of British colonial power in India (King 1976; Vale 1992). The design of the new Australian Parliament House has been interpreted as a response to the constitutional crisis of 1977 (Weirick 1989).

The symbolic legitimation of state authority may be linked to the periodic legitimation 'crises' which Habermas (1975) suggests afflict the capitalist state on a periodic basis. Such crises occur when subjects of authority lose faith in its fairness. The system then tends to correct itself, reorganizing power at one level to preserve it at another. However, as legitimacy weakens, authority may come to seem more oppressive since the need for self-deceit also weakens (Wrong 1979: 111); what was once seen as a natural order of things comes to seem unfair and unbearable. There are many responses to such crises but the renewal of the trappings of power is common. The capacity of buildings and urban form to stabilize identity and symbolize a 'grounding' of authority in landscape, nature and 'timeless' imagery means that architecture is regularly called on to legitimate power in a crisis.

MEDIATING 'POWER OVER'

Power is not lodged inertly in built form. Force, coercion, manipulation, seduction and authority are forms of everyday practice which are inevitably mediated by built form. Such mediations are inherently complex and multi-dimensional and as a beginning I suggest the following set of dimensions of place/power mediations. These dimensions do not constitute a theory and they should not be read as deterministic. They are dimensions along which the dialectics of power in places are played out.

- *Orientation/Disorientation*: Built form can orient, disorient and reorient its subjects through the spatial framings of everyday life. Cities and buildings structure the cognitive maps through which we imagine our world and give it our attention.
- *Publicity/Privacy*: Built form segments space in a manner that places certain kinds of people, places and actions under conditions of surveillance while privileging other kinds of people, places and actions as private. Spatial segmentation mediates social encounter.
- *Segregation/Access*: Boundaries and pathways can segregate places by social status, gender, race, culture, class and age, creating privileged enclaves of access, amenity and community.
- *Social/Universal*: Built form is socially produced, yet it has a particular capacity to make the contingent appear universal, to make socially constructed history appear natural.
- *Stability/Change:* Built form has great inertia, generating illusions of permanence – a stable social order and the impossibility of change. Paradoxically, constructed images of dynamism and innovation can produce illusions of progress.
- *Authentic/Fake*: The quest for authenticity is a quest for the original and the real in a world of simulation and fakery. Yet authenticity is wrapped up with authorship and the idea of original authority; the quest is enmeshed in practices of power.
- *Identity/Difference*: Buildings and places inevitably construct and symbolize socially constructed identities and differences – of persons, classes, cultures, institutions and nations. The politics of identity in built form mediates who we are and where we belong.
- *Dominant/Subservient*: A large-scale built or urban form, in mass or volume, inherently signifies the power necessary for its production. The juxtaposition of large and small inherently signifies a relation of power and may be linked to discourses of domination and intimidation.
- *Place/Ideology*: The experience of place has the capacity to move us deeply, to 'ground' our being, to open the question of 'spirit'. Yet the very potency of place experience renders it particularly vulnerable to the ideological appropriations of power.

These are some of the practices of power in built form, but they are neither discrete nor complete. Like Hydra the nine-headed water serpent, power has many faces and its practices and mediations are slippery and hidden. When Hercules severs these heads we can never be sure they will not re-emerge; nor indeed that Hercules is not the new tyrant. There is no eradication of power and we are always already engaged in its practice.

Chapter 2: Program

How are power relationships mediated through spatial programming? I want to begin here with the social theories of Giddens, Bourdieu and Foucault with a link to the spatial syntax analysis of Hillier and Hansen. The focus here is on analysing and understanding power as mediated by spatial programs and spatial practices. I will turn to issues of representation in later chapters.

STRUCTURATION, *HABITUS* AND GAZE

Giddens' theory of structuration is based on a differentiation between 'agency' and 'structure'.[1] 'Agency' is simply the 'capacity' to transform our world. 'Structures', on the other hand, are the organized properties of social systems in the form of rules and resources, the frameworks of possibility within which our capacities are realized or not. The relations between structure and agency are primarily those of 'enabling' and 'constraining'. Structure both enables and constrains the forms of agency that are possible. And at the same time structures are constructed by agents.

From this view architecture can be considered as a form of structure, and the social action it 'frames' as a form of agency. Architecture evokes and enables certain forms of life while constraining others with both walls and sanctions. Yet Giddens' notion of structure should not be considered as physical; language is also a form of structure, and speech is a form of agency. Without the structure of syntactic and semantic rules we call 'language' we cannot speak. The structure enables the agency of speech. Yet speech is also constrained by language and its structuring of reality. For Giddens, structure is not simply external to agency; indeed structure has a 'duality' wherein it is 'both the medium and the outcome' of social practice or agency (Giddens 1979: 69). Thus when we speak we simultaneously contribute to the reproduction of the language. This complex interaction of structure and agency is what Giddens calls 'structuration'.

Giddens gives spatial relations a key role in structuration theory. Spatial structure is one form of structure, and design is one kind of agency. Power is spatialized in the sense that all agency is situated in time/space 'locales' – kitchens, board meetings, cities, neighbourhoods, lectures and clubs. 'Locales' are akin to 'places' inasmuch as they are meaningful centres of everyday life. Everyday life is described by Giddens as a serial time/space path, marked by opening and closing brackets in both space and time which define 'situations'. Thus the 'board meeting' is framed temporally by its time-slot and spatially by its entry sequence, enclosure, art works and outlook. Situations are also framed by clusters of rules which help to constitute and regulate activities, defining them as actions of a certain sort and subject to given sanctions. Thus 'the predictable character of the social world is "made to happen" as a condition and result of the knowledgeable application of rules and resources by actors' (Giddens 1979: 64). Giddens sees issues of privacy, rules about who shares space or crosses paths with whom, as a key to understanding structures of domination in space. Drawing on Goffman (1959) he gives special significance to the spatio-temporal opposition of front and back regions. Locales are places and settings which structure institutionally embedded practices, including practices of power.

Bourdieu's early work can be seen as parallel to much of Giddens. He wants to understand the practical mastery that people have of their situations in everyday life, constrained as they are by structures which are not of their own choosing. From scholastic philosophy Bourdieu borrows the term 'habitus' to refer to the complex net of structured predispositions into which we are socialized at an early age. The sources of this early work are largely architectural – the Berber house and the Gothic cathedral.[2] The 'habitus' is a set of practical taxonomies, divisions and hierarchies which are embodied in the everyday lifeworld of experience and action. These divisions of space and time – of objects and actions, of gender and status – are at once forms of 'habit' and of 'habitat'. Thus the *habitus* is embedded in familiar forms of dwelling and the house is a very important ideological construct as the first such *habitus* (Bourdieu 1977). The *habitus* is thus a form of knowledge, a set of structured beliefs about reality. While it is a set of acquired dispositions, it is also necessary to any world view, as Bourdieu (1990a: 210) puts it: 'A vision of the world is a division of the world'. The *habitus* is the way the 'arbitrary' is constituted as the 'real', culture seen as nature, ideology inscribed in habit and habitat. *Habitus* constructs the sense of one's 'place' in both the social and physical senses:

> the habitus produces practices and representations which are available for classification
> . . . Thus the habitus implies a 'sense of one's place' but also a 'sense of the other's
> place'. For example, we say of an item of clothing, a piece of furniture or a book: 'that's
> petty-bourgeios' or 'that's intellectual'.
>
> (Bourdieu 1990b: 113)

The *habitus* is both the condition for the possibility of social practice and the site of its reproduction. Social practice then is a form of 'game', framed within the *habitus* and its rules, which are rarely written but most often learnt through social practice as one develops a 'feel for the game'. Whether in a meeting, dinner party, playground, beach, lecture, seminar or restaurant, a set of spatio-temporally structured rules operates. The power dimension of the *habitus* derives largely from its thoughtlessness; it operates beneath consciousness. The domin-ant modes of thought and experience are not cognitively understood but rather internalized and embodied. Bourdieu refers to the dialectical relationship between the body and space as a form of 'structural apprenticeship' through which we at once appropriate our world and are appropriated by it: 'the "book" from which the children learn their vision of the world is read with the body' (Bourdieu 1977: 89) and *habitus* is society written into the body (1990b: 63). Everyday life in architectural and urban space is a product of history which pro-duces more history. As Bourdieu (1977: 188) puts it in an often used quote: 'the most successful ideological effects are those that have no words, and ask no more than complicitous silence'. The ideological effects of built form lie largely in this thoughtless yet necessary complicity.

Foucault argues that fundamental transformations in power relations have taken place since the eighteenth century, linked to the Enlightenment and the parallel rise of scientific rationality, the nation state, modern institutions, capital-ism and industrial technologies.[3] For Foucault, the Enlightenment, shining its searchlight of knowledge and truth, brings new forms of domination mas-querading as liberty. This is a new knowledge/power regime which requires that we replace the notion of power as a relation of dominance of one person over another with a concept of power dispersed throughout the social body. Such power is not something 'held' by agents; rather it constructs 'subjects'. Power operates through social and spatial practices and is embedded in institutions. It is called 'disciplinary power' because it operates through regimes of normalization and the eradication of deviance. It is a 'bio-power', since it acts on and through the body to constitute docile subjects. Such power is productive; it produces and harnesses human agency. To Foucault, such power is dispersed and exercised through micro-practices of everyday life where it spreads by a kind of capillary action.

The most important of the spatial micro-practices whereby disciplinary power transforms human beings into subjects is the 'gaze', a practice of discipli-nary control through asymmetrical visibility. This is at once the gaze of science and of the State, the knowledge/power regime. Foucault speaks of the complici-ties of architecture in a 'long elaboration of various techniques that made it pos-sible to locate people, to fix them in precise places, to constrict them to a certain number of gestures and habits' (Foucault 1988). A normalizing regime is estab-lished and the gaze of surveillance controls deviations from it. The easiest way to understand the spatial dimension of Foucault's work on power is through his account of the growth of disciplinary institutions from the eighteenth century. Around that time he notes that prisons turned their efforts from spectacles of punishment to techniques of normalization and 'cure'. The coercion of surveil-lance began to replace the force of violence. Bentham's invention of the panoptic prison serves as an ideal for Foucault's concept of this new form of institutionalized power (Foucault 1979). Not knowing whether a guard is present, the subject must always act as if it were so. Herein lies the key to efficiency – the discipline is self-enforcing, power relations are internalized. Power is taken for granted because it is embodied in spatial relations. In one sense the agents of such discipline can see without being seen while the subjects are seen but cannot see (Dandeker 1990). Yet the very notion of 'agency' is effaced since the enforcers have scarcely any power and are under surveillance themselves.

Foucault argues that such bodily discipline structured through space/time organization has spread from the early institutions to become a dominant feature of industrial capitalism. It included the partitioning of space according to rank, class and grade along with temporal regulation of ritual, routine and marching in time (Dandeker 1990: 25). Such a form of power has major advantages over the force which it often replaces. It drives power underground, makes its operations invisible as it utilizes the subject's capacities in the task of their own oppression. It is continuous, cheap, decentralized, efficacious and difficult to target (Fraser 1989). Bio-power holds its subject at a deep biological level, controlling bodily gestures, habits and desires. It disciplines both body and soul.

Foucault's insights have been profound, yet his conclusions are mostly pessimistic. For Foucault we are broadly implicated in a kind of internalized 'fascism' that infects us all: 'the fascism that causes us to love power, to desire the very thing that dominates and exploits us' (quoted in Miller 1993: 369). Yet this Nietzschian notion of an all-pervading 'will to power' need not be seen as negative; the ideas of Gilles Deleuze would lead us to focus on the production and flow of desire.[4] The Deleuzian world is a difficult one to grasp; indeed launching oneself into it would seem to be the metaphor. This is a world formed by 'flows of desire', where 'lines of flight' take precedence over points of order or stability. What we call buildings and cities, identities and institutions are effects of these flows of desire. In this sense a 'program' is a constellation of congealed desires – for space, privacy, shelter, views, light, amenity, social distinction, profit. Desire is the immanent productive force of life itself; without desire there is no city.

For my purpose here in understanding spatial programming I want to use the distinction outlined by Deleuze and Guattari (1988: Ch. 14) between what they call 'striated' and 'smooth' space. The term 'striated' captures the etymological links to the Latin *stringere* – 'to draw tight', linked to 'strict' and 'stringent'. This is contrasted with the 'smooth', which they intend to be read not as homogeneous, but rather without boundaries or joints. Smoothness implies a slipperiness and movement where one slides seamlessly from one site (place, meaning, image) to another. These are not different types of space so much as spatial properties. Striated space is where identities and spatial practices have become stabilized in strictly bounded territories with choreographed spatial practices and socially controlled identities. Smooth space is identified with movement and instability through which stable territories are erased and new identities and spatial practices become possible.

The smooth and the striated are not types of space or place so much as conceptual tools for thinking about space. Every real place is a mixture of the two in a reciprocal relation where they are constantly 'enfolded' into each other. 'Folding' is a key term for Deleuze (1993); it involves a focus away from things, elements or points of stability and onto the movements and 'foldings' between them. This focus on the 'between' is a way to rethink binary and dialectic oppositions as an enfolding of each other; for our purposes here this entails the enfolding of different spaces and functions, of public with private space, and of inside with outside. For Deleuze, concepts such as 'smooth space', 'flows of desire' and 'folding' are intellectual tools; the test is whether they are useful in enabling new ways of thinking and understanding practices of power in built form. Striated space is often structured like a tree; hierarchically organized and deeply rooted. Smooth space is identified with the 'rhizome' – a largely underground and horizontally migrating form of life that thrives within the interstices of a larger order. Spatial structure can be analyzed in terms of this distinction between smooth and striated space, between rhizomatic networks and tree-like hierarchies.

SPATIAL ANALYSIS

While one may usefully explore differences between these theorists, my interest here is in their complementary contributions and in the overlapping focus on ways in which power relations are embedded in spatial programs. I would suggest a pluralistic epistemology which acknowledges the inhabitants of buildings as both 'subjects' and 'agents', and seeks to understand the multiple ways in which buildings both empower and disempower. But how are we to specifically investigate such issues in relation to built form? With some important reservations I believe that methods of space syntax analysis, developed by Hillier and Hanson (1984), are useful for the analysis of programmatic issues of power in architecture.[5] Hillier and Hanson suggest that architectural discourse, with its roots in representational critique, has bypassed a deeper social structuring of architectural space because these structures are not visible. They seek to uncover deep socio-spatial structures, the 'genotypes' of architecture. Genotypes are not formal 'types' or 'archetypes' as often debated in architecture. Rather they are clusters of spatial segments structured in certain formations with syntactic rules of sequence and adjacency. Genotypes are institutionally and epistemologically embedded. Thus shops, factories, schools, offices, libraries, houses, suburbs will be reproduced from a limited number of spatial genotypes each linked to specific social institutions with forms of knowledge and production. This is the sense in which Hillier and Hanson suggest that genotypes embody a 'social logic of space'.

Beyond such a general recognition of these claims I want to adapt one of the methods of space syntax analysis while maintaining some distance from the methodology. One primary form of syntax analysis (gamma analysis) proceeds from a technique of mapping buildings into a cellular structure using the external entry points as a base. The building plan is translated into a structural diagram of how life is framed within it. In Figure 2.1 three similar plans with different doorways yield three quite different syntactic structures.[6] The linear structure is a string of spatial segments in sequence, known in architecture as the enfilade. There is no choice of pathway from one segment to another. The ringy structure or network is the opposite inasmuch as it connects segments to each other with multiple choices of pathway. A fan or branching structure controls access to a range of spaces from a single segment, like a corridor or hallway. In practice nearly all buildings are structured in combinations of these basic syntactic structures.

Hillier and Hanson identify a range of properties, applying to any syntactic structure and which are argued to be of social significance. First, the 'depth' or 'shallowness' of any segment from the external entry can be determined, along with the overall depth of the structure. A deep structure requires the traversing of many segments. This has implications for how many boundaries and points of control one crosses in penetrating into the building. In Figure 2.1 the linear structure is twice as deep as the fan or the network.

Another key dimension of syntactic analysis is the degree of 'ringiness' versus 'control'. To what extent are spatial segments interconnected by networked pathways as opposed to being controlled by a linear or branching syntax? The networked structure is defined by its multiple and lateral connections, many possible pathways through it and dispersed control. The linear or fanned structure controls circulation and social interaction in certain key spaces. The degree of 'control' of a given cell is the degree to which access to other cells must pass through it. Thus a hallway or foyer which is the only access to a cluster of rooms has a high level of control over the flow of everyday life. The linear structure produces a spatial narrative with very strong levels of control in all cells except the deepest. The branching or fan structure gives access to many segments from a single segment of control. The networked or ringy structure offers many possible pathways and diverse encounters – the flow of life through space is only loosely controlled.

According to Hillier and Hanson, spatial syntax structures social relations of two primary kinds: those between inhabitants (kinship relations or organizational hierarchies); and those between inhabitants and visitors. For instance, in the western cultural context domestic space is primarily segmented along age and

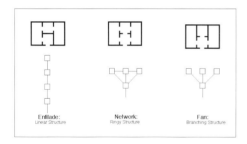

Figure 2.1
Primary spatial structures.

Enfilade:
Linear Structure

Network:
Ringy Structure

Fan:
Branching Structure

gender lines. The genotype of the three-bedroom house operates to enable sex between adults and constrain it between children. The domestic syntax also mediates relations between insiders and visitors in spaces such as living, dining and family areas. However, these spatial mediations are not simple since higher levels of segmentation and privatism in domestic space also enable increasing levels of sexual assault and domestic violence to proceed, unconstrained by the social gaze.

A key issue for Hillier and Hanson is the depth to which visitors are permitted to penetrate into the structure. Traditionally, the deeper cells of the structure were occupied by the inhabitants or controllers and the shallower cells by visitors. Positions of power were then located deep within a tree-like or linear structure. Traditional centres of power often developed an enfilade of rooms, framing a spatial narrative through which visitors were led. The depth of the inhabitant was an indicator of status, and the depth to which visitors were permitted to penetrate also indicated their status. Figures 2.2 and 2.3 show the plan and spatial syntax of the ceremonial entry to the palace at Versailles under Louis XIV which developed a very deep lineal sequence of cells (Berger 1985; Perouse de Montclos 1991). This building frames a representational narrative as visitors proceed through the salons of Venus, Mars and Mercury in the approach to the throne room of the Sun King. The path then turns at the Salon of War (the 'turn' of history) to enter the Gallery of Mirrors, which places the gardens on display whichever way one turns. A similar sequence for the approach to the queen is mirrored on the other wing of the palace. Like most such deep structures, Versailles had a 'stage door' to enable private entry and exit without traversing the deep structure. A similar syntax can be detected in the English country house where an enfilade with a back entry developed in the seventeenth century as a distinctive architecture of individual power (Girouard 1978). During the eighteenth and nineteenth centuries the formal choreography of individual contact was replaced by the informal social networking of the gentry and the architectural enfilade was replaced by a networked plan form.

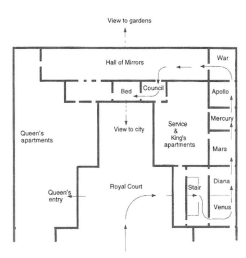

Figure 2.2
Versailles Palace c.1701.

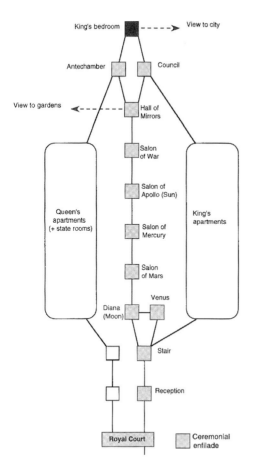

King's bedroom ----→ View to city

Antechamber   Council

View to gardens ◄----/---- Hall of Mirrors

Salon of War

Salon of Apollo (Sun)

Queen's apartments (+ state rooms)   King's apartments

Salon of Mercury

Salon of Mars

Venus

Diana (Moon)

Stair

Reception

Royal Court   Ceremonial enfilade

Figure 2.3
Versailles Palace c.1701: spatial analysis.

The relation of power to depth is not simple and a key insight of Hillier and Hanson's work has been to identify what they call the 'reversed building'. The syntax of such buildings 'reverses' the traditional power relation by locating their powerless 'visitors' in the deepest cells within the structure where they are placed under surveillance. This is the structure of Foucault's disciplinary institutions (prison, hospital, asylum, school and factory) which establish a new kind of interface between controllers and visitors, linked to new forms of knowledge and practice. Hillier and Hanson's work is an advance on Foucault inasmuch as they distinguish between a diversity of reversed buildings and different degrees of reversal. Prisons, hospitals, factories, schools and offices can all have different forms and degrees of institutional control.

The primary architectural achievement of spatial syntax analysis has been the interrogation of the plan through which buildings reveal a social ideology embedded in structural genotypes. For Markus (1987) buildings are 'classifying devices' which reproduce such classes through the framing of social relations. In general terms he suggests that buildings locate classes of similar status at a similar depth, with their members located one segment deeper. He analyses the asymmetries of power embedded in a large range of institutional building types emerging from 1750–1850: town halls, baths, markets, libraries, galleries, schools, factories, prisons, hospitals, asylums (Markus 1993). While the mapping of these genotypes is historically important, Markus also raises theoretical issues relevant to further work. Drawing upon Gorz (1989), he suggests that social relations in buildings can be construed along an opposition of power versus bonding. 'Power' is here construed as a form of constraint; 'bonding' is about love, friendship and solidarity – a liberating and possibly subversive unity of interest. From this view buildings both embody and reproduce various distributions of power, and they can affirm or deny the development of bonding:

> Spaces can be so linked that communication is free and frequent, making possible dense encounters between classes, groups and individuals. These are the basis for community, friendship and solidarity. The alternative is controlled movement, under surveillance, for narrowly defined purposes of production . . . buildings always have double meanings in making concrete both power and bonds.
>
> (Markus 1993: 25)

I suggest that Markus is right to theorize this tension between the quest for control and freedom, and to suggest that a networked structure is one condition of solidarity. Yet as he points out in relation to the airport terminal, buildings are increasingly called upon to produce an illusion of freedom of movement, coupled with the reality of control and surveillance. The freedom of movement enabled by the 'open plan' office and school also enables new higher levels of surveillance and control (Hillier and Hanson 1984: 195). As I shall show in a later chapter, the deep but ringy structure of the private shopping mall is conducive to certain forms of pseudo-solidarity framed by the instrumental imperatives of consumption. Any deterministic conflation of physical enclosure with social constraint, or of open space with liberty, is a dangerous move. An open syntax can operate as a powerful signifier of solidarity and democracy in the absence of the practice.

The key structural distinctions outlined here between controlled and networked structures on the one hand, and between deep and shallow structures on the other, can be mapped against Deleuze and Guattari's distinction between 'smooth' and 'striated' space outlined earlier. Strictness of control through spatial structure is a form of striation and in general terms linear and branching structures are more striated while ringy networks can be identified with smooth space. Deleuze and Guattari deploy the metaphors of the 'tree' and the 'rhizome' to distinguish between 'tree-like' structures of control (where a stem controls the branches) and the multiple lateral flows of a 'rhizomatic' system.

A few words are in order with regard to the ways in which I have used spatial syntax methods in this book, and about the status of the spatial analysis diagrams. Hillier's work is at times highly difficult to understand. This is a language of 'distributed' and 'non-distributed' structures which reveal 'integration' values measured by a formula for 'relative asymmetry' with evidence in the form of complex mathematical tables. Hillier's more recent book (1996a) extends his arguments, transforming the modernist metaphor of architecture as a 'machine for living' and applying it to the analysis of the effects of spatial structure on social behaviour. His work has gained increasing currency in fields of practice such as the programming of large facilities, urban design (Hillier 1996b; Hillier *et al.* 1993) and crime control (Hillier 1988). However, this work is widely regarded within the design professions as positivist, determinist and a return to the 'scientific' approaches of the 1960s (Holyoak 1996). Much of such disparagement stems from the inaccessibility of the work, a rather blind anti-determinism and a pursuit of formal issues to the exclusion of program.

I believe that such disparagement is wrong and that spatial syntactic analysis is a major advance in our understanding of spatial structure. However, I would also suggest some important limits.[7] While cellular analysis is not the only method of syntactic spatial analysis, it is the primary one for interior space, which is presumed to be fundamentally cellular: 'by and large, a building consists of well-defined spaces with well-defined links from one to the other' (Hillier and Hanson 1984: 16). Cellular analysis then enables exact measurement of structural properties to be determined. While the maps of traditional centres of power such as Versailles are relatively unproblematic, many contemporary buildings defy clear segmentation. Many of Hillier and Hanson's key insights have been into new open-plan genotypes such as the school, office, factory and hospital, but these insights still rely upon a certain measureable clarity of enclosure and segmentation. How do we generate a social understanding of the spatial syntax of flowing and fragmented spaces which deploy security cameras and new forms of transparency and opacity? What are we to make of trends in architecture which pursue deliberate ambiguities of enclosure, visibility and permeability? Is there scope for a 'liberation' from the architecture of ideological control in a systematic disdain for the program or are we encountering new forms of ideology, new spatial genotypes? Such questions are raised in relation to Deleuze and Guatarri's distinction between smooth and striated space, and between tree-like and rhizomatic practices. Cellular spatial structures based on socially constructed genotypes can be seen as highly striated spaces with a strict choreography of everyday life. The distinction between deep and shallow structures on the one hand, and between ringy and controlled structures on the other, raises significant questions about the prospects for spatial structures that are more 'smooth', enabling new kinds of spatial practice and meaning. Such analysis needs methods that can map and clearly communicate the emerging production of space with all its ambiguities, fragmentations and layering of the virtual and the real.

I would not wish to predict the future of syntactic analysis yet I would argue that the more complex its mathematics the more difficult it becomes to use in design practice. And as technical difficulty increases, so does the danger that such approaches may be appropriated as 'instrumental reason' into new practices of power – defended from everyday critique by their technical 'difficulty'. I am by no means suggesting any such complicity within Hillier's work, but

I am interested in the prospects for its use in practices of empowerment through what Habermas (1984) terms 'communicative action'.

With this in mind, my use of such methods departs from those of Hillier and his colleagues in some important ways. I do not find the numerical values useful, but I suggest that the diagrams themselves have the potential to reveal structural properties of ringiness, depth and control in a more immediate manner as a language for communicative action in spatial programming and interpretation. There is an earlier and somewhat parallel precedent for such a view. Alexander was the leading proponent of mathematical approaches to design methodology in the 1960s with his seminal text *Notes on the Synthesis of Form* (Alexander 1964). Yet in a later preface to that book he rejected the focus on mathematical method in order to deal directly with spatial 'patterns' as design discourse, a move which led to the well-known 'pattern language' (Alexander *et al.* 1977). With all its problems, the pattern language approach to design has had enormous impact, largely because of its usefulness as a base for communicative action. This is not the place for a critique of the pattern language (Dovey 1990), yet many of these patterns are fragments of spatial syntax. And a great deal of everyday spatial programming is 'patterned' in such a manner. Codes and standards for institutions and building types often incorporate what can be construed as syntax diagrams. Hillier (1996a) himself suggests that his is a non-discursive spatial theory, which does not lend itself to lineal explanation. One primary potential, in my view, lies in the diagrams themselves as modes of communicative action.

My aim in using spatial analysis diagrams is to build some bridges between the different forms of analysis which inform this book – spatial programming, representation and lived experience. The syntax diagrams are useful not only because they reveal a deeper structural program, but also because of the manner in which they structure representational regimes and construct experiences of place. In other words, places are framed syntactically; it is necessary to look beyond the form of the plan, to how spatial segments are named and given meaning. To return to the Versailles plan, it is the representational narrative enfilade of planetary rooms which indicates its importance as an approach to power. Neither the representations nor the spatial structure can be privileged here; they operate in an integrated manner. A technically 'correct' syntax diagram, including all servant and private access, would be impossibly complex. And it would not show the forms of control and representational framing designed into the building.

It is important to note that the diagrams are not plans; they are designed to reveal depth or shallowness, trees or networks – the modes of access and control through the spatial structure. Differences in cell size are to facilitate labelling and do not reflect spatial size. Lines occasionally cross to achieve accuracy of depth in multi-storey buildings, they do not indicate points of social encounter. Clusters of cells may be grouped in rounded boxes for purposes of clarity. Finally, I suggest that there are prospects for basing methods of spatial analysis in the social theories introduced earlier. What makes space syntax analysis potent as a method is that it maps the ways in which buildings operate as 'structuring structures', it maps the *habitus*, the 'divisions and hierarchies' between things, persons and practices which construct our vision of the world. Building genotypes are powerful ideological constructs which frame our everyday lives. They are at once the frames and the texts, in which and from which we learn spatial practices. Our 'positions' within buildings lend us our 'dis-positions' in social life. The spatial 'di-vision' of our world becomes a 'vision' of our world. The buildings we inhabit, our habitat, our spatial habits, all reproduce our social world. Syntactic analysis opens up questions – what kinds of agency are enabled and constrained by the particular building genotype within which it is structured? And whose interests are served? How is everyday life 'bracketed' and 'punctuated' into socio-spatially framed 'situations' and 'locales'? In relation to the gaze, how does architecture frame realms of asymmetric visibility? What regimes of normalization are enforced and in whose interest? To what degree are spatial practices striated by tree-like or linear spatial structures and to what degree are new social relations and rhizomatic practices enabled by open plans or networked spatial structures?

Beyond our position as mute subjects, framed within such genotypes, we are also and at the same time agents producing these programs and structures, changing their forms, uses and meanings. There are lessons here for both disempowerment and empowerment. In this regard there is potential to breathe new life into theories of human–environment interaction as a base for design programming. Studies of privacy, territory, proxemics, cognitive mapping and behaviour settings have all been attempts to develop a humanist base for environmental design research and practice.[8] However, in my view much of the theory developed within the human–environment paradigm has not realized the early promise. For instance, Altman's (1975) seminally important dialectic model of privacy regulation is thoroughly based in the construction of 'identity' through the dialectics of 'boundary control'. Such theory is saturated with questions of power – who controls which boundaries, constructing which identities and in whose interest? Likewise Rapoport's nonverbal communication approach shows how effectively architectural settings can be 'coded' to produce 'appropriate' behaviour (Rapoport 1982). Yet questions remain of how and in whose interest the 'appropriate' is framed. Spatial analysis can reveal ways in which built form marks territory, enables and constrains proxemic relations, frames behaviour settings and constructs cognitive maps. Much of the work in these areas could benefit from being situated in relation to recent social theory and their critiques of power relations.

If grounded in a broad range of current social theories, space syntax analysis has the potential to revolutionize architectural programming. The prospect is to build a more critical context within which one might judge the spatial construction and reproduction of social practices. Yet any attempt to transform the practices of spatial programming will have to deal with the fact that designers are generally not in charge of it. Markus (1993: 317) argues that there has been an unwritten historical pact formed between the architecture profession and its client groups whereby control over the building program has been traded for control over formal imagery. In other words, the architecture profession has defined itself primarily as a practice of representation. This division between formal and functional issues in architecture diminishes the engagement of architects with issues of power. It enables the 'brief' to be written in a technical and value-free language, placing its decisions and elisions beyond debate (Markus 1993: 152). This division between form and program is an ideological division which is ultimately untenable. It serves to sustain the illusion that architecture can be practised in a realm of autonomy from social power. While this division between function and form also marks these early chapters it will then disappear. In the experiences of place in everyday life there is no clear distinction between the ways our lives are programmed and the socially constructed meanings of built form.

Chapter 3: Representation

I now want to turn to issues of representation in built form, to the ways in which the meanings of places are constructed in text. Such theory stems largely from the discursive turn in social theory and the realization that language is not a transparent medium through which we view the world, rather language constructs the experiences of those who use it. To understand place as text involves a focus on the modes of representation or webs of discourse through which the world is encountered. The central role of individual agency is thrown into question; concepts such as 'culture', 'nature', 'identity' and 'community' are seen as social constructions. The 'human being' as 'agent' is in this sense replaced by the 'subject' who is enmeshed and constructed in discourse. Discourse embraces all of the practices through which meanings are communicated, not just speech and writing. The built environment, like food, fashion or film, is a primary form of discourse. Discourse is entangled in power relations since 'subjects' are constructed according to certain interests. These include the interests of the state in maintaining power and social order; private interests in stimulating consumption; and those of dominant classes, cultures and groups in the maintenance of privilege. Forms of discourse and representation construct desires, joys, fears and identities. They construct oppositions between the normal and the deviant. Truth-effects are produced in representation, the 'real' becomes a social construction.

MYTH

The early work of Roland Barthes on the semiotic construction of mythology remains highly useful for readings of architecture and urban form.[1] This work derives from the semiotics of de Saussure and the attempt to construct a general science of signs. For de Saussure the 'sign' is a conjunction of 'signifier/signified', like two sides of a coin considered as form/content or image/meaning. The red light is a signifier, the imperative to stop is the signified. It is axiomatic to early semiotics that the relationship between signifier and signified is arbitrary – there is no necessary relationship of image to meaning. While this arbitrariness is contentious, confusion of a particular social meaning with the universal or natural is fundamental to Barthes' political interpretation of sign systems. For Barthes many signs are not innocent – they problematize relations with our world. Meanings may be 'cooked' to produce truth effects and his call is to enter the 'kitchen of meaning' (Barthes 1988).

Barthes' concerns are with the way society produces self-effacing signs that do not look like signs, linked together in 'codes of domination' which sustain authority and which he calls 'mythologies'. The promise of his early work was that by decoding myth one can strip it of its power; that to bring such symbolic power into the light is to dissolve it. For Barthes myth is structured out of the distinction between denotative meanings (red light means 'stop') and connotative meanings (red rose means 'passion'). The connotative signified is slippery, indeed easily slips into a chain of meta-signifiers such that the meaning becomes 'a fragment of ideology'. He uses the term 'myth', because such signs evoke a way of seeing or making sense of the world and tell us a story. Most importantly myth enables arbitrary meanings to appear natural: 'myth has the task of giving an historical intention a natural justification, and making contingency appear eternal' (Barthes 1967: 91–92). Myth is the use of language to depoliticize speech; myth transforms history into nature.

In this early work Barthes recognized a world beyond textual analysis upon which myth is constructed: 'Wine is objectively good, and at the same time, the goodness of wine is a myth: here is the aporia. The mythologist . . . deals with the goodness of the wine, not with the wine itself' (Barthes 1973: 158). The 'aporia' here is the theoretical impasse to which we are led if we follow the implications of semiotic analysis – we cannot discuss 'the wine itself' except as text. The attempt to explore the limits of the text through textual analysis leads to an endless chain of signifiers and to the semiotic adage that 'there is nothing outside the text'. There is then no escape from the chains of language, and Barthes focuses on the need to 'cheat speech' from within, to dislocate and displace its operations and closures. This is the deconstructive turn.

DECONSTRUCTION

In his later work Barthes (1974, 1976) distinguishes between what he calls 'readerly' versus 'writerly' texts. A readerly text has pre-given meanings, is popular, easy to consume and requires little effort. By contrast, writerly texts invite the reader to construct meaning, subvert passive consumption and challenge the reader into consideration of its code of construction. Such a text unsettles cultural assumptions and tastes; it brings our relations with language and our own subjectivity into focus. The writerly text is related to the experience of *Jouissance*, a state of bliss or loss of 'self' that can come from the reading of a writerly text. This is not the easy pleasure of the readerly text but the almost erotic joy of complicity in the undermining of language and meaning. *Jouissance* is seen as a form of resistance to the socially constructed self and an evasion of ideology. By contrast, the pleasures of the readerly text are seen as the pleasures of surrender to a dominant ideology.

This later work by Barthes suggests that western discourse has a tendency to privilege a closure of meaning, the closure of 'truth' over the openness of metaphor. Readerly texts, he suggests, have a tendency 'to arrange all the meanings of a text in a circle around the hearth of denotation (the hearth: center, guardian, refuge, light of truth)' (Barthes 1974: 7). The deconstructive task is to undo this closure. Barthes' use of the spatial metaphor of the circle and hearth parallels the manner in which the deconstructive move in architecture has targeted the meanings of architecture as an enclosed and stabilized sense of place.

Deconstruction is more commonly associated with Derrida, for whom it is a more fundamental attack on western metaphysics and a set of tactics for the destabilization of meaning (Derrida 1974). There is an avowed aim to expose any buried metaphors and conceptual oppositions in a text, and in general to pull the rug from under any presupposed correlation between language and reality. Deconstruction in this way is intended to open up a text to multiple interpretations wherein any definitive meaning is forever deferred. Thus deconstruction opposes any notions of structure, unity, identity or authority that serves to immobilize the play of meaning. Derrida draws on Heidegger (1962) who refers to language as the 'house of Being', and who invented the practice of writing words like ~~Being~~ 'under erasure' – the score marks intended to signify that ~~Being~~ is framed but not revealed by language.

These attempts to 'cheat speech from within' have been given a new twist by Derrida and others but there is an earlier precedent in the critical aesthetic theory of Adorno (1974). For Adorno the culture industry brings aesthetic production into complicity with forces of domination. The 'aura' of aesthetic production becomes manufactured and geared to a standardized market (Adorno and Horkheimer 1993). The culture industry forges an alliance of art with advertising and political propaganda. It involves the colonization of the psyche as the unconscious is manipulated for purposes of seduction and dreams are appropriated for profit (Arato 1987). Thus there is a stimulation of desire producing a market that is never satisfied: 'The culture industry perpetually cheats its consumers of what it perpetually promises . . . the diner must be satisfied with the menu' (Adorno and Horkheimer 1993: 35).

Adorno saw the task for aesthetic practice as a critique of the conditions which produce it. Emancipatory thought must think against itself, to illuminate truth through what he termed a 'negative dialectic' (Jay 1973). He proposed an aesthetic which divests itself of complicity with power by becoming a kind of weapon: 'A successful work of art . . . is not one which resolves contradictions in a spurious harmony, but one which expresses the idea of harmony negatively by embodying the contradictions, pure and uncompromised, in its innermost structure' (Adorno 1974: 224). One can read here the seeds of the decentring deconstructive move, a claim for the power of aesthetic discourse to disrupt ideology and to generate critical thinking. Adorno also privileges the writerly over the readerly text – the reception of 'critical' work is limited to experts and must protect itself from the appropriations of the culture industry by its 'difficulty'. The aesthetic task is not the production of harmony but of dissonance, utopian visions that meet audience desires are seen as complicit with the dominant order (Heynen 1999: 186–188). Thus cultural production resists complicity with power only by a retreat from public engagement and popular reception (Arato 1987: 219). This critical distance also entails a severing of form from function that becomes particularly problematic for architecture. For Adorno it is the useless-ness of art, its exemption from instrumental function, that gives it subversive potential. The retreat to an elite aesthetic code can become a masking process; the power of aesthetic form is defended by controlling access to its meaning.

A famous debate between Adorno and Benjamin hinged on this question of an elite versus popular art. Benjamin (1978, 1992) agreed with the attempt to shock the audience out of aesthetic ideology but differed on the issue of popular recep-tion. He believed in the capacity of popular dream-like images to generate a revolu-tionary aesthetic through the commodity forms themselves. He saw a power in 'dialectical images' to turn aesthetic ideology against itself and break the spell of desire (Gregory 1994: 231). Unlike Adorno's retreat to an inaccessible formalism, Benjamin recognized a role for figurative and mimetic representation. Dialectical imagery comes from taking fragments of the past out of their contexts and forming new juxtapositions, 'wish images' which can awaken collective memory (Jay 1973).

From the mid-1980s until about 2000 deconstruction was applied with dra-matic impact through the work of architects such as Eisenman, Tschumi, Libe-skind, Hadid, Koolhaas and others (Jencks 1988; Wigley and Johnson 1988). As a formal style it was identified by warped planes, oblique angles and exploded parts. It explored an aesthetic of discord, discontinuity and distortion with a goal to construct a decentred subject and confound the idea of architecture as pure form or stabilized presence. As Wigley and Johnson (1988: 91) put it: 'Decon-struction gains all its force by challenging the very values of harmony, unity and stability, and proposing instead a different view of structure: the view that the flaws are intrinsic to the structure'. Deconstruction offered a challenge to the taken-for-granted language of built form and place. It called such language into question, often using the Heideggerian tactic of writing under erasure, produc-ing images like the 'stair' that leads nowhere or the 'door' that does not open. Functional signifiers were used for play, supposedly without signifieds. The role of architecture in the grounding of social order and the signification of function was thrown into doubt. The promise of deconstruction in architecture lay in the challenge to spatial ideologies, to social ideas about the use of space.

There is no doubt that the deconstructive turn reinvigorated the forms of architectural and urban discourse. While any argument for emancipatory poten-tial is usually tacit, King sees such work as part of a long-standing quest for spaces of emancipation, conducted through architecture and urban design. The claim is that new forms of representation bring new worlds into existence and that 'a new social order – and experience of space, time and the self – can come about' (King 1996: 168). The potential of deconstructionist design lies in a kind of 'shock value' – the capacity of built form to challenge deeply held ideologies and belief systems, and to thereby create a space for the new.

Yet inasmuch as such work carries an implicit claim to address issues of power, emancipation and social change, there are reasons to be sceptical. Eagle-ton (1990: 360) has written of Adorno's aesthetic that he offers 'as a solution what is clearly part of the problem . . . sickness as cure'. Such a charge might be extended to some deconstructive work in architecture and urban design. Werck-meister (1991) suggests that deconstructive thought has developed a 'citadel' mentality by retreating into an elite realm of discourse wherein 'aesthetic lament and political apathy feed upon one another' (Werckmeister 1991: 18). The aes-thetic of crisis, alienation and violence makes horror acceptable; an 'aura' of top-icality and resistance is coupled with a neutral political stance. In this view deconstruction is a new orthodoxy posing as emancipation: 'deconstructive thinking has reached an autonomy which reinforces the self-assurance of its lib-erating role' (Werckmeister 1991: 20).

Saul (1997) has suggested that while deconstructive critique demonstrates how language is enmeshed in self-interest, it becomes complicit with a corporat-ist ideology that there is nothing other than self-interest. In a world where public debate is paralyzed by a mix of propaganda, rhetoric and private dialect, decon-struction further undermines the debate and adds new dialects. In a similar vein Hughes argues that deconstruction breeds a paralyzing 'culture of complaint':

> The intellectual . . . is thought to be as helpless against power and control as a salmon in a polluted stream, the only difference being that we, unlike the fish, *know* the water is poisoned . . . We hold it true that truth is unknowable; we must suspect all utterances, except the axiom that all utterances are suspect. It would be difficult to find a worse – or more authoritarian – dead end than this.
>
> (Hughes 1994: 63)

There are clearly no easy escapes from the complicities of language with power; 'difficult' discourse can be a cover for new forms of power. In this vein Ghirardo (1994) has suggested that Eisenman's enormous influence within archi-tecture has rested on a chameleon-like ability to remain one step ahead of the ability of his audience to understand and critique his work. Indeed she suggests a political conservatism in the practice of the most 'radical' of architects:

> Eisenman's formalism [is] . . . an ideological manouver that deflects attention from the other factors involved in the production of building, in order to ensure the survival of a notion of architecture that transcends history, social circumstance, and politics by excluding such matters from consideration . . . it effortlessly summons nostalgia for the days when architecture was a gentleman's enterprise rather than a profession.
>
> (Ghirardo 1994: 73)

She suggests a hijacking of the liberating impulse in architecture under cover of the very discursive spaces made available by deconstruction. Eisenman defended himself from this attack by organizing seventeen responses from his supporters.[2] Ghirardo clearly pressed a raw nerve and the marshalling of numbers suggests an ossification of deconstructionism into orthodoxy. The retreat of deconstruction into an abstract vagueness was exacerbated by the collaboration of Eisenman with Derrida (Derrida and Eisenman 1997), where the book is punched with a grid of holes. The argument is literally full of holes as Heidegger's tactic of 'writing under erasure' is pursued into a theoretical cul-de-sac. But *Chora L Works* surely 'works' in one sense – it liberates its market from the obligation to read.

The claims of deconstructive designs can be tested, I suggest, only when they are built. The 'shock value' needs to be judged in the everyday lifeworld rather than the coffee table books and design magazines. I shall return in the final chapter to some of the prospects and problems of deconstruction in design. But for now I would make a distinction between deconstruction as a form of discursive analysis and as a form of aesthetic discourse. As analysis – the unpacking, decoding and unmasking of the texts through which places are constructed and experienced – deconstruction is a primary method in what follows. However, this is only one method among several. As aesthetic discourse we need to take care since it is clear that the formal styles of deconstruction are as easily appropriated as any other language. From the 1970s to the 1990s Eisenman inspired a generation of younger architects with the hope for a 'critical architecture' that could resist and deconstruct a dominant social, political and economic order. In a more recent interview he is quoted as follows:

> most of my clients are Republicans . . . And I have the most rapport with right-leaning
> political views, because first of all, liberal views have never built anything of any value,
> because they can't get their act together.
>
> (Eisenman 2004)

It is a paradox, as Pecora points out, that symbolic capital can be 'used simultaneously to signify both the exchange or commercial value of the architect's skills and the architect's ability to renounce all mere exchange value' (Pecora 1991: 46). There is nothing new in this role for architecture, nor in the illusion of autonomy from the market. Designers are the suppliers to a 'meaning market' and the avant-garde have a key role.

THE MEANING MARKET

The shift from modernism to postmodernism has been broadly characterized by Lyotard (1984) as a loss in the credibility of universal theory (metanarratives), coupled with increased attention to difference (local narratives). While this shift has embodied liberating aspects, in Jameson's terms it also brings a new wardrobe of cultural clothes for capitalism and a new 'depthlessness' of cultural life (Jameson 1984). It involves a triumph of surface over depth that in architecture has detached built form from its social context. At the same time the economic value of aesthetics, of architecture as 'symbolic capital', has increased. Architectural style has become both a form of currency and a decisive component of political life. This new politics of the image permits the aesthetic surface to subsume matters of substance. The detachment of form from social life has allowed a seemingly radical break with modernism to mask a deeper conservatism – a commodification of meaning under the aesthetic guise of a revival of meaning. The interpretation of postmodernity as a new conservatism was led in 1980s architectural critique by Lipman and his collaborators. Through a range of critiques – from Venturi in the USA (Lipman and Parkes 1986), to rationalism in Europe (Lipman and Surma 1986) and historicism in the UK (Harris and Lipman 1986, 1989) – the production of meaning under postmodernity was argued to be a new incorporation of aesthetics into older structures of power. Architecture became enmeshed in a 'meaning market' (Harries *et al.* 1982; Lipman and Harries 1984).

Baudrillard (1975, 1981) has long pointed to the ways in which the commodity has become a self-referential sign whereby 'use value' becomes displaced by the 'exchange value' of the sign. In this view the production of things is displaced by the production of signs – it is the meaning which is produced and consumed. This triggers effects of hyperreality wherein the distinction between real and imaginary disappears (Featherstone 1991: 69). There are important lessons in the early Baudrillard, yet claims for the disappearance of use value are exaggerated and dangerous. The semiotic adage that 'there is nothing outside the text' can become self-fulfilling. The depthlessness which Jameson points out in urban experience is evident in much of the representation of built form in design magazines, studiously replicated by design students across the globe. Architectural drawings have gained value as art, as the 'end' rather than the 'means' of architecture. Free-floating signifiers which do not signify a lived future are thereby depoliticized and insulated from social critique. Architects and students alike are inducted into a kind of commodity fetishism, a focus on formal imagery and away from the site, program and social context. The *significance* of places in people's lives is often reduced to the *signification* of meaning, a 'text' to be decoded. There is clearly a congruence between shifts in the marketplace and in architectural ideology. The market for new meaning creates an appetite for distinction and therefore for increased turnover in fashion. A voracious meaning market demands of architects both the manipulation of taste and new images to feed it. In this market, as Ewen (1988: 52) puts it, 'Style is something to be used up, part of its significance is that it will lose significance'.

TASTE AND SYMBOLIC CAPITAL

Within this context I want to return to the work of Bourdieu on 'fields' of cultural production and 'symbolic capital' (Bourdieu 1984, 1993). Unlike the *habitus* which is a 'feel for the game', the 'field' of social practice is like a game board wherein agents are positioned with certain forces available and resources at stake at any given moment. The field differs from the *habitus* as the arena differs from the rules; however, the 'field' in this sense is discursive rather than spatial. For our interests here there are overlapping fields of cultural production such as art, education, housing, urbanism and architecture. The definition of the 'field' is often part of what is at stake. Can a urinal become 'art'? Is a bicycle shed 'architecture'? The resources at stake in these fields of cultural production are defined as cultural, social and symbolic capital – significant forms of capital based on the economic but not simply reducible to it (Bourdieu 1993; Jenkins 1992: 85; Dovey 2005a). 'Economic capital' is any form of wealth that is easily and immediately turned into money: buildings, shares, land and cars. There is a good deal of definitional confusion surrounding these terms in writing both by and about Bourdieu. Cultural capital is the accumulation of manners, credentials, knowledge and skill, acquired through education and upbringing (Bourdieu 1993). It may be 'embodied' as a form of presence based in the *habitus*; the confidence of bodily language and facial expression that engenders authority in social situations. Such capital is often acquired so young that it appears to be innate or natural. Cultural capital may also be 'objectified' in things such as art objects, food, dress and buildings. But the capital in this sense does not lie in ownership but in the capacity to choose and consume them – the objects can be bought but this capacity cannot. Cultural capital can also be 'institutionalized' in educational degrees and academic titles. University fees transform economic capital into cultural capital as an investment in socially valued knowledge.

Social capital inheres as a form of supportive trust in social relations or networks of family, friends, clubs, school, community and society. It differs from cultural capital by being collective rather than individual; if you leave the group you lose the capital. What is often called 'networking' can be construed as building social capital; when architecture commissions are won through social connections, social capital is transformed into economic capital. Trust, solidarity, community and class are all forms of social capital while fear, alienation and isolation indicate its absence. This definition of social capital as reciprocal trust and solidarity is widely shared (Portes 1998; Putnam 1995); Bourdieu's account of it is notable for its focus on the negative solidarity of privileged networks. Social capital is strongly geared to the social connections of place and community, often inherited through class membership. Symbolic capital is the most problematic form of capital to define and there is considerable slippage in Bourdieu's use of it. In his early work (Bourdieu 1977) it is defined as the symbolic component of goods which demonstrate the aesthetic 'taste' of the owner, a form of honour closely linked to objectified cultural capital as a resource which accumulates in objects and individuals. In later work 'symbolic capital' is defined more as a form of legitimation:

> Every kind of capital (economic, cultural, social) tends (to different degrees) to function
> as symbolic capital . . . symbolic capital is not a particular kind of capital but what every

> kind of capital becomes when it is misrecognized as capital . . . and therefore recognized
> as legitimate.
>
> (Bourdieu 2000: 242)

Symbolic capital slips between formal and social distinction. It circulates through built form as symbolic value – in this sense a painting is all symbolic capital and a factory is mostly economic capital; architecture ranges across a continuum between the two. Yet symbolic capital also circulates as the social distinction which accrues through aesthetic 'taste'. Symbolic capital is not something one possesses so much as something which infuses the field, similar in some ways to the Foucaultian (1980) notion of power with its capillary actions and micropractices. Bourdieu is interested in fields of cultural production such as literature, painting and architecture, which are defined in terms of an opposition between a popular mass culture and an esoteric avant-garde. The avant-garde occupies a sub-field of restricted production wherein work is largely defined by its opposition to popular culture for mass consumption. One of Bourdieu's key contributions has been to identify this sub-field as a primary source of symbolic capital (Bourdieu 1984, 1993). Within this sub-field, popularity and economic profit are disavowed. Indeed the prestige of an avant-garde producer is diminished by popular success, since it is sustained by symbolic opposition to the mainstream. The avant-garde sub-field of restricted production has a certain autonomy from the market, which is necessary to its radical innovations. Popular culture, being geared to the market, has less autonomy, yet it relies upon the avant-garde to supply new meanings for this market. For Bourdieu art is neither socially determined nor autonomous. He sees a certain autonomy for aesthetic producers, but only within a social framework which authorizes and legitimizes. The supposedly autonomous formal properties in art are shown to be a key source of symbolic power.

A key point for Bourdieu is that fields of cultural production are generally structured in a manner which sustains the authority of those who already possess it. The legitimacy and value of the symbolic capital at stake in the field is at once presupposed and created through the operations of the field. 'Symbolic domination' is the power of a dominant class to frame the field in which symbolic mastery will be determined. Within this field, the criteria of symbolic distinction favour those who have already imbibed a basic disposition towards it through the *habitus* of home, school, gallery and theatre. To achieve success in such a field one must possess the cultural capital and the 'feel for the game' of investing it. The social power of one class over another is sustained by coercing the other into a field and a *habitus* in which they cannot win.

In such a context, according to Bourdieu, aesthetic 'taste' is 'misrecognized' – first as a universally legitimate criteria and second as an inner quality of the individual rather than a product of the discursive field. A key part of the definition of symbolic capital is that it is 'denied capital'; it is not seen as a form of scapital (Swartz 1997: 43; Stevens 1998). The potency of symbolic capital lies in this masking effect; the difficulty of definition is not coincidental. For Bourdieu the production and circulation of symbolic capital is a key to the way social divisions become naturalized (Bourdieu 1984: 172). Like social capital, symbolic capital infuses a field rather than simply accumulating in individuals. Unlike social capital, of which more or less may be produced, symbolic capital is a fixed resource, a zero/sum game. There is only so much distinction and prestige to be distributed. If everyone gets 'good' architecture, no one wins the symbolic capital. For Bourdieu, all forms of capital are closely linked and partially convertible into each other. An architect will inherit a certain disposition towards architecture through the *habitus*, will develop cultural capital through education and social capital through family, profession and other networks (Stevens 1998; Rüedi 1998). This will enable the architect to play the field wherein the production of symbolic capital is the architect's key market niche.

Bourdieu's (1984) book *Distinction: A Social Critique of the Judgement of Taste* is an oblique attack on the primary canon of aesthetic philosophy, Kant's *Critique of Judgement* (Kant 1974, 1979). For Kant, aesthetic value is transcendent and universal. Art is not that which simply gives pleasure or serves any personal interests – aesthetic experience transcends human interest, indeed it requires a 'disinterest' in merely human affairs. For Bourdieu the ideal of aesthetic experience identified as universal truth is a paradigm case of ideology – the social misperceived as natural; a conflation of 'taste' with 'truth'. He wants to expose the Kantian view as based in class domination. 'A work of art has meaning and interest', he argues, 'only for someone who possesses the cultural competence . . . The "eye" is a product of history reproduced by education' (Bourdieu 1984: 2–3).

For Bourdieu, a primary social function of art is to divide its audience into those who do and don't understand and appreciate it. A key social function of 'taste' is to establish this social distance; aesthetic judgements which appear to mark distinctions between things turn out to mark distinctions between people (Featherstone 1991: 18). Social classes pursue aesthetic strategies to distinguish themselves from the class below and to identify with the class above. These distinctions are constructed upon a set of binary schema such as: difficult vs. easy, unique vs. common, original vs. reproduction and form vs. function. In each case the former term is privileged over the latter, not by argument but by ideology. The difficult, complex and unique are judged more highly by legitimate taste which is also characterized by a contemplative distance from everyday life. The Kantian paradigm is particularly problematic for the aesthetics of place because it implicitly privileges 'looking at' over 'living in'. Legitimate taste is characterized by a privileging of form over function – a contemplative distance that only some people can afford. For Bourdieu (1984: 469) these are structures of domination wherein distinctions between people, based in cultural capital, are made to appear as pure aesthetic judgements. Interest is seen as disinterest.

The traditional role of the avant-garde is to overturn codes of aesthetic taste through semantic inversion. To place a urinal on display as sculpture, or a

blank canvas as art, is to invert the schemas of unique/common, original/repro-
duction, complex/simple and formal/functional. These are paralleled in architecture by deconstructive designs which look unfinished or under collapse –
attempts to defy the alliance of architecture with authority and social order. Yet
Bourdieu's point is that the radical aesthetic can only achieve success within the
field as already constituted. Thus the urinal becomes 'unique' when framed for
contemplation, the blank canvas becomes 'difficult' as a painting. The social distinction becomes drawn between those who do and don't understand.

This phenomenon is evident in the way the avant-garde uses popular
imagery. When popular symbols are appropriated into legitimate taste, as with a
Warhol painting, a contemplative distance between the subject and the work,
never present with the original soup can, is introduced. For Bourdieu the avant-
garde fulfils a role in the system of keeping the images within the market from
becoming stale; it changes and enlivens the field without disturbing the founda-
tions. The appropriation of popular and even vulgar images can be incorporated
into the dominant aesthetic if they are properly framed for contemplation and consumption. Thus art produced as resistance against a dominant class can be framed,
emptied of subversive power and appropriated as a means of further demonstrating distinction. From Bourdieu's position those who answer Adorno's call to use
the autonomy of the aesthetic to develop weapons against it are entering into
complicity with it. Symbolic power is the power to appropriate radical images
designed to unsettle and to use them to reinforce the field (Bourdieu 1984: 254).

Bourdieu does not refute the value of Kantian aesthetics so much as he
shows its complicity with the production of symbolic capital. The field of cultural
production is structured such that the cultural capital necessary to legitimize aesthetic appreciation can be acquired only by freedom from economic necessity.
Thus the aesthetic power of legitimate taste is based on the economic power to
keep necessity at arm's length (Bourdieu 1984: 55). A building which violates its
own function or metaphorically places its meanings 'under erasure' will appear
senseless to many but does make sense within the field of architectural production and its avant-garde. Within such a field the new imagery at once reinvigo-
rates the meaning market, redefines symbolic capital and constructs the
identities of its agents. At the same time it also reproduces and legitimizes the
definition of the field – celebrating the architect's control over form while often
abrogating responsibility for the program. The relative autonomy of the avant-
garde, its symbolic opposition to the mainstream, is structurally necessary to its
role as the primary source of new symbolic capital. However, once the field legitimizes a new form of expression the architect's reputation as avant-garde is
thrown into doubt and a gap re-emerges in the 'meaning market'. The apparent
autonomy of the avant-garde is geared to its structural role in keeping the field
supplied with a stream of new images. While the avant-garde have the key role
of overturning arbitrary aesthetic codes, finding or forging art out of that which
had been considered artless, they can do this only within the field as already
constituted.

Symbolic domination operates by relegating distinctions of taste to the taken-for-granted, making class distinctions appear natural. Thus the symbolic capital accrues to those who inherit the social capital and imbibe the cultural capital (Jenkins 1992: 139). Without the necessary cultural capital, imbibed through the *habitus*, attempts to climb the aesthetic hierarchy can lead easily to kitsch – the badge of the nouveau riche. Thus the difficulty and complexity of high art maintains its superiority to low and obvious easy art; the superiority of legitimate taste is naturalized. Thus dominated classes make symbolic choices and identify themselves within a field of values which are constantly redefined negatively in relation to their own values (Bourdieu 1984: 250).

Bourdieu's work can be seen to suggest a rather dismal prospect for designers who seek a retreat from codes of aesthetic domination in the private language of 'writerly' texts. And this problem is most apparent in architecture, the least autonomous of the arts. The complicity of architecture with the mediations of power cannot be overcome and indeed can be fueled by a retreat to the supposedly autonomous field of aesthetic representation. Once reduced to text, all architectural signifiers are available for appropriation into new codes of domination. Lest Bourdieu's critique sound too totalizing, there is surely a residual autonomous capacity within aesthetic production. Despite the machinations of the meaning market, the aesthetic of built form retains a capacity to 'change the world'. Yet to understand this capacity we must understand the world as more than text and representation.

The primary method for understanding representation as a practice of power is discourse analysis, a complex and contentious set of research practices that seek to expose the constructions of meaning in a text (Fairclough 1995; Rose 2001). My primary task in this book is to engage with such representations as they operate through built form; discourse analysis is a key method in the case study chapters. Such methods are also useful in the interrogation of those non-built texts that are crucial for the production and reception of buildings; practices of power that operate through building programs and professional journals have been investigated to considerable effect.[3] In relation to built form the task is to understand the ways in which constructions of meaning intersect with the practices of everyday life – a key task of the next chapter.

Chapter 4: Place

Authenticity comes from a single faithfulness: that to the ambiguity of experience . . .

John Berger (1992: 216)

The concept of 'place', so central to this book, is difficult to define and deploy in any clear and widely shared manner. It is common to see 'place' as an experiential phenomenon defined in opposition to 'space': a location experienced as meaningful within a larger spatial context. While such a view makes sense in everyday life it is ultimately too narrow, stable and closed to capture an understanding of place. The concept of 'place' is aligned with a group of terms, such as 'identity', 'community', 'character' and 'home', that perform key roles in our everyday lives yet are tantalizingly difficult to define. How is it that these terms all resonate at different scales from local to global, as we move from body to room, building, neighbourhood, city, nation and planet? While most theories of place stem from philosophy, social theory and geography, my interests here are focused on the nexus of built form and power. Ultimately any useful concept of place in this sense will encompass both the programs and representations outlined in Chapters 2 and 3 – places frame and construct social programs and representational narratives, as they are framed and constructed by them. Place is not the third in a series that proceeds from program and text, rather it is the practice of their intersections and much more. I will begin with the phenomenology of place and its critics, proceeding to ideas of place as an assemblage of socio-spatial dialectics, and as a product of practice rather than an effect of built form.

ONTOLOGIES OF DWELLING

Place theory in architecture gained currency and popularity from the 1970s–1990s largely through the propagation of Heideggerian phenomenology, particularly through the work of Frampton (1983) on 'critical regionalism' and Norberg-Schulz

(1980, 1985) on the notion of a 'genius loci'.[1] This material has now percolated through the profession and in some mainstream international journals has become a dominant ideological framework. At the same time various post-structuralist critiques have rendered such concepts, along with 'sense of place', 'spirit of place', 'authenticity' and 'home', problematized. The desire for some simple return to authentic local roots in 'place' has been shown to be enmeshed in practices of cultural domination. Ideologies of essential, deep and unchanging meaning have a conservative and stabilizing effect on formations of identity, they are repressive of difference. 'Authenticity' is connected in more than its etymology to 'authority' – the discourse of authenticity is a legitimating discourse which authorizes certain meanings while repressing others. From such a view concepts of 'place', 'home' and 'authenticity' are often condemned as essentialist. Yet such concepts are not so easily discarded; they remain to haunt the field and need to be re-theorized.

The understandings of place that I want to sketch here have their beginnings in both Heidegger and Merleau-Ponty. The key Heideggerian contribution lies in his claims about the ontology of dwelling and the spatiality of being. For Heidegger there is no existence separate from practices of dwelling; there is only 'Being-in-the-world'. Most phenomenological theory within architecture and urban design has focused on this ontology of dwelling. For Norberg-Schulz (1980) the primary functions of buildings are to 'orient' and 'identify' – architecture tells us where we are and who we are. In this view buildings are seen to 'ground', shelter and stabilize a fragile sense of being.

Much less used within such fields is the work of Merleau-Ponty (1962), who established a phenomenology of space based in the body. Lived space (as opposed to the abstract space of geometry) was fundamentally embodied, grounded, constructed and perceived through the human body. For Merleau-Ponty the body is a 'bridge' between 'being' and 'world' – the lived experience of the body-in-space is the primary relation from which all conceptions of space are constructed. Our understandings of space emerge from action, indeed space is to be defined as 'a certain possession of the world by my body, a certain gearing of my body to the world' (Merleau-Ponty 1962: 250). From such a view the concept of 'space' and the experience of 'place' are products of the dialectics of body and world in everyday practice. This idea of space as 'embodied' means that any experience of place has an indeterminate and virtual dimension because it is always open to a range of actions and practices (Casey 1997: 235). From this view place experience is not a subjective encounter with an objective world but cuts across the binary division between subject and object: 'One does not first have a subject that apprehends certain features of the world in terms of the idea of place; instead the structure of subjectivity is given in and through the structure of place' (Malpas 1999: 35).

The critique of phenomenology has been characteristic of the 'discursive turn' in social theory that developed through Barthes' semiology to Derridean deconstruction. Thus 'place' is interpreted as a 'myth' (in Barthes' terms) or a 'transcendental signified' (Derrida). Such discursive analysis of the discourse of place has been very useful but it has also served to reduce 'place' to 'text', a repression of all that stands 'outside the text'. This reduction to text has had the effect of purifying the concept of 'place', stripping it of some fertile complications. Consider the following quote from Barthes' early work:

> If I am a woodcutter . . . The tree is not an image for me, it is simply the meaning of my action. But if I am not a woodcutter . . . this tree is no longer the meaning of reality as a human action, it is an *image-at-one's-disposal*. Compared to the real language of the woodcutter, the language I create is a second-order language . . . This second-order language is not entirely mythical, but it is the very locus where myth settles . . . There is therefore one language which is not mythical, it is the language of man as producer: wherever man speaks in order to transform reality and no longer to preserve it as an image, wherever he links his language to the making of things . . . myth is impossible.
>
> (Barthes 1973: 145–146, original emphasis)

This talk of action as a 'real language' and contemplation as 'second-order' disappears from Barthes' work with the deconstructive turn, but the questions are not resolved. There are some clues here in Heidegger's (1962: 97–102) distinction between active and contemplative modes of dwelling, which he terms *Zuhandenheit* and *Vorhandenheit*.[2] The former is a mode of active engagement with the world, while the latter requires a certain contemplative distance from which we might 'read' it. While both modes are necessary, our active engagement with the world has primacy in the construction of place (Casey 1997: 283). This does not suggest that meaning can be reduced to function, but rather that some primary meanings of place stem from what and whom it is 'for'. It follows that representations are not simply 'read', but are constructed through dwelling. There is a parallel here with Wittgenstein for whom language is a 'game' with meanings of words constructed through the uses to which they are put; to paraphrase him: 'let the use of (buildings) teach you their meaning' (Wittgenstein 1967: 220).

There have been two main lines of critique of Heideggerian thinking. The first is his guilt by association with Nazism. If this connection were simply coincident there would be little concern – philosophy is not necessarily underwritten by morality. In this case, however, the idea of authentic dwelling was a key component of both Heideggerian philosophy and Nazi ideology where ideas of racial purity were enmeshed in the connection to place (see Chapter 5). The lesson here is that place attachment can be narrow, parochial and politically potent. Heidegger's Nazism illustrates the dangers of romantic phenomenology and the complicities of place with power; it does not follow, however, that he was wrong about the ontology of place and the spatiality of being.

The second line of anti-Heideggerian argument in architecture is a more direct attack on the notion of a spatially rooted ontology. For Rajchman the 'grounding' of dwelling in place is a source of false naturalism and a constraint on freedom: 'we need to get away from the picture . . . that the lifeworld is in the first instance a grounded world' (Rajchman 1998: 86). From this view, the gravitas and heaviness of the earth is to be overcome in a Nietzschean spirit of freedom; 'place' is a centre of orientation and identity is an 'anchor' which weighs us down. As Rajchman (1998: 88) puts it: 'Once we give up the belief that our life-world is rooted in the ground, we may thus come to a point where ungroundedness is no longer experienced as existential anxiety and despair but as a freedom and lightness that finally allows us to move'. There is here a desire to sever the connection of building with site and place, a privileging of movement over stasis, of 'wings' over 'roots'.

In the provocatively titled book 'Non-Places', Augé (1996) portrays the increasingly fleeting and fragmented nature of 'supermodernity' as a disappearance of place: 'If a place can be defined as relational, historical and concerned with identity, then a space which cannot be defined as relational, or historical, or concerned with identity will be a non-place' (Augé 1996: 77–78). Included as 'non-places' are spaces of transit and temporal occupation such as freeways, transit lounges, aircraft cabins, supermarkets, hotel rooms, leisure parks, shopping malls and the informational spaces of telepresence. Koolhaas has given architectural expression to such desires of lightness, an un-grounding of architecture, which he has written about as a form of 'freedom' from place and its grounded critiques – the 'non-place', the 'generic city' (Koolhaas 1995). Some of these ideas appear to mesh well with Deleuzian thinking about 'lines of flight', 'folding' and 'smooth space' (Deleuze and Guattari 1988).

While I am sympathetic with such critiques, questions about the ontology of dwelling are not so easily wished away. The 'non-place' is another kind of place experience geared to a new form of identity production with certain classes of people who feel quite at home in them. Rootlessness is most easily embraced by those whose ontological security is assured. The common ground of most such critiques of place is to select the stabilizing tendencies of Heideggerian dwelling as the point of critique, seeing it as the propagation of illusions of stable identity. Yet I would note a crucial point of agreement between many phenomenologists and deconstructionists in this field – it is that built form does operate to stabilize identities, the disagreement is over whether it should do so. Such stabilizations seem to me unavoidable; the question is not whether 'place' is a good or bad concept but how good are our theories of place. In this view the concept of 'place' should be approached dialectically as a set of practices, and as the product of conflict, contradiction, resistance and the play of difference.

The question of the ontology of dwelling is crucial to issues of power and place. Acceptance of a universal impulse or structure of dwelling may seem like a turn backwards to a prison-house where culture masquerades as nature. The desire for place may at times be conservative but it also harbours the progressive desire for a better future. For Benjamin the experience of dwelling is linked to desires for return to the closure of the mother's womb as a form of idealized paradise (Heynen 1999: 117–118). There is a recognition that this ideal lies in a

lost past but an ambivalence about the way the openness, transience and transparency of modernity promises freedom but threatens the loss of security. Benjamin's famous figure of the angel of history can be read in this context of a
desire for a return to paradise; the angel is blown backwards into the future by a
storm he calls 'progress', which could also be called capitalism (Benjamin
1992: 257).

SPATIAL DIALECTICS

This capacity of built form to ground and shelter, to orient, to stabilize and
protect a fragile sense of being and identity, is the primary connection of place
to power. Place establishes the order of the world and our place within it. It also
establishes who and what is 'out of place'; it constructs the infinite other against
which the closures of place are defended. In what follows I want to frame the
experience of dwelling and the mediations of power in terms of a series of
dialectics beginning with two spatial dialectics. In 'The Poetics of Space'
Bachelard suggests that the house is imagined in accordance with 'two principal
connecting themes: 1) A house is imagined as a vertical being. It rises upward
. . . 2) A house is imagined as a concentrated being. It appeals to our consciousness of centrality' (Bachelard 1969: 4). In a manner that can be linked to Jungian
psychoanalysis the garret is associated with dreams and the cellar with the sub-
conscious. Bachelard writes also of the way that the horizontal distinction
between inside and outside constructs the meaning of the house, the ways that
the larger world is present in the intimate spaces of dwelling. Bachelard's book is
based in French poetry and is highly ethnocentric yet what is at issue here is not
the existence or value of cellars or garrets but the dialectics of place.

   The dialectic of vertical/horizontal emerges from a lifeworld that is structured as a largely horizontal plane between earth and sky. The vertical dimension, reflecting the body, is decidedly asymmetrical. Vertical symbolism
permeates the language of power and domination: the 'highness' of kings, the
'upper' classes, the 'high' table, social 'climbing' and so on. We construct theories (like buildings) on a solid 'base' – our ideas like our lives are 'grounded'.
Such a symbolic dimension is linked to the upright stance of the body. The word
'stand' shares a root with 'stasis', 'stable', 'state', 'statute' and 'establish'. The
vertical 'stands' against the horizontal as a form of aspiration. This does not
imply that the meanings of vertical forms are determined by the structures of
lived-space, only that such meanings are constructed within the context of this
dialectic. The idea that a taller building is better than a lower one is entirely irra-
tional at one level yet vertical prominence reads as dominance in social space.

   Diagonal forms play upon this tension between vertical and horizontal,
embodying a certain perceptual dynamism. A predominance of diagonal forms is
characteristic of the dynamic architecture of revolution (constructivism, futurism)
but also marks the expression of tension and disorder (deconstruction). The
pyramid is a potent formal type in which diagonal forms are stabilized – it

embodies the capacity to represent both dynamic aspiration and stability at the same time. While the meanings and materials change, the persistent use of the pyramid at centres of power is more than arbitrary: stretched into an obelisk (Washington Monument, Place de la Concorde), a symbol of modernity (Eiffel Tower) or a transparent jewel-like presence (Louvre). Bataille (2005) suggests that the pyramid and obelisk identify the centre of power with the heavens and work to stabilize the idea of power flowing downwards and outwards like the sun's rays: 'the obelisk was to the armed sovereignty of the pharoah what the pyramid was to his dried out corpse. It was the surest and most durable obstacle to the drifting away of all things' (Bataille 2005: 18). Clearly the pyramid does not have a consistent meaning for pharaoh, slave, tourist, citizen and consumer, yet it would appear to have a potent and persistent capacity as a grounding of central-ized power.

The vertical/horizontal dialectic lends meaning to metaphoric expressions of aspiration and grounding in architecture from the detached house with pitched roof to the capitol, cathedral and corporate tower. Wright's prairie houses were both hearth centred (vertical) and earth hugging (horizontal) – they constructed a range of potent meanings about democracy, landscape and individuality. Tatlin's famous, albeit unbuildable, design representing the new Bolshevik state was composed of diagonal forms spiraling into a tower, its potent expression of a lib-erating spirit relied strongly upon a vertical/horizontal tension.

The second of Bachelard's dialectics is the inside/outside dialectic. This dialectic is founded on the distinction between 'here' and 'there', between place and its context, between place identity and its 'other'. It can be linked to what Douglas (1966, 1973) long ago theorized as an opposition between purity and danger; a place of purity, strongly identified with the human body, is defended by socially mediated (yet universally prevalent) spatial rituals. Key examples are the symbolic rituals associated with bodily orifices and passage across them – food, sex and ablution (Douglas 1966). Such rituals identify a zone of purity and order while ritually defending the body against the perceived dangers of dif-ference. This inside/outside dialectic is at once personal and social: 'The rituals enact the form of social relations and in giving these relations visible expression they enable people to know their own society. The rituals work upon the body politic through the symbolic medium of the physical body' (Douglas 1966: 128).

This dialectic projects into the built environment which becomes a kind of prophylaxis – it mediates the penetrations of 'otherness' into our lives; it keeps 'difference' and 'dis-ease' at bay. The inside/outside dialectic becomes ordered along the lines of enclosure/openness, safety/danger, home/journey, familiar/ strange, self/other and private/public. Practices of 'entering' bodies and build-ings are universally given ritual meanings about social identity and threats to it, thus they are also necessarily mediations of power. As Douglas (1966: 3) puts it: 'the laws of nature are dragged in to sanction the moral code'. The inside/outside dialectic structures the lifeworld with boundaries and thresholds, all strongly linked to the construction and protection of identity – it structures social relations between insiders and outsiders; between identities and differences. The dialectic of inside/outside is crucial to identity formation and role performance because it is also a dialectic of private and public. Goffman (1959) has shown the importance of back and front zones in the negotiation and performance of public and private identities; and Altman (1975) redefined the concept of privacy from something that was somehow held in things to a dialectic process.

The inside/outside dialectic may be manifest in other ways, such as Appleton's (1975) prospect/refuge theory, which suggests a general spatial preference for edge conditions where one can see without being exposed. When manifest in built form this is clearly geared to practices of social power – the 'commanding' view of the corner office or the panoptic guard tower, seeing without being seen. There are obvious connections here with the theories of *habitus* and spatial syntax. The segmentation of space structures the lifeworld with boundaries and thresholds, all strongly linked to constructions of identity. The inside/outside dialectic is a fundamental dimension of spatial programming – it structures social relations between insiders and outsiders.

The formal and social potency of these two dialectics can be illustrated in key works of architecture. Le Corbusier's famous Villa Savoye is a modernist icon where the Bachelardian schema of the typical French house seems to be completely abolished – cellar, attic and roof are gone along with most of the ground floor which became an entry with a hand-basin – the purification rite. Having largely severed relations with the earth, Corbusier established a new relationship with the sky (the roof terrace) and a new inside/outside dialectic (the transparency of strip windows). This was a very potent architectural type precisely because it operated upon the vertical/horizontal and inside/outside dialectics. This design suggested a new mode of dwelling – playing upon a dream of liberty in a purified upper world, where one washed one's hands of the earth on entering. The meanings of Villa Savoye are by no means exhausted by such interpretation; the design is inconceivable outside its class and gender relations and the struggle for professional reputation that are mapped onto it (Colomina 1992: 98–104; Ballantyne 2005: 165–167). The maid's room finds its place within these two dialectics, starved of sunlight on the recessed ground floor. Yet without the symbolic potency of the vertical/horizontal and inside/outside dialectics this building would be reduced to an arbitrary play of imagery.

In a more recent play on a similar theme Koolhaas has designed a house at Bordeaux where the cellar becomes an entry, the main floor is almost transparent and dissolves inside with outside and the attic floor seems to float above this new space of 'freedom' (Dovey and Dickson 2002). The lesson here is not that we should or should not have glass walls or garrets but in the ways in which dreams of self and home, of being grounded or liberated are constructed in relation to these dialectics of vertical/horizontal and inside/outside. Urban types such as the detached house, housing enclave, shopping mall and corporate tower are linked to them, incorporating problematic mediations of power which I shall describe in later chapters. I do not suggest that such types are in any way natural; they have emerged as global types in response to historical conditions of capitalism. While recognizing the primacy of social constructions of meaning, the universal dialectics outlined above cannot be disregarded. The social maps onto the spatial and it does so in a way that is structured by the spatial ontology of dwelling. Questions of the ontology of dwelling will continue to haunt social theory until the intellectual polarization of essentialism and anti-essentialism dissolves.[3]

SOCIAL DIALECTICS

This notion of space as produced through the dialectics of everyday social life is a key to Lefebvre's social theory which couples a concern for the social constructions of spatial ideology with the importance of lived experience (Lefebvre 1971, 1991, 1996).[4] For Lefebvre the concept of 'space' defies traditional categories – it is at once a means of production and a commodity; both a social product and a medium of social reproduction and control. For Lefebvre the production of space is a series of dialectics between space as practised, conceived and lived. The production of the 'lived' is the result of struggle between appropriation and expropriation of space (Lefebvre 1971: 88). He criticizes phenomenology for a limited focus, constrained within the immediacy of the lived. The dialectic of lived/conceived is close to the Heideggerian contrast of engagement/contemplation and with a similar warning of the tendency to reduce the lived to text. Lefebvre wants to reconcile the lived and the everyday with the lessons not only of Marx, but of Nietzsche and Barthes. His call for the 'right to the city' (Lefebvre 1996) is not only about rights of access but about rights of appropriation.

The work of de Certeau is also useful in this regard. For de Certeau, like Lefebvre, the meanings of place are continuously constructed and reconstructed through action in everyday life: 'Like words, places are articulated by a thousand usages' (de Certeau 1985: 131). Places are the warehouses of memory, always haunted with a myriad of possibilities for meaning and behaviour. Against Foucault, he celebrates the possibilities of resistance to any disciplinary regime. As disciplinary power in space becomes more totalizing, it also becomes more available for subversion: 'The surface of this order is everywhere punched and torn open by ellipses, drifts, and leaks of meaning: it is a sieve-order' (de Certeau 1984: 108). De Certeau makes the distinction between 'strategies' of power adopted by institutions and the 'tactics' of resistance that are utilized in everyday life. Through the dialectics of strategies and tactics, mediations of power can be reversed and meanings inverted. Like the rhizomatic practices that Deleuze and Guattari (1988) contrast with strategic striations, the tactics of resistance and appropriation can insinuate themselves into the very pathways of discipline, manipulation and authority.

Deleuze and Guattari relate body to space not through bilateral symmetry but through the act of dwelling and appropriating; one dwells by moving (Casey

1997: 307). Such thought unsettles the paradigm of the settled place that dominates the work of Heidegger and Bachelard. While it valorizes the smooth over
the striated there is also the understanding that the smooth is always being
striated, that these are not different spaces (Deleuze and Guattari 1988).
While Deleuze and Guattari oppose binary thinking, their work is replete with
oppositions such as territorialization/deterritorialization, being/becoming,
sedentary/nomadic and arborial/rhizomatic, all of which resonate with the
smooth/striated distinction and that of home/journey. These should not be seen
as mutually exclusive binary opposites since the ways they fold into each other is
one of the keys to understanding place.

GLOBAL SENSES OF PLACE

An understanding of the nexus of place and power requires that we move
beyond philosophical conceptions of place to an understanding of how such
place experience has been transformed under conditions of global capitalism.
There is not scope here for a detailed account of globalization, which is generally
understood as a cluster of interrelated conditions, two of which are particularly
pertinent here: the collapse of lived distance through accelerated global flows of
capital, people and information (Appadurai 1996); and the production of global
cultures (King 2004).[5] Globalization has transformed place experience and
fuelled a proliferation of global place types (discussed in Chapters 8–11).

Based in Heideggerian notions of being-in-the-world, Giddens argues the
importance of 'ontological security' under conditions of global place production.
Ontological security is defined as 'the confidence that most human beings have in
the continuity of their self-identity and the constancy of the surrounding social and
material environments of action' (Giddens 1990: 92). This is strongly embedded in
place, not necessarily as enclosure but as 'a defensive carapace or protective
cocoon which all normal individuals carry around with them as the means whereby
they are able to get on with the affairs of day-to-day life'. (Giddens 1991: 40). Sustained by the routines and habits of a familiar world this figurative 'carapace'
brackets out aspects of our world which would otherwise engulf us and cause
paralysis of the will. This is clearly resonant with the inside/outside dialectic.

Giddens suggests that globalization and modernity have transformed the
very tissue of place experience. In the modern world local/global tensions infuse
all places. But this does not signal a loss of 'place' any more than it is a loss of
self-identity. Rather it is the end of the closed local place; the romantic view of
the harmonious village is in many ways a nostalgic response to this loss. For
Giddens the importance of local place relations rests in the necessity for ontological security within a world which has been transformed by globalization. Such a
construction of place has a collagist character; a collision of practices and images
rather than one narrative replacing another. It gives the experience of place a
phantasmagoric character wherein the global and local, the familiar and the
strange become inextricably intertwined (Giddens 1990: 108).

For Harvey conceptions of space need to go beyond the lived and the material to be seen in relational and dialectic terms: 'If I ask the question: what does Tienanmen Square or Ground Zero mean, then the only way I can seek an answer is to think in relational terms' (Harvey 2006: 125). The answer to how one defines space or place lies in practice. The relation between 'space' and 'place' is characterized as a dialectic of global and local (Harvey 1996: 316). Harvey wants to reconcile differences between Marxian and Heideggerian approaches to place. The concern for the particularities of place is linked to the manner in which place is the site for dwelling, the locus for collective memory. He echoes Heidegger in basing social and community life in dwelling practices and suggests that place becomes more important in a world where the authenticity of dwelling is increasingly enmeshed in global commodity culture.

Place experience gains importance in a globalizing world for several reasons (Harvey 1996: 297–298). The threat of homogenization produces a re-evaluation of local differences. Yet at the same time the greater mobility of capital produces a greater choice of location and more sensitivity to the qualities of place. And finally the market responds with investment in constructions of place identity, fuelled in turn by an over-investment in the property market. One result is that we cannot understand urban development unless we understand both the phenomenology of dwelling and its ideological constructions across broader spatial fields. Harvey argues for the pursuit of a dialectic between the 'places' of everyday dwelling and the 'spaces' of global production, calling attention again to the myopia of the lived:

> what we learn from sensuous interaction with the things we touch and the processes we directly encounter is different from what we need to know to understand the processes of commodity production and exchange that put our global breakfast upon our individual tables . . . immediate experience is so authentic as to permanently tempt us to regard it as all there is and so ground our sense of being, of moral responsibility, and of political commitments entirely within its myopic frame.
>
> (Harvey 1996: 313)

The uniqueness of place is a form of monopoly advantage that globalization threatens to erase through homogenization and commodification (Harvey 2001). The market's pursuit of such monopoly entails 'seeking out criteria of speciality, uniqueness, originality and authenticity'. A key contradiction is that in pursuit of profit globalizers are often driven to support local places even when they embody antagonism to globalization. Thus capital opens up spaces of antagonism to its own processes; for Harvey these are spaces of hope for social transformation: 'The spaces for transformational politics are there because capital can never afford to close them down' (Harvey 2001). The local capacity to win battles in defence of place is considerable, yet the politics of place alone is doomed to failure if it remains trapped within the myopia and parochialism of the local.

Massey has been the key proponent of a 'global sense of place' that embodies a dynamism towards a better future, is open to difference, outward looking and globally connected (Massey 1995, 2005; Cresswell 2004). There are three key propositions underlying such theory. First is that space is the product of interrelations, there can be no claim to essential meanings or authenticity based on a pre-given identity. Second is that a condition of multiplicity is integral to the concept of space. Third is that space is dynamic and open to the future. Such theory counters the sense of rootedness and closure often identified with Heideggerian approaches. For Massey notions of place identified with stasis, nostalgia and enclosure are limited and problematic because they privilege singular identities deeply rooted in singular histories; they are inward-looking and backward-looking with robust boundaries (Massey 1993: 64). The 'progressive sense of place', by contrast, is multiplicitous and open. This is not an abstract ideal and Massey offers her local high street in London as a model:

> while Kilburn may have a character of its own, it is absolutely not a seamless, coherent identity, a single sense of place which everyone shares. . . . If it is now recognized that people have multiple identities, then the same point can be made in relation to places.
>
> (Massey 1993: 65)

Such a place cannot be understood without a global perspective: 'the identity of a place does not derive from some internalized history. It derives in large part precisely from the specificity of its interactions with "the outside" ' (Massey 1992: 13). Massey's ideal sees place as process rather than product; local places are forged from the encounter with a global space of flows: 'the identity of place is always and continuously being produced' (Massey 1992: 14). In this view 'place' can have a complex and unique 'character' without the Heideggerian characteristics, even a role in stabilizing dwelling practices in a sense of home that is neither inward- nor backward-looking.

This is a sense of place that valorizes routes rather than roots, journey rather than home, flows rather than stasis. Such a sense of place 'is absolutely not static and in no way relates to the Heideggerian view of space/place as Being . . . places are processes' (Massey 1993: 66–67). While this desire to liberate place from its Heideggerian roots is understandable, the phrase 'in no way relates' implies that place can be severed from the ontology of dwelling. This denies the role of place in establishing ontological security. It is as if place is always and only social – constructing a polar opposite to the essentialist and asocial theories of place that have proven so dangerous.

Thrift shares with Massey the valorization of an open and dynamic sense of place. This is again a theory of place as produced through practice; places are never finished because they are continuously performed (Thrift 1997). He argues for 'non-representational' theories of place that he links to a range of thinkers from Heidegger, Merleau-Ponty and Wittgenstein to Deleuze. These he opposes to the long tradition of Kantian thought which sees space as transcendental and intuitive. People and places are connected by various 'hauntings'; we are haunted by the memories of places and they are haunted by our practices. Perhaps the most evocative aspect of Thrift's essay entitled 'Steps to an Ecology of Place' is the title, which he does not theorize except to pay tribute to Bateson's 'Steps to an Ecology of Mind'. It is worth noting, however, that the title of Deleuze and Guattari's 'A Thousand Plateaus' is drawn from the same source. The 'plateau' is a spatial metaphor deployed by Bateson to refer to the ways in which certain stable systems emerge from a context of difference and the practices of social life. The plateau is a level of stability derived from movement and legitimated as culture, although often understood as nature (Bateson 1972: 113). The word 'plateau' shares its etymology with 'place' – a sense of a socially constructed experience framed in the form of a horizontal surface or territory.

AMBIGUITIES OF PLACE

It follows from much of the above that place can be construed as an assemblage of interrelated dialectics: local/global (Harvey, Giddens, Massey); striated/smooth (Deleuze and Guattari); strategies/tactics (de Certeau); lived/conceived (Lefebvre); home/journey; private/public (Altman); up/down (Bachelard); and inside/outside (Douglas). These should not be seen as mutually exclusive opposites since the ways they fold into each other is one of the keys to understanding place – tactics become strategies, the lived becomes conceived, private becomes public, smooth becomes striated, the journey becomes home and local becomes global.

In the end the concept of place remains an enigma and our inability to nail it down is essential to its meaning. At one level the dialectics of place are driven by an essentialist desire for a space of purified cultural identity and an exclusion of difference. Yet it does not follow that the quest for place can be conflated with such exclusion. The dialectic is always two-sided and constructions of place are equally a product of difference. Within such dialectic thinking if place embodies 'identity' then it also embodies 'difference'; and a rejection of 'place' is a rejection of 'difference'. The idea that the grounding of identity in place stands in opposition to the proliferation of cultural difference ignores the key role of place in establishing ontological security as a basis for difference. The mistake is often to identify place with form rather than social process, the reduction to text.

Within a conception of place as an assemblage of dialectic processes, places of hybridity and impurity become sites for new spatial practices, for the production and performance of new identities and cultures in everyday life. The unstable, the nomadic, the slippery can be seen as authentic – not in the sense of a quest for essences but as an opening up of new forms of authority and authorship. For Berger the quest for authenticity is not a quest for essences but for ambiguities: 'Authenticity comes from a single faithfulness: that to the ambiguity of experience' (Berger 1992: 216). And for Benjamin the ambiguity is often revealed in 'dialectic images': 'Ambiguity is the figurative appearance of the dialectic, the law of the dialectic at a standstill' (Benjamin 1974: 171). Berger draws a distinction between 'mystification' and 'mystery': 'Mystifications protect power. Mysteries protect the sacred' (Berger 1992: 218). The 'mystifications' of place share a good deal in common with Barthes' 'mythologies' and are ripe for deconstruction. Yet there are also mysteries of place of which textual analysis says little.

There is a crucial distinction to make here between two kinds of difference – differences between places and differences within places.[6] 'Differences between places' are what distinguishes one room, building, neighbourhood or city from another. Such distinctions are firmly embedded in practices of power and they may well be driven by the quest for purification and exclusion of difference. 'Differences within places' are about the degree to which difference is permitted to intrude into a place. To what degree does a place embody difference and to what degree is it purified? Purified places (such as housing enclaves) have a capacity to limit identity formation while differences within places (such as mixed neighbourhoods) open up new possibilities. Places of difference are those where the encounter with difference is structured into the life-world both spatially and representationally. Places of difference become valorized as sites for new spatial practices, for the production and performance of new identities and cultures in everyday life. In this view the unstable, the nomadic and the slippery can be seen as authentic – not in the sense of a quest for essences but a quest for new forms of authority and authorship. The difference that makes a difference (to revive a phrase from Bateson) is that between places of difference and places of purity; between places which give voice to the displaced, and places where identity formation is fixed and finished.

In his evocative book *Invisible Cities*, Calvino (1979: 30) asks us to divide cities into two types: '*those that through the years and changes continue to give their form to desires, and those in which desires either erase the city or are erased by it.*' The city that is erased by or erases desires is where the creative destruction of unregulated capital or political tyranny transforms all in its path. The question of whose desires prevail brings me to ponder the resonance between Deleuzian notions of 'desire' as the lifeblood of existence and the Habermasian notion of 'interests' as the foundation of politics and communicative action.[7] The ideal of a progressive sense of place is one where interests are diverse and there can be no singular 'public interest'. These diverse interests, however, are bound together by a common interest in shared use of public space even where desires for its future may not be shared. While desires and interests are coupled as motivating forces in placemaking, there are important differences. Interests are more public than desires in the sense that they can be identified while desires are private and may remain secret. Interests are more strategic than desires, which are more tactical. Interests are more striated while desires are smoother; interests are more stable and desires more fleeting. The relationship between the production and flow of desires and the negotiation of interests, particularly public interests, is another dialectic. This is a dialectic between the stabilizing structures, strategies and practices of urban planning and the fluid and tactical desires and designs that bring change.

The idea of place as a phenomenon that integrates issues of representation and spatial practice can be linked to the work of Arendt, who defines power as a communicative agreement on collective action: 'Power corresponds to the human ability not just to act but to act in concert. Power is never the property of an individual; it belongs to a group' (Arendt 1986: 65). This brings us back to the distinction between 'power *over*' and 'power *to*'. Arendt reasserts the primacy of 'power to' as a collective social capacity that unites issues of practice and representation:

> Power is actualized only where word and deed have not parted company, where words are not empty and deeds not brutal, where words are not used to veil intentions but to disclose realities, and deeds are not used to violate and destroy but to establish relations and create new realities.
>
> (Arendt 1958: 200)

I want to conclude this theorizing with a return to where I began in Chapter 1, with the primacy of power *to*, in relation to which all forms of power *over* are parasitic. While many of the case studies that follow can be construed as negative critiques of the framings of place, all questions about power as mediated by built form ultimately return – as I will in the afterword – to those of empowerment.

Part II

Centres of Power

Chapter 5: Take Your Breath Away

Berlin

> When one enters the Reich Chancellery, one should have the feeling that one is visiting the master of the world. One will arrive there along wide avenues containing the Triumphal arch, the Pantheon (the domed hall), the Square of the People – things to take your breath away.
>
> Hitler (quoted in Hochman 1989: 260)

The Brandenburg Gate was built in 1791 on the site where the major entry to the old city of Berlin intersects the former city wall. This east–west axis began as a seventeenth century 'Royal Way' from the medieval castle to the royal gardens, the Tiergarten. The axis became symbolic of the rise of the Prussian State, lined with military and cultural buildings along the Unter den Linden. The design of the gate was modelled on the Grecian Propylea but the urban location sites it as a triumphal arch in the Roman tradition, framing the victorious return of troops from war. It does not face outwards as a city gate would, but inwards. It is not a fortified part of a city wall but a representational 'frame' for the victorious 'return'. The gate is surmounted by a statue of the 'Goddess of Peace' driving a four-horse chariot into the city. She holds the symbols of Germany and victory: oak leaves, spear, eagle and iron cross. Napoleon stole the statue after his victory over Germany in 1806 and the denuded gate became symbolic of resistance to France until Napoleon was defeated and the statue returned in 1814. Ritual marches through the gate were enacted for victories over Denmark in 1864, Austria in 1866, and especially the French in 1871. The gate is a symbolic punctuation mark on the Berlin–Paris axis.

The Reichstag, housing the German Parliament, was built nearby in 1894. Funded from French war reparations, it was sited facing west (towards France) across a military parade ground called the Platz der Republik. The building was modelled on a neo-Renaissance palace and later inscribed *Dem Deutschen Volke* (To the German People) on its entablature. In the centre of the plaza the Victory

Column was erected, a 90 metre shaft with a golden winged 'Victory' statue clutching the same symbols of war and German unity as found on the gate. She also faced France, on a plinth incorporating captured and melted cannons. The ensemble of axis, gate, Reichstag, plaza and column was symbolic of both the Reich and its domination over France (Figure 5.1).

In January 1933 Nazi stormtroopers held a torchlight procession through the gate to mark Hitler's appointment as Chancellor. They marched towards the

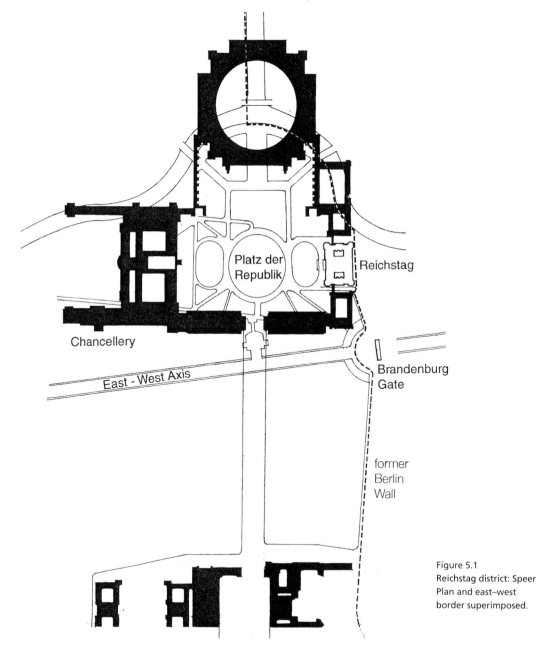

Figure 5.1
Reichstag district: Speer Plan and east–west border superimposed.

city, echoing the idea of the 'return' and 'victory'. Within a month the Reichstag building was largely gutted by fire. Immediately blamed on members of the Communist Party, the fire was used by Hitler as a pretext to suspend constitutional rights on the following day. This and the later Enabling Act, on the same pretext, opened the door to political persecutions which continued all the way to the holocaust. Responsibility for the arson has never been fully resolved, since the communists were acquitted and there is evidence that Goering was involved.[1] The Reichstag was a repository of substantial popular emotional investment. The razing of the national icon touched a deep nerve in the German people and unleashed a reservoir of power which Hitler harnessed. The emotional investment in architecture was cashed in the form of legitimation for tyranny.

COMMUNITY ARCHITECTURE

There is ample evidence of Hitler's fetish for architecture and urban design. He spent large portions of his early life designing and building models for the transformation of Linz and Vienna. Twice rejected for architecture school in his youth, he reportedly told his flatmate: 'I'll show those incompetent senile fools that I can go ahead without them' (quoted in Hochman 1989: 183).[2] During the 1930s, while Chancellor, he spent up to a day per week on architectural matters and even during the war he leafed through architecture books before going to bed. Hitler developed coherent theories of architecture and urban form which he saw as an expression of the spiritual and psychological condition of the people. This was more than the representation of culture or *Zeitgeist* for him. Architecture stimulated community spirit, inspired patriotism and a faith in the future. But it also inspired a belief in leadership. Hitler understood that power is not a zero-sum game, but lay in the capacity to generate a sense of empowerment in his subjects. He believed in what he called 'community architecture' as a product of collective effort, to be used by and embody the spirit of the 'community' (Taylor 1974). Buildings and cities not only housed but also 'represented' this community/nation/race.

Hitler believed that insufficient money was spent on the public realm. He was inspired by and envied Paris in this regard. Disdaining the economic rationalism of the market, he believed that public buildings should be more imposing than those of private capital. He loved the monumental neo-classical for its 'timeless' values of imperial power. It was a plank of Nazi propaganda that Greeks and Aryans were racially linked but Hitler was also much influenced by Roman history. He wanted buildings that would outlast the Reich, believing that architecture had inspirational inertia which could carry a national spirit through periods of decline, and retain its meaning in decay. This was what Albert Speer termed the 'theory of ruin value' whereby the inspirational power of architecture transcended any utilitarian or instrumental purpose.

Speer built his reputation designing stage sets and choreography for Nazi rallies, initially in Berlin and later in Nuremberg. These culminated in the rally grounds with up to a quarter of a million people in the Zeppelin Field stadium, built in 1936 (Blomeyer 1979; Taylor 1974). The design, modelled on the Greek Pergamon altar, was in the form of a 400 metre square of open space, framed by neo-classical stands on all sides. The main stand to the north had a central rostrum for the Führer and was backed by a massive colonnade. This is where the famed 'cathedral of light' effects were achieved with anti-aircraft searchlights shining columns of light 15 kilometres into the sky to create an ethereal glow. These night rallies showed that the monumental Nazi architecture was based on more than classical nostalgia. While Hitler was not impressed by the forms of gothic architecture, he admired the mysterious light, the sense of awe and vertical aspiration evoked in the cathedral interiors (Taylor 1974). The 'cathedral of light' effect was an eclectic fusion of the most potent elements of both the classical and the gothic.

The rallies exemplified Hitler's notion of community architecture. 'Why always the colossal?' he once asked rhetorically; 'Because I want to build self-awareness into every German' (quoted in Dal Co 1981: 105). The Zeppelin Field embodied a sense of enclosure and togetherness within. The rallies were bonding ceremonies between the Führer and the 'community'; they embodied the paradox of feeling stronger by submerging personal identity into a larger whole (Adorno 1991). At the rallies and marches the blood red banners with their orderly but dynamic swastikas established a congruence with the orderly and disciplined, but emotionally charged and dynamic, troops. The flat floor of the arena was a signifier of order in space, 16 hectares of disciplined helmets and weapons. The rallies were multi-dimensional spectacles where 'People, buildings, flags, insignia, acoustics and light were essential elements of the whole' (Blomeyer 1979: 59). As aestheticized displays of disciplined power in space, these rallies have no equal.

The swastika was a particularly astute choice as a Nazi icon. This archaic symbol has its roots in Jain, Buddhist, Hindu and Native American traditions, among others. Jung suggests that such mandala symbols are pervasive cultural symbols which construct images of social and religious unity; they have a therapeutic role for people in chaotic psychic states (Jung 1972: 36, 96). The swastika is a particularly potent mandala which embodies both the stability of the square and the dynamic wheeling movement of the circle. Adapted to the Nazi context it evoked the historic German cross but gave it a new 'turn'. Poised on the diagonal, black on white against a blood-red ground, this was a logo that was congruent with a state on the move and with the human choreography of jackboots on stone in monumental space.

BLOOD AND SOIL

Despite the focus on the public realm, Nazi ideology was profoundly anti-urban. Urban life was portrayed as rootless and racially mixed, whereas the true Aryan blood was to be found in the purified rural community; the regional *völkische* ideal was one of deep connection to the German soil – a conflation of the authenticities of 'soil' and 'soul'. Art and architecture were seen as stemming from these deep roots in place attachment, a chthonic 'spirit of place'. The blood and soil ideology has its roots in German literary and landscape painting traditions and it resonates with Heidegger's ontology of dwelling which identifies 'building' with 'Being' (Heidegger 1971).[3] The significance of the blood and soil component of Nazi ideology was precisely that it managed to appropriate such architecture and gear it to the politics of nationalism. The 'other' to these 'authentic' modes of dwelling was the rootless urban dweller and particularly the urban Jew. Without an authentic architecture one did not really dwell nor belong.

Hitler's rural retreat at Obersalzberg in the Bavarian Alps was a cottage in vernacular style, enlarged according to his own design. A 650 hectare fenced enclave for the party elite was established around it with many buildings added during the 1930s, including a mountaintop 'eagle's nest'. The entry to this eyrie was literally through the mountain, via a large stone archway, a tunnel and then an elevator 150 metres to the top (Speer 1970: 85; Taylor 1974). Here one literally entered the German 'soil' in order to metaphorically become the Germanic eagle with a commanding view of the landscape. The Bavarian retreat helped to construct the myth of the romantic Hitler. In 1938 Britain's Prime Minister Neville Chamberlain was charmed into appeasement at Obersalzberg.

SLIPPERY SURFACES

In 1938 Hitler commissioned Speer to design and construct a new Chancellery in Berlin. This building was a tour de force in terms of both design and Speer's capacities in organizing the design and construction of the building within a year. Speer designed a 400 metre long building, entered at its end from next door to the old Chancellery in Wilhelmstrasse. The plan (Figure 5.2) was organized along a 'diplomatic promenade' from the old to the new, along a carefully orchestrated narrative enfilade that led for 230 metres to Hitler's study (Goodsell 1988: 4). The Palace at Versailles (Figure 2.2) was a primary source for the planning, with a similar enfilade leading from the Royal Court to the Hall of Mirrors before turning and terminating in the King's bedroom. The diplomatic promenade of Speer's Chancellery began adjacent to the old Chancellery with two giant bronze drive-through doors into a Court of Honour (60 by 28 metres), designed for a processional loop in one door and out the other. The dimensions are important here because Hitler memorized and boasted of them (Speer 1970: 114–115). The processional path led up some steps to a Doric portal flanked by nude male statues representing the party (legitimacy) and the army (force). This portico led to a marble walled antechamber decorated with flowers. Beyond the antechamber a vestibule led to the Roman inspired Hall of Mosaics. This was a large (37 by 20 metres) windowless but skylit hall, decorated with German symbols of eagles and oak leaves in the marble walls and floor. Beyond the hall some more steps and a vestibule led to a rotunda, skylit from above. Figures of the German cross and swastika were woven together in the floor mosaic. The rotunda was an entry space to the huge Hall of Marble which, at 146 by 12 metres, was designed to dwarf the Hall of Mirrors at Versailles.

While the hall was terminated at its far end by a formal reception hall, a second axis bisected the gallery. Here the diplomatic promenade turned to enter Hitler's office, framed by motionless guards. This room of 27 by 14 metres overlooked the gardens. It was furnished with a desk in one corner, a circle of easy chairs around the fireplace and a map table. The room was decorated with tapestries, paintings, floor rugs, plants and a globe of the world.

This building needs to be understood as a form of symbolic choreography where the spatial structure operates to control the framing of a series of representational themes. Germany as a one-party state was signified in almost every space through the image of the eagle above the swastika, and naturalized through the oak and eagle icons. The narrative pathway constructed a myth of the progression of history through links to Greece, Rome and Paris, punctuated by a mounting of steps. The use of materials such as bronze, stone and marble evoked a sense of timeless immortality.

The building also served to signify the controlled force of the nation state. The scale of both the vast and useless voids and the formal designs that enclosed them were designed to belittle the human subject. The building signified the force necessary to produce it, as the motionless armed guards signified the discipline and order to which this force was subject. The intimidating effects of the gigantic chambers were enhanced by being punctuated with smaller spaces such as the antechamber and the rotunda. These smaller spaces were decorated with flowers, the sublime tempered by the beautiful. This produced an intimidation/seduction dialectic akin to the hard cop/soft cop routine of police interrogation. The subject is intimidated by the implied force, yet seduced into admiration; one is either empowered by acceptance into the Reich or crushed by its force.

Figure 5.2
Berlin Chancellery and bunker.

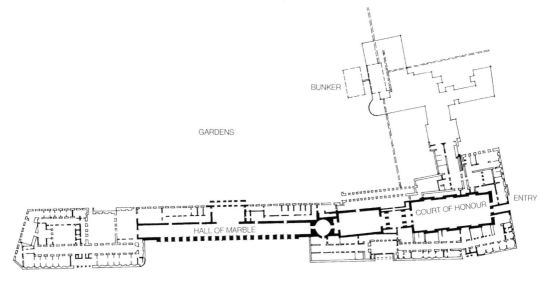

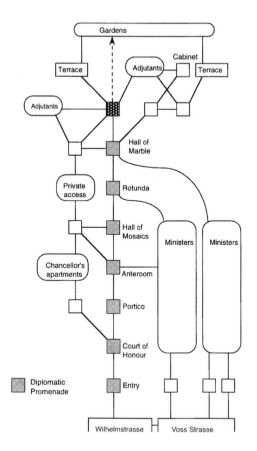

Figure 5.3
Berlin Chancellery:
spatial analysis.

The spatial analysis (Figure 5.3) shows that the long approach to Hitler's office was a ten segmented enfilade (including vestibules). The deepest realm of the building incorporated the formal Reception Hall, the Cabinet Room and some assistants' offices. Yet all formal access to the inner realm was through the controlling segment of the Hall of Marble. Ministers, heads of state, officials and visiting dignitaries were all subject to its intimidating volume. Beyond the Hall of Marble, the inner realm was ringy in structure, and softened with garden views.

Speer's enfilade delighted Hitler, who especially liked the long march diplomats would have to take: 'they'll get a taste of the power and grandeur of the German Reich!' (Speer 1970: 103). He ordered the marble floor left exposed since 'diplomats should have practice in moving on a slippery surface' (quoted in Speer 1970: 113) (Figure 5.4). There is little evidence of how the Chancellery worked in practice since diplomacy was displaced by the war that quickly followed its completion.[4] However, it was the setting for Hitler's triumphant intimidation of the ageing President Hacha of Czechoslovakia in early 1939. With German troops already occupying part of his country and poised to invade the rest, Hacha was formally received late at night by an SS guard in the Court of Honour and escorted along the enfilade to Hitler's office. He was assured of Hitler's determination to maintain peace and urged to sign a document agreeing

Figure 5.4
Hall of Marble: slippery
surfaces for diplomats.

to full German occupation. In an adjacent room he was threatened by aides with the alternative of turning Prague into ruins. Hacha suffered a heart attack, was revived with an injection, and signed the document (Jarman 1956: 245; Speer 1970: 115–116).

GERMANIA

The constructed Chancellery was but a provisional building, a prelude to the larger transformation of central Berlin, which was to be renamed 'Germania' and developed largely in secret by Speer from 1936 to 1942.[5] Speer's planning office was set up as an independent 'research' institute, isolated from the Berlin city government. The plan, which entailed removal of parks and huge sections of the urban fabric, was inconsistent with public planning (Helmer 1985). The old east–west Berlin–Paris axis was to become subsidiary to a new north–south axis signifying the 'turn' of history. Hitler visited Paris with Speer in June 1940 and is quoted as saying: 'In the past I often considered whether we would not have to destroy Paris. But when we are finished in Berlin, Paris will only be a shadow' (quoted in Speer 1970: 172). The Berlin scheme was conceived in global competition with historic centres of power. It was to be capped with a domed hall or *Volkhalle*, which was to dwarf both St Peter's basilica and the US Capitol. The ceremonial way was to be wider and longer than the Champs Elysées with an arch higher than the Arc de Triomphe. The new axis was to be aligned with the historic Platz der Republik in front of the Reichstag and was to extend for 5 kilometres to the south. The ceremonial entries to the city were to be a new railway station at the southern end of this axis, and the nearby Templehof airfield, which was connected via a diagonal axis. The two major architectural pieces of the plan had been sketched by Hitler in prison in 1925 – the triumphal arch and the domed hall. Both were to be visible on exiting the railway station where, in Speer's words (1970: 134–135), visitors 'would be overwhelmed, or rather stunned, by the urban scene and thus the power of the Reich' (Figure 5.5).

Figure 5.5
Proposed north–south axis: 'things to take your breath away'.

In front of the station was to be a 330 metre wide avenue lined with captured cannons and enclosed by hotels, opera and municipal buildings. This section extended for over a kilometre and encompassed the triumphal arch, a copy of Hitler's clumsy design from 1925, which was to be 115 metres high with a plaza on top about the size of a football field. The huge Roman inspired arch was to frame a much smaller gateway of a similar scale and design to the Greek inspired Brandenburg Gate. This designed juxtaposition can be read as both Rome surmounting Greece and the new Reich surmounting the old. The path underneath was to be the path of history and the arch was but the beginning. The central segment of the vista was to be lined with ministries, cultural institutions and industrial corporations. Adjacent to the existing Potsdammer Platz, the busiest intersection in Europe at that time, a grand roundabout was planned. Beyond this, the path penetrated the Tiergarten parkland before entering the forecourt to the *Volkhalle*. The principle of spatial manipulation here was like that of the Chancellery/Versailles but incorporating ideas that were developed later in the suburban shopping mall. It established a magnet and an extended path of approach to be used for symbolic display. The subject was to be led past displays of German products, military force, culture, nature, history and industrial technology on the way from the entry to the centre of power. This is the spatial principle of the chancellery writ large.

Capping the 5 kilometre axis, the *Volkhalle* was to be a giant domed hall for 180,000 people modelled on the Roman Pantheon. The idea and initial sketch were Hitler's but the design was Speer's and under his hand it was influenced by Boullée's 1792 project for a National Assembly Hall in Paris, the great rationalist symbol of emancipation. The dome was to be surmounted by a bronze eagle spreading its wings with its claws enclosing a globe of the earth. The Platz der Republic was to become a grand forecourt enclosed by the domed hall, new Chancellery, Führer's Palace and the existing Reichstag (Figure 5.1). Speer wanted to demolish the old and fire-damaged Reichstag, but Hitler, alert to the powers of juxtaposition, insisted that it be retained and dwarfed under the wing of the new scheme (Figure 5.6). In order to achieve the setback of this hall from the plaza, the Spree River was to be diverted underneath its entry court. The Platz der Republik was to be a paved square of about 20 hectares fully enclosed by buildings. Variously named both the 'Square of the People' and 'King's Plaza', it was to be defended against insurrection with large steel gates. The Führer's Palace was to face the plaza with a 240 metre long façade penetrated only by a single arched gateway surmounted by a balcony where the Führer could address over half a million people in safety. This proposed plaza was to be the culmination of the rally ground designs.

The south-western wing of the palace complex was to become the new Chancellery. Buoyed by his success with the provisional Chancellery, Speer simply enlarged the design for this project – the diplomatic promenade was to be extended to half a kilometer, the Court of Honour to 180 metres and the Hall of Marble to 216 metres. These giant segments were interspersed with smaller halls

Figure 5.6
Proposed hall from
Brandenberg Gate:
belittling the past.

and vestibules generating a similar spatial dialectic. Once again Hitler's office was on a cross-axis, overlooking the palace gardens and scaled up to about 900 square metres.

BUNKER AND WALL

Hitler's use of architecture changed as the war progressed and his needs changed from visibility, legitimation, seduction and intimidation to protection.[6] The Chancellery was camouflaged against Allied bombers and from early 1945 Hitler retreated to a newly constructed bunker under the Chancellery gardens (Figure 5.2). This was, both literally and syntactically, the deepest in a connected series of bunkers that housed hundreds of guards and officials, plus medical facilities, canteens and garages (O'Donnell 1979). Access to Hitler was subject to three layers of guards. His personal apartment formed a string of cells with a private exit stair to the Chancellery gardens and a concrete lookout tower which offered a protected view. Thus the bunker with its linear string of rooms coupled with the private rear exit and garden view was a structurally congruent but shrunken version of the Chancellery above. Marble was replaced by concrete and the study was one-thirtieth in size. Hitler's retreat underground was also a retreat into unreality, as he pored over his beloved urban designs while blocking out the destruction of the real Berlin above. Jung has interpreted Hitler's final days as a retreat into the 'cellar' as metaphor of the unconscious (O'Donnell 1979: xi) – a final and literal retreat to 'blood and soil'.

Soon after the war, the marble from the bombed Chancellery was used to construct the Soviet Memorial at Treptow Park. The site of the Chancellery was transformed with housing, a children's playground and the nearby Berlin Wall from 1961. By a coincidence of bureaucracy and imagination, the official boundary between East and West Berlin ran through the centre of where the *Volkhalle* would have been, had history taken a different turn (Figure 5.1). As a practice of power the wall was archaic, a return to the walled city of force rather than seduction and intimidation. Technically it was modern, developing from barbed wire and brick beginnings to prefabricated concrete sections slotted together and locked with a tubular section on top. The floodlit 'death-strip' on the east was under permanent panoptic gaze from concrete towers. Never designed in representational terms, the wall developed a semantic life of its own in the 1980s, gathering an extraordinary collection of graffiti on its western surface as an endless public billboard. This graffiti was whitewashed at times by both the eastern and western authorities. The wall ran along the old city limits directly past the Brandenburg Gate and the image of the gate sealed by the graffiti covered wall became a potent symbol of the Cold War. This dialectic image – a gate without a wall sealed by a wall without a gate – was one that Walter Benjamin would have appreciated.

Ladd (1997) suggests that the wall was a division in time as much as in space, embodying a denial of history on both sides. Maps in East Berlin erased West Berlin and its street patterns, a denial of any place beyond the wall. It was not called a 'wall' but an 'anti-fascist protective rampart' or simply the 'border'. Yet in western maps the wall appeared as the minor municipal boundary it once was, a denial of the wall (Ladd 1997. 18, 28). The collapse of the wall in 1989 was due in part to its failure to stop the flow of information – the gaze of television defeated that of the watchtower (Wark 1994). The prefabricated wall has now been fragmented and commodified, a metaphor for the shift from the modern to the postmodern. Graffiti coloured chips, with newly inverted meanings, adorn window sills and mantels across the globe, although only the graffiti covered western surface has exchange value. A cottage industry produces graffitied chips of concrete with certificates of authenticity (in English). Larger stretches of wall have been marketed as a way to 'decorate the entrance hall of your corporate headquarters' (Ladd 1997: 10).

Similar ironies and transformations of meaning have also played out through the 'Goddess of Peace' statue surmounting the gate, which was destroyed in the war. Anticipating this the Nazis had made a cast, yet with the division of the city in 1945 the cast was in the west and the gate was in the east. A rare example of cooperation in the 1950s saw the west supply a new copy of the statue. Insisting that it should be a symbol of peace, the eastern authorities severed the German cross and eagle before they mounted it. This severing then

1961 1962 1963 1964 1965 1966 1967 1968

21 46 29 16 14 17 5 9

Figure 5.7
Berlin Wall memorial
1991.

became symbolic of the East German state and after another debate they were restored in 1991 (Ladd 1997: 74–80). Such struggles over meanings have since been played out along the length of the former wall and its blood-stained death-strip; struggles between memory and forgetting, between profit and the public interest (Balfour 1990; Ladd 1997). The great striation of the Berlin Wall became for a time the smoothest of spaces, a *terrain vague* colonized by gypsies, guest workers and artists. One of the more poignant memorials was the use of wall segments to mark the numbers who died trying to cross it (Figure 5.7). The void at Potzdamer Plaz temporarily housed a café enclosed by wall sections from which patrons could chisel fragments for a fee. This site has since become one of the largest urban redevelopments in Europe, re-territorialized by a series of corporate towers (Sony, Daimler-Chrysler) with their signature architects (Piano, Kolhoff, Jahn). The nearby bunker has proven almost impossible to demolish with its 2 metre thick concrete walls, and even more difficult to erase from memory. It has a growing virtual presence as the subject of films, books and websites while the real place lies unmarked and unopened – the collapse of one practice of power in space is always the beginning of another.

STYLES OF TYRANNY

Despite the massive transformations in Berlin since the war, Nazi architecture lives in the imagination and debate has not resolved its lessons. It remains diffi-cult to discuss because we are still dealing with the aftermath of the regime and its forms of representation remain stained – the swastika remains unusable outside neo-Nazi politics. In architectural discourse, debate has raged over Hitler's allegiance to the neo-classical and vernacular. And his disdain for the modern has been used to boost the idea that modernism is an architecture of liberation. Leon Krier has been the most articulate defender of Speer's work. He suggests that architecture is autonomous from politics, that one cannot blame the power of architecture for its misuse by a tyrant.

> There is neither authoritarian nor democratic architecture, no more than there are authoritarian or democratic Wienerschnitzel. It is just as childish to read a particular color or the immanence of a political system into a row of Doric columns as it is to accept kidney shaped tables and tensile structures as the authentic expression of a libertarian and democratic regime. Architecture is not political; it is only an instrument of politics.
>
> (Krier 1981: 37)

In this view, Nazi architecture was a form of deceit, a civilizing façade for the legitimation of terror: 'Classical Architecture was . . . the civilized and well mannered face of an empire of lies' (Krier 1985a: 223). For Krier, Hitler was just a tyrant with taste, and he turns this preference for the neoclassical into an argument for its status as the highest form of architecture.

In countering Krier, Ockman (1981: 39) has argued that there is a 'well established linkage between . . . the tradition of classicism and a calculating and cold instrumentality . . . It is precisely this inherent aspect of order in classicism which renders it so potent as a political instrument'. The classical is an architecture of regularity, symmetry, hierarchy and a harmony of parts to whole. It is easy to read such architecture as a metaphor for similar qualities in the political order. The classical language legitimizes authority. But authority is not the same thing as tyranny, and order cannot be simply conflated with any single style. Coaldrake (1995) shows how the same characteristics of regularity, symmetry, harmony and hierarchy are used without the western classical traditions to legitimize authority in Japanese architecture. Those who seek to problematize certain styles of architecture because of their complicity with power may simply be engaging in a new round of such complicity. It is necessary to accept some of the logic of Krier's defence while rejecting the claims of autonomy. While we cannot recognize tyranny from the form of its cultural clothes, the production of built form is strongly complicit in such practices.

The claim for the autonomy of architecture rests upon a separation of form from instrumental function. And it also rests implicitly upon a broader Kantian aesthetic of universal judgement. Kant's transcendental aesthetic is an a priori judgement which is at once both universal and subjective. The uselessness of art coupled with the subject's disinterest in its function are the conditions for aesthetic judgement (Kant 1979). Yet it is precisely this sense of timeless and permanent aesthetic value, the presumed autonomy of architecture, which makes it so useful to the practices of power. For Eagleton such an aesthetic is a paradigm case of ideology, an 'experience of pure contentless consensus' (Eagleton 1990: 96) which resonates with Bourdieu's 'complicitous silence' and with Hitler's well-known quote about the instrumental power of buildings: 'Their word is more convincing than a spoken one: it is the Word in stone' (quoted in Taylor 1974: 30). The greatest instrumental effects of architecture lie in this silence, the power to convince without debate.

The claims for architectural autonomy are by no means limited to particular styles. The assertions which issue from Speer and Krier echo those from Mies van der Rohe who was a key agent in asserting the autonomy of modernism. In Berlin in the early 1930s Mies depoliticized the Bauhaus school in his zeal to make modernism palatable to the Nazis (Hochman 1989: 222). He publicly declared support for Hitler and of one of his designs he wrote: 'This clear and striking language corresponds to the essence of German work . . . This hall of honor . . . serves to accommodate the national emblems and the representations of the Reich' (Hochman 1989: 226). Mies's work had a strong sense of order, well suited to colossal scale, and scarcely bereft of roots in the history of empire. Hughes was writing about Speer, but it could have been Mies, when he argued: 'Authoritarian architecture must be clear and regular on the outside, and let the passing eye deduce nothing of what goes on inside. It must be poker faced to the point of immobility; the mask must not slip' (Hughes 1991: 105). Mies was a more skilled designer than Speer but lacked political loyalty and had a well-known disdain for clients. He left Berlin in 1937, having built very little, his reputation luckily unstained by Nazism.

Modern architecture did not suit Hitler's theory of 'ruin value'; steel and glass lacked the sense of timelessness. But his disdain for the modern is no argument for its autonomy from tyranny; indeed, his dismissal of it as suitable only for 'functional' factories was based on an inability to see the potential. 'Futurism' was the chosen style of Italian fascism, expressing the dynamic and youthful image of a new order (Etlin 1991). While traditional styles can be enlisted in support of power, it does not follow that formal novelty has any necessary link to liberation, nor that tradition cannot be used against authority. During the Free Speech movement in Berkeley in the 1960s the neo-classical façade of the administration building (Sproul Hall) was mobilized as a setting for demonstrations. It was depicted in murals with the columns as canons trained on demonstrators. All architecture represents some social order and style is its language of expression. All styles mediate practices of power. The attribution of tyrannical power to a particular formal style is a dangerous practice since it lures architects into the false hope of a stylistic escape from complicity and a blindness to new styles of seduction.

Having said this, there are some important ways in which contemporary styles are at an ideological disadvantage in practices of power. Most importantly they lack semiotic connections to the history of empire. As Hughes (1991: 102) puts it, the neo-classical works metaphorically as 'the past underwriting the present'; it is difficult for the new to establish a linkage with the history of empire. Yet the capacity to construct historical narratives through stylistic revival is not limited to the neo-classical, hence the use of the vernacular to sustain the Aryan myth. The 'cathedral of light' at Nuremburg tapped a traditional idea of 'gothic' community spirit; and here the effects were created with modern technology rather than formal style.

Another major disadvantage of contemporary styles is that they cannot easily play upon the fear of change. Propaganda is most effective when it reinforces and twists prevailing values and ideologies, rather than displacing and replacing them (Thies 1983). Revival styles can play upon the fear of change. But once again the corollary does not hold – the refusal to play on such fear does not constitute a liberation from it. Contemporary forms can equally play upon the desire for liberty and progress, and illusions of liberty and progress are easily appropriated to political ends. Hitler's disdain for the modern was a gap in his understanding of its potential.

It was not the fact of Nazi use of tradition but the manner and scale of such use that set it apart. The historic urban axis was to be turned into a minor axis as a signifier of the turn of history. The Brandenburg Gate, the Reichstag and the old Chancellery were to be belittled in the same manner. Hitler's fetish to 'outdo' earlier regimes, whether in Berlin, Paris, Washington or Rome, marks this as a global discourse that enables a utilization of history in more than style. Existing symbols of power are stripped of symbolic capital and converted into 'has beens' through the productions of ever larger buildings and urban spaces (Canetti 1979).

These were not matters of style but of scale and urban form. Hitler understood the power of the dialectical image in the construction of narrative. The aesthetic lure of the major Nazi projects had more to do with scale than with style – the sublime rather than the beautiful. While beauty is a pleasure into which we enter willingly, the sublime is 'aestheticized danger'. This is the awefull pleasure of submission to that which overwhelms us – a mix of reverence, fear and an almost phallic pleasure inspired by grandeur (Eagleton 1990). The sublime is an aesthetic of quantity – it is that which makes everything else seem small, as when confronted with the immensity of nature (Kant 1979).

Krier (1985a: 49) recognizes that more than design skill was evident in the Berlin scheme: 'The very immoderate size of the buildings and monuments would have given this avenue an air of grandiose intimacy which can be found in nature'. The monumental architecture was designed, as Hitler affirmed, 'to take your breath away'. The experience of the sublime forms a thread connecting the mountain eyrie to the Chancellery, and the gothic-inspired 'cathedrals of light' to the neo-classical Hall of the People. The theory of ruins and the use of stone was a means to sustain this immensity across time.

Hitler was highly attuned to crowds and how to work them. In his well-known book *Crowds and Power*, Canetti (1962) distinguishes between the 'open crowd' that grows by absorbing allcomers and the 'closed crowd' with limits to access, boundaries and containment. While the open crowd can fall apart or out of control at any moment, the closed crowd has staying power and can be repeated. Canetti argues that Hitler's urban schemes show a sophisticated understanding of how to frame and to hold a crowd: 'Hitler's constructions are meant to attract and to hold the greatest crowds. The creation of such crowds is what brought him to power, but he knows how easily such crowds tend to fall apart' (Canetti 1979: 146). The proposed boulevard is for open crowds with direction and movement through the triumphal arch towards the closed crowds of the forecourt and Volkshalle. The Berlin urban design scheme was in part an assemblage for the production and reproduction of crowds. For Canetti, Hitler's architecture is a production of 'crowd containers'; not so much a crowd that cannot escape as 'a crowd that cannot crumble' (Canetti 1979: 148).

Interpretations of the Nazi use of architecture need to also go beyond style and spatial practices. Jaskot (2000) has shown how the illusion of aesthetic auto-nomy operated to mask a deep complicity that integrated the architecture with the violence of SS control in forced labour camps. Through Speer, Hitler main-tained an aesthetic veto over all major building designs; he had the materials changed to stone from steel and glass for several buildings in the mid to late-1930s (Jaskot 2000: 91). These projects were given top priority, the stone indus-try was reorganized and new quarries were opened up. Speer's office (GBI) became interdependent with the SS as new concentration camps were set up to work the quarries and raise production to almost impossible levels. The punishing and violent conditions under which forced laborers suffered and died were seen as necessary to the supply of stone (Jaskot 2000: 141).

Speer's career was based in much more than design skill, particularly his personal rapport with Hitler and a technical and managerial capacity to organize production (Sereny 1995). The Chancellery was completed at an extraordinary speed and his 1942 promotion to Armaments Minister – from architecture to weaponry, stone to steel – was based on management skill. According to Sereny (1995: 551), Speer was torn by an inner conviction that he was not the great architect that Hitler believed him to be. One of the lessons of this era is the degree to which production and destruction of architecture and cities were dif-ferent outcomes of the same assemblage (Canetti 1979). Speer's defence at the Nuremburg trials was based on a limited admission of responsibility with a clear line between his architectural and armaments work: 'I, as an important member of the leadership of the Reich, therefore share in the total responsibility, begin-ning with 1942' (quoted in Jaskot 2000: 143). He suggests that before 1942 his work was merely aesthetic, with no involvement in planning or conducting the war. These assumptions about the aesthetic autonomy of architecture were accepted by the Nuremburg judges and played a key role in his defence (Jaskot 2000); in a twist on the typical 'Nuremburg defence' he wasn't following orders because he was an autonomous artist.

There were many strands to the Nazi uses of architecture – gigantism, timelessness, history and authenticity – deploying neo-classical, gothic and ver-nacular styles. These were often coupled with ritual displays of force, discipline and community; using the spatial structure of the enfilade as a temporal and spatial narrative. And while projects were undertaken in the name of the 'people', the design/construct process was often secret and geared into oppressive modes of production. The lesson in the Nazi use of architecture and urban design is that such practices are multi-dimensional and promiscuous with regard to style. All dimensions of built form are available to appropriation in the service of tyranny. If there was a thread connecting the various Nazi uses of architecture and urbanism, it was a capacity to produce places of closure with deep roots in space and time where there is but one way to be and one way forward. An inside of community, uniformity, empowerment, enlightenment, tradition and pride was inscribed against an outside of weakness and difference. The tyranny is not found in style but in the closures of placemaking.

Chapter 6: Hidden Power

Beijing

> The Way of the ruler lies in what cannot be seen . . . See but do not appear to see.
>
> Han Fei Tzu (quoted in Wu 1991: 88)

For much of Chinese imperial history the emperor ruled from within the nested walls of the Forbidden City in Beijing. Named 'forbidden' after its strict exclusion of the Chinese people, this was one of the most enclosed and segmented centres of power in urban history. The revolution of 1948 brought the construction of Tiananmen Square outside its entrance. Conceived as the antithesis of forbidden space, the square was a representation of the 'people', designed to contain over a million of them on its vast unwalled expanse. From April to June 1989 several thousand students camped out on Tiananmen Square, periodically joined by up to a million supporters. Under the gaze of global television the largest urban plaza in the world also became the most visible, the least hidden. So symbolically charged has this place become that the presence of the people in the people's plaza undermined the legitimacy of an empire.

The relations of place to power in this context are steeped in Confucian and Taoist philosophy which operates within Chinese civil and political culture as a form of ideology. From this view, for power to be effective it should remain hidden, as the canonical texts make clear: 'The best of all rulers is but a shadowy presence to his subjects,' says Lao Tzu (1963: 73); 'The instruments of power in a state must not be revealed to anyone' (Lao Tzu 1963: 95). The art of warfare is the art of deception, of feigning submission and disorder to entice the enemy out of hiding. This is an art of turning the enemy's anger and strength against them and one's weakness to advantage. Taoism is a philosophy of opposites subject to persistent inversion, where 'The most submissive thing in the world can ride roughshod over the hardest in the world – that which is without substance entering that which has no crevices' (Lao Tzu 1963: 104). This embodies a deep commitment to paradox, the effective action is non-action, the effective word is unspoken. The use of violence against subjects is the mark of a poor ruler; the successful leader rules without contention: 'it is because (the ruler) does not contend that no one in the empire is in a position to contend with him' (Lao Tzu 1963: 128).

The philosophy of concealment is reflected spatially in the symbolic importance of the wall and the gate that penetrates it. And it is reflected in the enclosed places from the traditional Chinese walled courtyard house to the walled city (Kahn-Ackermann 1980). Walls reflect the Chinese passion for clarity of human relationships and of status. Walls divide the civilized from the barbaric (as the Great Wall did), sacred from profane, safety from danger. In this, Chinese culture reflects a broad cross-cultural attention to the dialectic of inside/outside and the rituals of entrance (Douglas 1966). The gate or threshold finds its meaning in the conjunction of opposing realms.

FORBIDDEN SPACE

Imperial Beijing was a city defined by its walls and gates, structured as four successively nested walled cities – the Outer, Inner, Imperial and Forbidden Cities respectively.[1] The ceremonial approach to power was from the south to the north along an imperial axis which successively penetrated the city walls through a series of ceremonial gates. The gates to the Inner and Imperial cities frame the space that is now Tiananmen Square (Figure 6.1). The Gate of Heavenly Peace (Tiananmen) was the entrance to the Imperial City. It is in the form of a monolithic platform (part of the former city wall) perforated by five tunnelled entries at ground level and surmounted by a hall. While the emperor passed through the central tunnel in procession, he seldom appeared on this gate, which was used for passing down imperial edicts to the ministers and officials whose offices lined the intersection outside. About 400 metres and two segments beyond Tiananmen is the Meridian Gate, where the imperial axis enters the Forbidden City.

The Forbidden City is a rectangular compound of about 950 by 750 metres, enclosing about 72 hectares within its 8 metre high walls and 50 metre wide moat. The city is strictly oriented to the cardinal directions with a gate at each point. It is a Celestial City, an ideogrammatic connection of heaven to earth. The emperor's rule was legitimized by his role as a link between heaven and earth; the relation of the people to the emperor was congruent with that of the emperor to the deity. One approached the emperor as one approached a deity, from the south moving upwards. And the path to power crossed multiple thresholds – gates, steps and bridges – into the hidden depths of the city.

The main southern gate, the Meridian Gate, formed a U-shaped entry court across the broad moat, surmounted by a hall. The emperor would sometimes appear on this gate to accept captives after a successful war. The gate is penetrated by another five tunnels to a courtyard where five bridges cross the Inner Golden River. Beyond this courtyard is the Gate of Supreme Harmony, which is

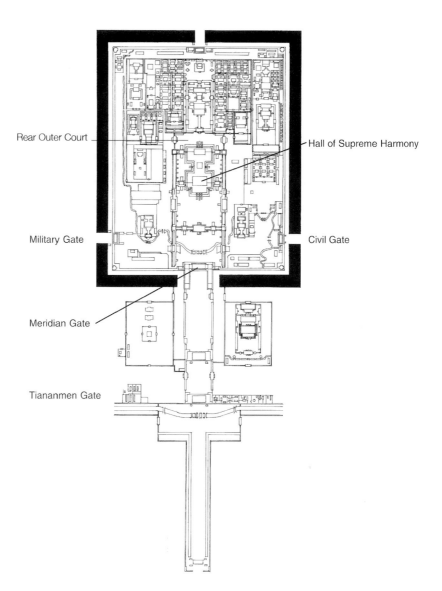

Rear Outer Court

Hall of Supreme Harmony

Military Gate

Civil Gate

Meridian Gate

Tiananmen Gate

Figure 6.1
Ceremonial axis and
Forbidden City, Beijing
(Qing Period).

the main entrance to the Outer Court, the primary ceremonial precinct of the Forbidden City.

The Gate of Supreme Harmony gives access to the primary ceremonial site and the termination of the ceremonial axis. It consists of an ensemble of gate and hall (sharing the same name) together with the (unnamed) courtyard they enclose. This ensemble is structurally congruent with the Chinese courtyard house but at a much larger scale. The courtyard of about 200 metres square is the forecourt to the Hall of Supreme Harmony, which is set upon a raised terrace and which houses the throne. To reach the hall one mounts several flights of steps to a large terrace, then up again to the hall, and up again to the throne on a 2 metre platform. The ensemble of throne/hall/terrace/court/gate was the primary site where the emperor's presence was made visible on ceremonial occasions. At about 4 hectares, this courtyard could hold very large numbers of people, for strictly choreographed rituals. The pavement was marked out with rank markers. On the east were the ministers and civil officials, ranked above the military officers to the west. Each of these groups was in turn ranked from north to south in diminishing status.

The ensemble was an ideogram of the world, of heaven and earth, reflecting the Chinese saying that 'heaven is high and the earth is broad'. The floor of the court represented the earth with the terraced hall in the heavens. Paintings of ceremonial occasions on this site often depicted the hall enshrouded in clouds, with the emperor hidden. This practice of hiding the emperor on occasions of highest visibility is evident in the spatial structure and ritual. The terrace is about 8 metres higher than the courtyard and the throne is about 50 metres back from the edge of the terrace. No one was permitted in the hall when the emperor was present and the 'kow tow' was a practice of averting one's eyes as he passed. The place of power was where one could see without being seen, a 'prospect' from on high coupled with multiple layers of 'refuge'.

The Outer Court as a whole is a 200 by 400 metre rectangular compound which encloses four courtyards and three major halls. The halls of Supreme Harmony, Complete Harmony and Preserving Harmony are all on axis and share the raised terrace (symbolic heaven) surrounded by lower courtyards. While the ceremonial ritual terminates at the throne, the flanking gates and courtyards give access to a rear courtyard beyond the Hall of Preserving Harmony. This hall was used for banquets and examinations and its rear courtyard was also used for ceremonial occasions. This court (which I shall call the 'rear outer court') also has a strong political significance since it was the only point of access to the everyday practices of power in the Inner Court of the Forbidden City.

The Inner Court was the inner sanctum of the emperor and empress, although not always used for living quarters. The spatial structure is essentially a half-scale replica of the Outer Court, a 100 by 200 metre enclosure, with another cluster of three buildings on axis. First among them is the Palace of Heavenly Purity, where the emperor received officials and emissaries; its square forecourt, with terrace and steps, replicates the ensemble at the Hall of Supreme Harmony at half scale. This palace forms a couple with the Palace of Earthly Tranquillity, symbolically the place of the empress with its bridal room. The small central building is called the Hall of Union, where sacred objects were stored. The three buildings together, also mounted on a single plinth, signify the union of heaven and earth, of male and female. Beyond the Palace of Earthly Tranquillity the axis continues through the Imperial Garden and the northern city gate to a small hill constructed from the excavated moat. Coupled with the river running through the outer courtyard, this establishes the geomantically propitious location of a dwelling with a hill to the north and water to the south.

Zhu (1994, 2005) has undertaken a spatial syntax analysis of the Forbidden City upon which Figure 6.2 is partially based. Such analysis identifies the

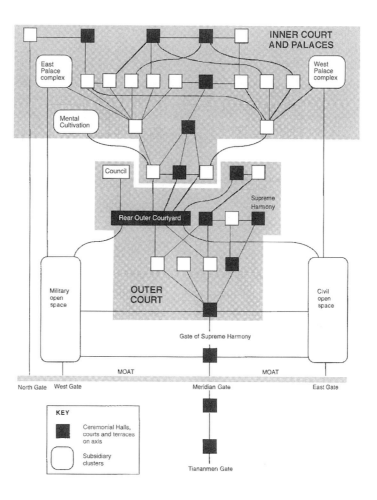

East
Palace
complex

West
Palace
complex

INNER COURT
AND PALACES

Mental
Cultivation

Council

Supreme
Harmony

Rear Outer Courtyard

Military
open
space

OUTER
COURT

Civil
open
space

Gate of Supreme Harmony

MOAT   MOAT

North Gate   West Gate   Meridian Gate   East Gate

KEY

Ceremonial Halls,
courts and terraces
on axis

Subsidiary
clusters

Tiananmen Gate

Figure 6.2
The Forbidden City:
spatial analysis (Qing
Period).

structure of the Forbidden City as four distinct spatial zones. The two major
zones are the ceremonial approach through the Outer Court and then the Inner
Court coupled with its flanking palaces. These two zones are augmented by the
south-western zone of military access near the west (military) gate and the
south-eastern zone of civil/ministerial access near the east (civil) gate. The city has
one key space of control linking all four zones – the 'rear outer court' behind the
Hall of Preserving Harmony.

Although ceremonies along the axis were important, they were also quite
rare. They were forms of legitimation of authority; the everyday exercise of
power followed quite different spatial circuits (Zhu 1994). The normal access to
the emperor for ministers and officials was an indirect path of about 3 kilometres
from their offices outside Tiananmen Gate. This approach skirted the eastern
edge of the Imperial City and entered the Forbidden City through the East (Civil)
Gate. From there they traversed a large, irregular open space of the civil zone
along the margins of the Outer Court to enter the rear outer courtyard in front
of the Gate of Heavenly Purity. This path to power was about twice as long as

the direct route up the axis and relatively unpunctuated with thresholds until it reaches the rear outer courtyard.

The Inner Court is flanked by clusters of six palaces on each side, housing a huge imperial household of concubines and eunuchs. Yet the lateral enclosing walls of the Inner Court are highly permeable, ensuring that the concubines and eunuchs were spatially integrated with the Inner Court (Zhu 1994). The patrol route which guarded and secured the inner sanctum encircled both the Inner Court and its adjacent palaces. Spatial control over this inner zone fell largely to the eunuchs. The eunuchs were the 'keepers of the bed', recruited because they were seen as neither a threat to, nor a subject of, the desires of the emperor. Regarded as basically *yin* (female) in nature, eunuchs could not bear a son to carry on wealth and power; they were therefore believed to be excluded from the struggle for power (Anderson 1990).[2]

Thus at its deepest realms the city was a relatively permeable spatial network for the circulation and interaction of the emperor, eunuchs and concubines. Yet the path into and out of this realm for ministers and officials was strongly controlled through the rear outer courtyard. So long as the eunuchs controlled this passage, they controlled imperial access. Zhu (1994) argues that this spatialization of power was linked to competing struggles for the emperor's body (by the concubines) and the emperor's mind (by the ministers and officials). The extraordinary power of the eunuchs was based on their role as mediators in these struggles – feeding the emperor's sexual appetite with concubines and his fears with stories of enemies beyond the walls. This power was reproduced across many dynasties through its embodiment in the spatial structure of the Forbidden City.

Zhu (1994) also theorizes that in addition to the everyday struggles for power between ministers and eunuchs, the city structure also served to mediate violent struggles, utilizing the enclosure of the walls and gates, enforced by the army who were otherwise confined to the military zone. The east–west opposition between the military and civil zones reflected these dual struggles for power – the violent and the legitimate. The power of the eunuchs, based in spatial control, was at the expense of both ministers and the emperor who became starved of information and advice. The Forbidden City became a refuge without prospect. The eunuchs are widely credited with the demise of the Ming dynasty when emperor Wan-Li lost control of the bureaucracy and retreated behind the inner walls for 25 years from 1595 to 1620 (Spence 1990: 16). The Forbidden City became a refuge without prospect. The celebration of the emperor's power through the architecture of the ceremonial axis had reinforced the power of the eunuchs – an illusion of control geared to a reality of isolation. Determined to gain closer control of his administration, Qing emperor Yong Zheng (1723–1735) renovated the Hall of Mental Cultivation as a new centre of power just beyond the north-west corner of the rear outer court. He set up a secret administrative council in the corner of the rear outer courtyard where his advisers were given direct access to him through the side gateway, bypassing the ceremonial axis

Figure 6.3
Rear outer courtyard
with Grand Council off
axis.

(Figure 6.3). This secret council became institutionalized as the Grand Council under the reign of his son Qianlong.

The Hall of Mental Cultivation has two wings in an H-shaped plan, with offices at the front and a bedchamber at the rear. The bedchamber is flanked by the Hall of Manifest Compliance (for the empress) and the Hall of Festive Joy (for the concubines). Here the struggle for the emperor's body and mind is evident in the plan and in the names of the halls. While the centre of power was moved off axis and informalized, a similar gendered spatial structure persisted.

When Tongzhi became emperor at the age of 5 in 1861, his mother, the empress dowager Cixi, ruled through him. She placed the child/emperor on a throne in front of a curtain. She received ministers and spoke through the emperor, from behind the curtain (Figure 6.4). The practice of power became quite literally hidden, even at its ostensible centre. The symbols of power in decline became mere propriety. Both Tongzhi and his pregnant wife died myste-riously when he was 18 years old. Cixi installed her 3-year-old nephew, Guangxu, as emperor, and continued to rule through the curtain. When Guangxu became a reformist in his twenties, he was placed under palace arrest for a decade. The meaning of the city inverted as the emperor was forbidden to leave. He died in 1908, followed within a day by Cixi, effectively ending imperial rule in China.

Despite its successive layerings and its spatial celebration as a centre of power, there was no ultimate place of power in the Forbidden City. Indeed this was part of its effectiveness, as Meyer (1991: 61) argues: 'Instead of overwhelm-ing the viewer with vertical monuments the Forbidden City hides in order to impress. One can never forget the power of the emptiness at the center because one is forever forbidden to see it.' Paradoxically, but consistent with the Chinese philosophies outlined earlier, in this empty centre of the empire power is both

Figure 6.4
Hall of Mental
Cultivation: screening
power.

marked and concealed. And the practices of power were subject to slippage, behind walls and curtains, off the imperial axis. These are traits that were to persist beyond the imperial era.

With the end of imperial power in 1911 the centre of power moved out of the Forbidden City and eventually moved in next door. Zhongnanhai, which means 'central and southern lakes', was a pleasure park for the emperor, developed outside the western walls of the Forbidden City from the tenth century (Figure 6.5). From the fourteenth century it was enclosed in the regal vermillion walls as an adjunct to the palace and a number of imperial halls and compounds were built within it. It was turned into a park for a short time after 1911 but was a government enclave by 1915 (Zhou 1984). After 1948 the compound became a residential and administrative enclave for party leaders. In the tradition of keeping power hidden, accurate maps of Zhongnanhai are difficult to find. Mao chose as his residence a traditional compound of several interconnected courtyards, built for the emperor in 1795 within what was then the walled park (Li 1994).[3] One entered this compound through a gate from the south into a courtyard called the Garden of Benevolence, the forecourt to the Hall of Longevity, which was used for banquets and receptions. Beyond this was another forecourt leading to Mao's library. His living quarters, called the Chrysanthemum Fragrance Study, were adjacent and to the east.

While the interior of the larger Zhongnanhai compound is unsegmented, Mao was very tightly guarded within it. His doctor (Li 1994) documents a climate of paranoia and mistrust within Mao's compound. Widely read in Chinese history, Mao identified with many former emperors and their traditional

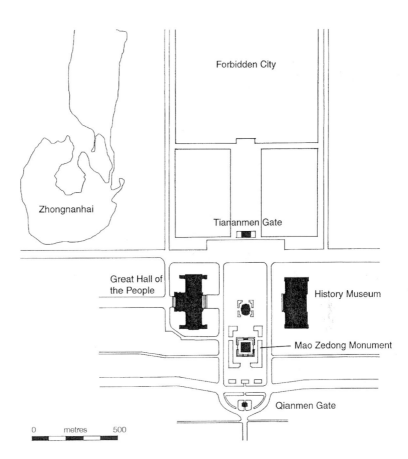

Figure 6.5
Central Beijing and
Tiananmen Square.

strategies of power, keeping his views hidden from colleagues. When under stress he retreated to his bed and feigned sickness, encouraging his enemies into the open. Isolated from senior colleagues and heavily dependent on guards, secretaries and attendants to keep him informed, he was told largely what he wanted to hear. Guards and secretaries also filled the roles of the former eunuchs, ensuring a good supply of young peasant women as modern concubines (Li 1994). His promiscuous sex life, which violated the Party line, required high levels of secrecy and spatial control over access, which in turn gave further power to his guards and minders.

In 1966, at the height of the cultural revolution, Mao discovered that the Chrysanthemum Fragrance Study had been bugged and he became paranoid. He abandoned Zhongnanhai and lived in four different places throughout Beijing in one year until he had some new quarters built adjacent to an indoor swimming pool at Zhongnanhai. Here he lived for the last decade of his life, conducting business primarily from his bed or the poolside. The spatial isolation necessitated by security and sexual promiscuity persisted and information flows were convoluted. While spatial structure did not play the prominent role in Zhongnanhai that it did in the Forbidden City, the parallels are uncanny. The power remains hidden, the aim of the ruler is to see but not be seen. Mao slipped neatly into the emperor's role, where he was badly informed and isolated at the apex of an empire of lies that produced the appalling famine of 1959–1962 and the cultural revolution soon after that.

LIBERATED SPACE

> The great square has no corners. The great vessel takes long to complete.
>
> (Lao Tzu 1963: 102)

On 1 October 1949 Mao Zedong mounted the Tiananmen Gate and proclaimed the birth of the People's Republic of China to a vast crowd gathered below in the T-shaped open space to the south (Figure 6.1). While this open space was the segment of the imperial axis between the Inner and Imperial Cities it is the gates of Tiananmen and Qianmen that were named; the 'square' was a modern and highly political invention in Chinese urban space (Wu 2005: 18–22). The choice of Tiananmen for a new centre was by no means arbitrary. Although the emperor had rarely appeared there, imperial edicts were issued from above the gate and received by officials below. The space in front of the gate was first identified as a site of resistance on 4 May 1919 when a spontaneous demonstration of 3,000 students gathered there in protest at the Versailles Treaty which ceded Chinese land to Japan. This 'May Fourth' student movement was followed by protests on the same site in 1926 and 1935 and became an inspiration to the later revolution (Steinhardt 1990: 179; Wu 2005: 15).

Mao's appearance on the gate carried two significant yet contradictory meanings. First, this was 'hidden power' revealing and submitting itself to the people.[4] Yet, simultaneously, the new leader appeared in an imperial relationship to the people – on a raised podium facing south on the imperial axis. There is a strong congruence between the orchestrated displays of obedience in front of the Hall of Supreme Harmony and those in front of Tiananmen Gate. The tradition of imperial rule was at once denied and affirmed. A similar contradiction was evident in much of the urban design which followed.

Throughout the 1950s and 1960s the traditional enclosing walls and gates of the Imperial, Inner and Outer cities were progressively demolished and replaced with ring roads. The walls, seen by the Party as archaic signifiers of the imperial order, also had a deeper ideological significance in sanctifying and protecting the city. No longer a gate, Tiananmen soon began to appear on coins and banknotes as a monument and an emblem of the new state. The central tunnel through it, formerly reserved for the emperor, became a public pedestrian path with Mao's portrait hung on axis above. Initially the portrait was the revolutionary Mao of the Long March, gazing on and upwards. It was soon replaced with an image staring down, meeting the gaze of all who passed before. The emperor became permanently visible.

Changan Boulevard (Avenue of Heavenly Peace), which runs east–west across the entry to the gate, was enlarged and extended, a move which added a new primary axis to the city at right-angles to the imperial axis. This fundamental twist of orientation operates as a metaphor for the revolutionary 'turn' of history. Yet this too evokes the ideal of the cosmic city which is centred on the intersection of the east–west and north–south axes. As Meyer (1991: 39) argues: 'This is the center, the fixed point in the turning of the world, the locus of the imperial throne. Power is concentrated at this point and, as one moves from center to periphery, the power "thins" '. Thus the denial of the Imperial City also became an affirmation of it at another level.

Tiananmen Square was Mao's vision for a fundamental recentring of the city and empire. The forbidden depths of imperial power were replaced by the 'democratic' expanse of the world's largest open plaza. Modelled in part on Moscow's Red Square, it was also much more than a parade ground. This was to be the antithesis of forbidden space – a square of the people, without walls, corners or rank markers. Here the people's power was to be dis-closed, its signifiers those of open access and visibility; open space as a metaphor of freedom. The dream was of infinite space; Mao spoke of it holding a billion people. Here the identity of 'the people' was constructed and displayed. This idea of urban open space signifying freedom and participation has a long tradition in the European city. Yet Sennett traces the ways the Roman Forum had already turned the democratic traditions of the Greek Agora into a space of spectacle rather than participation; the hierarchy established by the rostrum constructed a space where the signifiers of freedom were coupled with an imperative to 'look and obey' (Sennett 1994). With the gate as rostrum, this was the model for Tiananmen Square.

The development of the square over 30 years involved the demolition of former government ministries and the construction of new monuments and flanking buildings. The Great Hall of the People which lines the western edge is in the monumental neo-classical tradition, fronting the open space with a colonnade and expanse of steps. Built in 1959, this massive building has 17 hectares of floorspace, a 10,000 seat auditorium, a banqueting hall for 5,000 and a 3,000-seat parliament. The Great Hall is balanced on the eastern edge of the square with similarly scaled museums devoted to Chinese history and the revolution. Not all of the constructions were so visible and public. The Great Hall sat on top of a secret underground complex connecting to command posts, party leadership at Zhongnanhai and the military headquarters to the west of the city (Brook 1992; Li 1994).

The centre of the square is dominated by the Monument to the People's Heroes, also known as the Martyr's Monument. This 37 metre granite obelisk, completed in 1958, is set on a series of layered plinths with steps up from each of the cardinal directions. The central location of the monument deliberately blocks the imperial way, denying the idea of a southern entrance. Thus it established the square as the centre of power and not a pathway to it. The podium is lined with bas reliefs, including one depicting the May Fourth students demonstrating in the square. The inscription reads: 'Eternal glory to the people's heroes who from 1840 laid down their lives in the many struggles against internal and external enemies, for national independence and the freedom and well-being of the people' (Wu 1991). This generic dedication to the 'people's heroes' would later prove very useful.

By the 1970s the square had been formed as a single open space extending 900 metres from Tiananmen to Qianmen Gate, flanked by the hall and museums with the monument in the centre. This 40 hectare site held about 600,000 people for ceremonial occasions, which were limited largely to parades on Labour Day and National Day, when Mao and the leaders appeared on the gate to review military and cultural displays along the boulevard. However, the square became a key site during the cultural revolution, when large parades of Red Guards were choreographed to generate support (Wu 2005). These parades began to approach a festive version of the Nuremburg Nazi rallies; indeed the central section of the square is a similar shape and size to the Zeppelin Field. However, the meanings of Tiananmen are not so univalent; this is a more genuinely public place, legitimized on higher ideals, marked with monuments and memories.

In the aftermath of the cultural revolution any Party leader urging moderation became a 'people's hero'. Zhou Enlai qualified on these grounds, and when he died in January 1976 wreaths appeared on the Monument to the People's Heroes. Zhou's portrait was hung on the north of the monument, facing Mao across the square. The removal of the wreaths by authorities stimulated continuing resistance and by April large parts of the square were covered with flowers and banners, together with up to 100,000 people (Cheater 1991; Spence 1990; Wu 1991). To appropriate the monument and honour the dead as a form of protest was astute politics. It utilized the gap between the rhetoric of glorious revolution and the realities of the cultural revolution to resurrect revolutionary memory. The government, with Mao isolated and incapacitated, was directed through him by his wife Jiang Qing. The power of the resistance was paradoxically hidden in the light of the most open place in Beijing, under cover of grief and revolutionary loyalty.

This was a sophisticated form of identity politics, not quite camouflage since the Party leaders knew who they were and where they were. While these practices of power were strongly enmeshed within Chinese cultural norms, see here a shift from panoptic regimes of seeing without being seen more to Deleuzian conceptions of power as one spatial practice, meaning and identity 'folds' into another – in this case patriotism folds into protest. Power was established in the centre of the gaze and relied upon both the ambiguity of meaning and the public gaze for safety. The regime faced the dilemma that forcible suppression in such visible space must undermine its own legitimacy. To turn Lao Tzu around: 'because the people do not contend, the ruler is in no position to contend with them'.

Nevertheless, troops were ordered to remove the demonstrators by force and blood was shed on the monument for the first time in April 1976. But the role of the monument as a site of resistance was established, as Wu (1991: 105) argues: 'The meaning of the monument was never the same. This historical fabrication had come to life, and its empty inscription – "Eternal glory to the people's heroes" – had gained real meaning . . . Surrounding it a new public emerged.' Within 2 years these demonstrators were redeemed as patriots.

Mao also died in 1976 and his mausoleum, built a year later, became the final major addition to the square, on axis, south of the monument. The mausoleum is a square building of 105 metre sides facing north, set within a 5 hectare rectangular landscaped frame. Both Mao's body and a 3 metre marble statue of him are located on the imperial axis. Once again the design disrupts the imperial scheme yet utilizes it in another way. Against the avowed beliefs of the Party, the mausoleum incorporates geomantic principles (Cheater 1991). Trees and plants surround both the casket and the building to absorb the pollution of death. The permanent display of the chairman's body signifies power as both immortal and exposed. More people have seen him dead than ever saw him alive. But this too may be a deceit since there are suspicions that the body has been replaced with a wax replica.[5]

FORBIDDEN SPACE II

During the 1980s the square became a highly charged political space. Its role as a representation of the 'people' became tightly controlled. On New Year's Day in 1987, 2,000 students demonstrated in the square as part of the growing democracy movement. On that occasion police sprayed water on the freezing flagstones, rendering the square difficult to walk on in a new variation on the 'slippery surfaces' technique. By 1989, there were signs at the margins of the square saying: 'Without the approval of the People's government it is prohibited to parade, to hold rallies, to make speeches, to write, to distribute, or to put up any kind of propaganda' (quoted in Terzani 1986). The huge open expanse was framed with a grid of poles carrying lights, speakers and surveillance cameras. The people's space became forbidden space.

The student protest of 1989 began when the Party Leader Hu Yaobang died on 15 April.[6] Hu had never supported democracy; he merely opposed corruption, but he had been demoted for allowing the 1987 movement to spread, and he qualified as a hero. Upon his death many wreaths and mourners appeared in the square, and his portrait was hung on the monument, like Zhou's, facing Mao. In a repeat of 1976, the government order to clear the square stimulated a crowd of 200,000 including about 10,000 students, who set up camp around the monument, the base of which they used as a speaking podium. The camp, which occupied about a quarter of the square, was well organized by students, who cordoned off sections of it to prevent infiltration. The smooth space of the square was reterritorialized, striated with boundaries from inside which the protest was managed.

The students were a well-educated elite and many of their parents held influence; violence against them was politically difficult. Their primary policy was one of support for reformist elements within the current regime and an end to corruption at the top. It had little to do with universal voting rights. Their political tactics reflected the traditional approaches of non-contention and submission. Combining submission with irony, students 'kow towed' on the steps of the Great Hall, begging for an audience with Premier Li Peng as 'emperor'. When Mao's portrait on the gate was defaced in open defiance, the action was swiftly blamed by the students on provocateurs. On 13 May about 3,000 people began a hunger strike. This tactic of strength through non-action (not-eating), with its echoes of the 1959–1962 famine, struck a deep popular chord and further legitimized the resistance. Within a few days the spectacle of ambulances and medical staff caring for weakened students would dominate global news telecasts.

The demonstration and Hu's death were remarkably timed in the lead-up to the much heralded summit meeting between Deng and Gorbachev, scheduled for 15–17 May 1989. The number of foreign correspondents in the city increased about tenfold, offering unheralded access to the global telecommunications network. Student placards appeared in English and the reports that went out to the global media looped back on radio to all regions of China via the Voice of America, Radio Australia and the BBC – this is how the demonstrations spread throughout China. The local Chinese media also covered the demonstrations in order to maintain their own credibility. As Wark (1994) points out, the occupation of space in Tiananmen Square became increasingly geared to the occupation of time on television. The government opened up a gateway onto the global stage and the students appropriated the spectacle. The media exposure of the site made any hidden repression impossible. On 17 May numbers in the square reached 1 million people and another 2 million filled the streets. A proposal for Gorbachev to lay a wreath at the monument was abandoned as he was hustled into the Great Hall through a rear entry. 'I could not figure out who was in charge,' he said later (quoted in Salisbury 1989). It was an unprecedented loss of face for Chinese leadership.

On 20 May, with Gorbachev gone, martial law was declared, the press was banned from the square and all satellite links were severed. Electronic walls were constructed, but the telephones and tourists with videotapes went around them. Seven military divisions were sent into the city towards the square, but they were blocked by an extraordinary display of do-it-yourself urban design as residents spontaneously rebuilt Beijing as a walled city (Brook 1992). They erected barricades at all major access points using sewer pipes, loads of soil, existing traffic barriers, articulated buses and human shields. Within three days the paralyzed troops were withdrawn to the margins of the city.

Buoyed by success, some art students produced the Goddess of Democracy statute, which was installed in the square on 29 May (Figure 6.6). Often claimed to be modeled on the Statue of Liberty, it was adapted from a social realist statue of a man grasping a pole. The pole was replaced with the torch of enlight-

Figure 6.6
Goddess of Democracy
and Tiananmen Gate,
June 1989.

enment as the gender and gesture were reversed. She had neither the crown nor the chains of the US model. Young and fresh faced, her short hair was flying free as she held the torch aloft. If there is a model, it is the French revolutionary icon rather than its regal American appropriation.

The statue was placed on axis between the monument and the gate, facing north. While photos often show the statue as immediately under Mao's photo, it was located about 200 metres away across the broad boulevard. However, it was a gesture of open defiance which enabled the government to legitimize its position through the *People's Daily*. 'The Square is sacred,' they claimed indignantly, 'No one has the power to add any permanent memorial or to remove anything from the Square. Such things must not be allowed to happen in China' (quoted in Wu 1991: 112). The statue was also accused of being a sign of Western imperialism.

The statue represented a change in tactics by the students, designed to appear and be destroyed on global television. Hu Yoabang's portrait was hung on its base, which became a speaking podium. The focus of the demonstration moved half way across the space separating the monument and the gate, occupying the open centre. Some students occupied the south-facing rostrum at Tiananmen Gate, the preserve of top party leaders, as a speaking platform. Some began to call for the overthrow of the Party. Submissive tactics began to give way to the openly provocative.

In retrospect it is easy to judge these as tactical errors, but it is also clear that the State had also changed position. From 26 May the barricaded city was infiltrated by thousands of troops disguised as students and workers, who made their way by jogging, walking, riding and in single vehicles (Brook 1992).[7] These troops were massed in the Great Hall and behind Tiananmen Gate. The final assault came late on 3 June, under the darkness of the new moon, when

armoured vehicles with orders to shoot entered the city along the major boulevards. Most casualties occurred along these routes as residents flooded the
streets to enforce the barricades which had protected the city for two weeks. At
best estimate about 2,700 people were killed that night and over the next few
days.[8] Only a small percentage of those killed were students and few, if any,
were within Tiananmen Square.

Those planning the assault went to great trouble to avoid violence in the
square. Despite the massive infiltration of troops surrounding the square before
the assault, armoured vehicles were sent in first to capture the city and seal off
the square. Most casualties occurred before 4 a.m. on 4 June, at which time
student leaders negotiated the safe evacuation of the 3,000 remaining students
camped in the square. All left peacefully via the south-east corner. While there
was a good deal of slaughter on the fringes of the square, the open centre and
the monument became a relative sanctuary during the bloodbath.

Whatever combination of incompetence and state terrorism produced the
massacre, it did not extend to the sacred space of Tiananmen Square. The
problem for the leadership was not simply the student appropriation of the
square, but the 'hope' these events had awakened in the 'people'. While focus
was on the square as a signifier of this hope, it could not be destroyed by
turning the square into a bloodbath. The current regime has legitimized its
actions on the largely defensible claim that people were not killed in Tiananmen
Square. A new statue was briefly erected on the site of the former Goddess of
Democracy, portraying a steel worker, farmer, soldier and intellectual in a figure
of unity (Wu 2005: 50).

This story raises some general issues in our understanding of the spatialization of power. Urban form generally tends to legitimize the regime which produces it. Yet monuments and urban spaces express ideals of liberty, equality and
democracy which are thereby lent a certain reproductive inertia. When authentic,
popular and generic ideals are inscribed and represented in urban form and
public space, such sites may become potent places of resistance. Legitimizing
gestures have a potency which is available for appropriation, a potential linked to
both what they signify and the gap between rhetoric and reality.

Despite a rather banal design, the Monument to the People's Heroes res-
onated with the early hopes of the revolution as it remembered its martyrs. The
semantic breadth of its name, inscription and image contributed to its capacity
for appropriation. But it was the semantic gap between representation and
reality that generated the key opportunity for resistance. The site which served to
legitimize the authority of the regime was appropriated for the legitimation of
resistance. The new meanings of the monument and the open space around it
were constructed out of a dynamic social dialectic. Each move in the struggle,
the laying of wreaths and their removal, the demonstrations and repressions,
raised the stakes and added a new layer of meaning.

This tale is also one of the tension between this site and its various media
representations, between place and text. Issues of power in public space are now

thoroughly geared into control over the visual media. As Wark (1993: 141) rather optimistically puts it: 'New possibilities for constructing politics in the information landscape have momentarily been glimpsed'. Yet as he also points out, the same video footage which was beamed to a global audience was later edited and used on Chinese television as a means to identify student leaders. The information channels that incited resistance were available for the later repression.

Finally, there are questions raised by the inversion of the traditional enclosed spatial structure of the Forbidden City in the vast unsegmented expanse of Tiananmen Square. The Forbidden City largely reproduced its practices of power through a deeply segmented spatial syntax. An enclosed square such as the forecourt of the Hall of Supreme Harmony could never have permitted the 1989 scenario. Yet while the media focused on the bravery of the students in the sanctified open space of the square, the real bravery came from the spontaneous urban designers in the suburbs who enclosed the city against military invasion and 'forbade' access for two weeks. Forbidden space takes many forms. It is all too easy to identify the open/closed as congruent with liberty/constraint, or transparent/hidden. At the time of writing, Tiananmen Square has become a new kind of forbidden space.

In 1999 the square was closed for several months for resurfacing – widely believed to be a means of stopping demonstrations during the 10 year anniversary of the massacre. Low fences were constructed around the perimeter with entrance through small gates policed by guards and framed with large signs in English spelling out a strict choreography of public life (Figure 6.7). The rules are to keep the square 'solemn, silent, clean and (in) good order'. There is to be no 'parade, assembly, speech. No writing, distributing, posting, hanging and spreading and propaganda materials . . . No activities in any way which damage

Figure 6.7
Forbidden space, 2001.

the honour of our country, disturb the public order, obstruct the public security and the city sight'. The monument was also guarded and a large sign (in English) outlined a further set of behavioural restrictions:

> Presenting wreaths, baskets of flowers, garlands and small flowers to the Monument must be approved . . . Registration of formalities should be made five days ahead . . . No writing, carving, hanging or placing anything on the Monument. No sitting and lying down on the ground. No joking and playing . . .
>
> (Monument to the People's Heroes, June 1999)

Since the mid 1990s this newly forbidden square has stimulated new forms of resistance including Falun Gong breathing and avant-garde artworks ranging from performance to representation (Wu 2005: 195–233). Wu shows how such works deconstruct the meanings and myths of the square – the political tensions of the space and its iconic images have become grist for the artistic imagination. These works are based in the liberating impulse that flourished in 1989 and the attempt to keep it alive. Resistance continues under cover of art rather than grief, yet saturation surveillance of the square means that these practices are largely reduced to text as photographs of ephemeral events. Such work generally depends on its 'difficulty', which then limits both the audience and the political effects. Even in galleries some works have been banned for being 'too ambiguous' but of course it is the ambiguity in both the art and the grief that enables resistance.

These artworks are not the only ambiguous works in the new square. While the people cannot bring flowers, Wu (2005: 241–243) has also shown how official but ephemeral installations featuring grass, flowers, fountains and themed displays have become the key forms of symbolic representation in the square since the massacre. He terms these 'soft monuments' and argues that they are designed to depoliticize the square by reinforcing a festive holiday atmosphere. A network of water jets is hidden in the pavement to become instant fountains – also useful for dampening revolutionary enthusiasm. These tactics continue the struggle over control of public space and demonstrate again just how much is at stake in this public spectacle. While the rhetoric of revolution has been erased, the meanings of this square and monument are not settled yet and it remains available for resistance. In the sense that genuine public space and public art can be defined by the very contention over its meaning (Deutsche 1996), Tiananmen has become an increasingly public space.

Chapter 7: Paths to Democracy

Bangkok

The city [consists] . . . of relationships between the measurements of its space and the events of its past: the height of a lamppost and the distance from the ground of a hanged usurper's swaying feet . . . As this wave from memories flows in, the city soaks up like a sponge and expands . . . The city, however, does not tell its past, but contains it like the lines of a hand . . .

Calvino (1979: 13)

On my first visit to Bangkok in 1997 the taxi driver was crawling through the dense traffic choking the broad modern boulevard known as Ratchadamnoen near the Democracy Monument. He spontaneously pointed out an expanse of roadway and said that was where they killed the students in 1992. In case I couldn't understand his English he took his hands off the wheel and enacted a short spray of automatic fire. Several visits later I was teaching an urban design studio at a nearby university and regularly traversing Sanam Luang, the vast open space ringed by Tamarind trees adjacent to the Grand Palace. This is one of the world's great urban spaces – variously used for royal cremations, ploughing cere-monies, temporary buildings, sports, kite flying, markets, public sleeping and political rallies (Piromruen 2005). A colleague pointed out one among many of the Tamarind trees and said that was where they hung and beat the students in 1976. In class as an Australian student drew a pencil line across the plan of Sanam Luang a Thai student gasped in horror – only the King can cut this royal ground. This chapter portrays a city rendered rich by the play of meaning and memory, a city of collective memory (Boyer 1996: 68). It is also a story of the ways a particular part of the city was given meaning as a path to democracy, and of struggles over the right to the city and over the excavation of repressed and misrepresented stories.

In Bangkok, as elsewhere, the political dimensions of urban space become dependent on local nuances of culture, nationalism, religion and authority. The legitimation of authority – the belief in the state's right to rule – is a slippery concept and the struggle for legitimacy is played out in a field of culture and tradition (Alagappa 1995). Introducing aspects of Thai culture and traditional belief systems into this discussion can be dangerous if they are seen as totalizing or reducing contemporary Thai society to some kind of traditional straightjacket. This is not my intent, which is rather to view the urban field of modern Bangkok, the meanings of places and dispositions to act within them, in the light of such traditions.

Thai social structure is traditionally ordered by hierarchical oppositions of older/younger; parent/child; higher rank/lower rank. Principles of deference permeate social practice (Morell and Chai-anan 1981).[1] At the top of this hierarchy is a formation of Nation/Buddhism/King. The King is father of the nation and the head of the community. Buddhism is the national religion and the source of moral order and merit. These three lock together ideologically in a manner where to oppose one is to oppose them all (Tambiah 1976: 482). The order of the three is important and is reflected in the national flag of red (nation), white (religion) and blue (King) stripes – where the central blue stripe is framed by the smaller white and then red stripes. All forms of political power, including military coups and democratic constitutions, need to honour this triumvirate of Nation/Buddhism/King to succeed. Military power in Thailand has been based in a capacity to harness authoritarian governance to this legitimating triumvirate (Reynolds 1991). The harness, however, is unstable and there have been seventeen military coups and fifteen constitutions since 1932 (Sukatipan 1995). Thai Buddhist belief is also linked to community, justice and democracy, from which view authoritarianism is a perversion of Thai identity (Jackson 1991).

The social hierarchy is also geared to a conceptual opposition of order versus confusion (Morell and Chai-anan 1981: 29–30). *Woon wai*, which translates loosely as 'confusion', is a state of nuisance, instability or anarchy; those who engage in conflict are said to be *woon wai*. Confusion upsets the gentle order of Thai society, it is un-Thai. By contrast *jai yen* is the highly valued 'cool heart' or calmness in the face of confusion or conflict. Any challenge to authority must be calm and gentle or it will lack legitimacy. The high value placed on the stable social order links to a belief that it is only superior force that can create and maintain stability (Aasen 1998: 8). Instability or confusion can then be explained in terms of too little force and military force can be legitimized in the public interest (Dhiravegin 1992). Such a social structure is often seen from the West as passivity and receptivity to control; the social structure seems to militate against participatory politics since debate is disdained and power is self-legitimating (Hindley 1976; Wilson 1962: 74).[2]

Thailand has generally been very open to Western ideas and technologies (Reynolds 1998); the culture is characterized by a remarkable capacity to absorb new ideas, beliefs, names and meanings without displacing existing ones. Thus, through layering and juxtaposition one can have both the traditional and the modern, Thai and Western, authoritarianism and democracy, inherited power and meritocracy (Wilson 1962). There is a great deal of slippage or fluidity in spatial discourse. Places often have several names, which persist in common usage (formal and informal; royal and common), serving different interests with contradictions left in play (O'Connor 1990). Oblique communication is often preferred to the direct, deploying allegory, parody and irony – privileging the ebb and flow of life, rather than the stabilization of identities (Aasen 1998). Thai architecture is often comprised of hybrid styles – the nineteenth century Grand Palace is a French import with a traditional Thai roof. This hybridity, fluidity and slippage becomes especially interesting in the light of Western critiques of 'essentialism' and deconstructionist challenges to the stabilities of meaning and identity.

THE ROYAL ROAD

Bangkok was established as the centre of power in Siam when the current Chakri dynasty was established in 1782. Within 15 days of this coup the city pillar of the new centre of Bangkok was inserted, marking the north-east corner of a new palace complex (Figure 7.1). The insertion of the City Pillar was also a symbolic re-enactment of a traditional Thai ritual of planting the first housepost near the north-east corner of the house with offerings to earth spirits (Turton 1978). The predominance of the north-east was established through cosmological oppositions along cardinal axes. The east was regarded as sacred and pure – temples faced east, as did one's head when sleeping; west is the direction of the head during cremation. The progression from south to north was one of increasing authority and power (Tambiah 1973; Turton 1978: 120). This socio-spatial hierarchy of the traditional household was reflected in the larger spatial order of the village and State where the King is seen as head of the community and 'father' of the people. The palace compound was flanked by the grand Chao Phraya river and the military headquarters. Sanam Luang – an open field to the north of the palace – became the royal ground, the site of fertility and cremation rites. Here the King still presides over the annual ploughing ceremony that links the monarchy to the Thai landscape as mediator of earth spirits and the cycles of birth and death (Wilson 1962: 75). Sanam Luang has long been not just a 'royal ground', but also a symbolic 'ground' of royal authority.[3]

From the turn of the twentieth century under King Rama V (Chula-longkorn) a major modernization plan was implemented which shifted the political map of central Bangkok from one entirely centred on the Grand Palace to one which was stretched between the old centre and a new centre of symbolic power around the new Dusit Palace about 4 kilometres to the north-east, connected by the new boulevard of Ratchadamnoen Avenue (Figure 7.1). This incorporated a radical transformation and enlargement of the 'royal ground' which doubled the size of the open space into a racetrack shape of 600 × 200 metres fringed with Tamarind trees at its edges. Sanam Luang became a giant rationalist geometric figure in the urban landscape but also an entirely new kind of urban

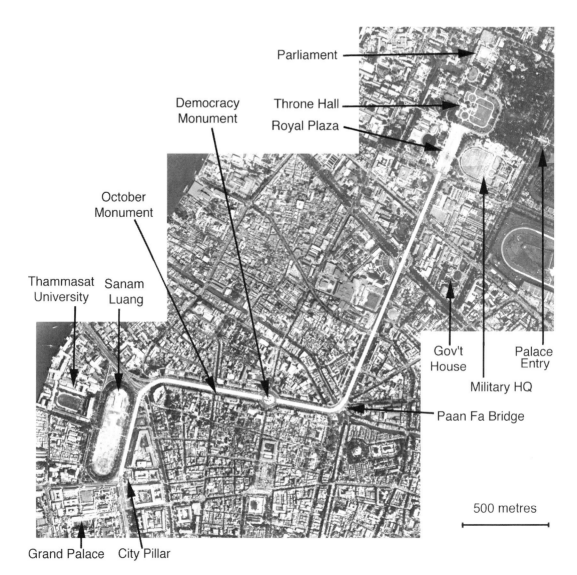

Parliament

Democracy Monument

Throne Hall

Royal Plaza

October Monument

Thammasat University Sanam Luang

Gov't House

Palace Entry

Military HQ

Paan Fa Bridge

500 metres

Grand Palace City Pillar

space – at once a park and a plaza, an agricultural field and a building site (Figure 7.2). It has become framed over the years by a series of buildings and institutions which form a symbolic constellation – the Grand Palace with its temple of the Emerald Buddha, the City Pillar, the Supreme Court, a Buddhist *wat* compound, two universities, the National Theatre and the National Museum.

Figure 7.1
The Royal Road.

The boulevard was inspired by a visit to Europe by Rama V in 1897 and fuelled by enlightenment thinking – visions of modernity, visibility and large scale geometric order produced a re-ordering of the city, with long vistas to symbols of power.[4] The antecedents of the urban design include the London Mall, Berlin's *Unter den Linden* and the Parisian boulevards. The name Ratchadamnoen literally means 'royal route' and the King rode in processions of cars which symbolized a monarch who was at the forefront of modernization. Ratchadamnoen Avenue

Figure 7.2
Sanam Luang and the
Grand Palace.

has three separate alignments, with the first beginning at the city pillar, the north-eastern corner of the Grand Palace (Figure 7.1). From the north of Sanam Luang the central section of Ratchadamnoen Klang turns east for about a kilometre until it meets the former city wall and canal. This is the stretch which is now strongly identified with the democracy movement. The northern section of Ratchadamnoen Nok commences after it turns north again, across the Paan Fa Bridge, and enters a one-and-a-half kilometre vista which terminates at the Royal Plaza in front of the Dusit Palace throne hall. The Royal Plaza is an open expanse of concrete about 150 by 500 metres centred on an equestrian statue of King Rama V (Figure 7.3). This is the key public site where the alliance of the military with the King is represented in urban space, framed on one side by the military headquarters and used regularly for military parades.

Unlike its neighbours, Siam was never colonized, yet the development of the nation state was heavily influenced by the colonial context. Indeed the appropriation of Western technology and models of urban development played a role in resisting colonization. Thongchai (1994) has argued that this reconstruction of the city was also a crucial period in the discursive construction of Thai identity and the emergence of what he terms the 'geo-body' – a construction of Siamese identity through the spatial technology of mapping. The nineteenth century threat of colonialism stimulated a crisis in Siamese sovereignty and identity. Maps were deployed to stabilize fluid boundaries and to identify the image of the nation with its territory. The re-development of Bangkok was a parallel phenomena of iconography and visibility. Ratchadamnoen Avenue re-framed the cognitive map of a new and modern Bangkok, stretching and stabilizing the royal territory across the city. Both the King and city, as icons of the nation, became more accessible, imageable and visible. The move to the Dusit Palace was at once a form of modernization and also a remaking of the traditional city with the King in the north-east (Korff 1993: 237). It was modern in the sense that the enclosing walls and canals of the traditional city were breached and

Figure 7.3
Royal Plaza and Throne
Hall.

bridged by the (then) fast-flowing traffic. The King was rendered visible in vast open spaces and motorized parades. Yet the alignments of the boulevard – north then east then north again – can be seen as reiterating and extending the traditional alignments with power and sanctity under the mantle of modernity. The new avenue also integrated monarchy and morality through the axes of power and religion. This reconstruction of the city was largely in place by the death of Rama V in 1910, and there was far less development under the following monarchs. Rama VI built a new palace, Chitralada, a little to the east of Dusit, as his residence which has been the King's palace ever since (Figure 7.1). The northern section of Ratchadamnoen Nok became lined with the palaces of the nobility, military headquarters and later government buildings as the new elite followed the King into the north-east.

An alliance of intellectuals and the military wrested power from the monarchy in a bloodless coup on 24 June 1932. The urban focus of this action was the new Throne Hall and Royal Plaza, an event now marked by only a small plaque in the plaza pavement over which military parades march and cars drive (Reynolds 1992). The coup was inspired by Western notions of democracy based in the 'People's Party' and the Throne Hall was appropriated as an Assembly building. The King was disempowered under a constitutional monarchy; he abdicated in protest and was succeeded by a young nephew who did not assume the throne for another 13 years. The Throne Hall fronting the royal plaza on the axis of Ratchadamnoen became the Assembly while executive power moved to Government House located in a former palace to the east (Figure 7.1). Within a few years of the coup tensions between the military and intellectual leadership led to a military dictatorship, aligned with Japan and inspired by the fascist politics of Mussolini. The intellectual leadership was sidelined, and its leader, Pridi, was eventually exiled.

DEMOCRACY MONUMENT

Under the military dictatorship in the late 1930s the central section of Ratchadamnoen Klang Avenue was widened for traffic and lined with four-storey buildings in art deco style. The centrepiece of this scheme was a commemoration of the 1932 coup known as the Democracy Monument (Figure 7.4). The monument was built by the military regime largely to legitimate a set of values they had already usurped. It is set on a circular plinth in a seven-lane traffic round-about on the axis of the royal road as the dominant visual symbol of this section of the boulevard. The monument combines images of the coup, the constitution, the military, Buddhism and nationalism.[5] The centrepiece is a small circular build-ing with six doors representing the six principles of the People's Party – freedom, peace, education, equality, economy and unity. On top of this building is an image of the constitution in the form of a folded document held aloft by two Buddhist offering bowls. This central figure representing constitutional values is framed by four slender vertical 'wings' with splayed striations representing the three armed forces and the police. These wing-like forms both guard and dwarf the central constitution as they represent the dynamism and futurism of the nation. The bas reliefs on the base construct a myth of the military seizing power on behalf of the people (Wong 2006: 65). The monument is surrounded by a

Figure 7.4
Democracy Monument.

circle of seventy-five half-buried cannons used as bollards with their barrels facing down, framing and 'grounding' the monument in military power.

In its early years the monument was also called the 'Thai Monument' to celebrate the change of the nation's name from Siam to Thailand – thereby conflating the concept of Thailand with that of democracy. The height, circumference (both 24 metres) and the number of cannons were representations of the day and year of the coup – 24 June was declared National Day. The monument has a rich layering of meanings including Buddhism, nationalism, militarism and democracy in a mix of styles from social realism to art deco and futurism. The most notable absence of signification is the monarchy – the monument disrupts the legitimating triumvirate of nation/religion/King, and its location interrupts the axis of the royal road. While there is a certain awkwardness in the attempt to meld its various significations, it is a splendid embodiment of the contradictions of its time. In its early years it was not well-loved because it became symbolic of the military dictatorship for which it served as propaganda, signifying fascism and the false promise of democracy (Thongchai 1999). The monarchy regained considerable power in 1956 after the current king (Rama IX) attained the throne when his brother (Rama VIII) was murdered. However, this was an uneasy balance of the military, civilian and monarchic power, punctuated by many military coups during the second half of the twentieth century.

THE PEOPLE'S PATH

The earliest place identified as a site of democratic resistance to the military regime was Thammasat University, established in 1933 by Pridi, the intellectual leader of the 1932 coup. *Thamma* is an ancient Hindu–Buddhist code of 'rights', or 'laws' and Thammasat University was conceived as an elite university for political and social thought. The site occupies the former palace of the 'Deputy King' between Sanam Luang and the river (Figure 7.1). A so-called 'Peace Movement' grew on Thammasat campus through the 1950s and spilled onto Sanam Luang in the form of protest speeches and marches along Ratchadamnoen Ave (Kwanjai 1998; Hewison 1997). The slippages of meaning that are so pervasive in this context proved useful; protests often began with everyday issues such as rising bus fares but then turned into a demand for a new constitution (Morell and Chai-anan 1981; Prizzia 1985). These demonstrations, however, were generally non-violent and often successful – resulting, for example, in a new constitution in 1969.

October 1973 marked the first really large demonstration, when 400,000 people marched from Sanam Luang to the Democracy Monument and filled that entire kilometre of the boulevard (Figure 7.5). They were well organized by students, supported by first aid and food crews, and carrying national flags and portraits of the King. A student leader of the time has likened the movement of the 'wave' of people up Ratchadamnoen to a dance or aesthetic performance in which this space of authority was transformed into a theatre (Kwanjai 1998). The

Figure 7.5
Ratchadamnoen and
Democracy Monument,
October 1973.

uninterrupted vista along a kilometre of Ratchadamnoen Klang Avenue enabled the spectacle of 400,000 people – a vision of the 'people' and 'nation' which had hitherto been something one only imagined. The 'imagined community' (Anderson 1983) and the 'geo-body' (Thongchai 1994) of nationalist discourse were thereby rendered palpably real.

The Ratchadamnoen spectacle opened up a new image of a participative community – a vision not of chaos and division, but of order and peaceful protest; not the confusion of *woon wai* but the cool heart of *jai yen*. The demonstrations were able to attach democracy to the same base of legitimacy that the military had appropriated, that of nation/religion/King. While the King had a long-standing alliance with the military (Hewison 1997), the demonstrators' support for democracy in the name of the King was crucial to their success. Instead of being seen as creating conflict, the spectacle was one of unity. Images of this spectacle were shared with the wider community through the mass media.

By appropriating Ratchadamneon Klang Avenue, the protest also caused a serious disruption to a major artery of city traffic. The heavily polluted traffic jams of Bangkok render much public space unlivable for pedestrians; the chaos also operates symbolically to signify a failure of urban policy to serve the public interest. The way in which the demands of demonstrators slipped from bus fares to constitutional reform is one indication of this link. The events of 1973 demonstrated both a new kind of community and a new kind of urbanism.

The Democracy Monument was initially a resting point for the demonstrators on the way to the effective centres of power to the north: the Parliament, Throne Hall, Royal Plaza, Government House, Chitralada Palace and Military

Headquarters. Yet beyond the Paan Fa Bridge large demonstrations became vulnerable, fragmented, less visible and ambiguous. The funnelling effect of the bridges created confrontation with police and military. And beyond the bridges the northern section of Ratchadamnoen Nok is lined with large fenced compounds and is highly impermeable. While the Royal Plaza is vast, it is an enclosed sector of the urban spatial structure where a large crowd can be effectively barricaded. By contrast, the central section near the Democracy Monument is a permeable street network with many access points which were useful both as points of access and escape, and for the supply of food and drink (Kwanjai 1998: 154).

In the northern sections of the boulevard the spectacle of the large crowd was also diminished due to the trees. Most importantly, the meanings of public action became confused; the pro-democracy spectacle here inverts to become a confrontation which could variously be seen, or portrayed, as anti-military, anti-parliament or anti-monarchy. In the early morning of 14 October 1973 students outside Chitralada Palace calling for the King's support were portrayed as anti-monarchist. Some of those trying to escape across the canal into the palace (where the King had opened the gates) were portrayed as attacking the King and were shot (Prizzia 1985). Attacks by the police and army then expanded to the Democracy Monument and surrounding streets; in the end over 100 people were killed and several government buildings were burned before the King intervened (Morell and Chai-anan 1981). The military leaders were exiled, and a more democratic (if temporary) constitution was established. Sanam Luang, generally reserved for royal cremations, was made available by the King for cremation ceremonies of many of the dead students (Charnwit and Thamsong 1999; Thongchai 1999).

As a result of these events, the potency of peaceful behaviour in public space became apparent and the string of urban space from Thammasat University through Sanam Luang and along Ratchadamnoen was established as the 'path of democracy' (Kwanjai 1998). This was a processional route from the bo-tree courtyard of Thammasat University, past a statue of Pridi, through the 'dome' building at the centre of campus to the university sports field, then to Sanam Luang and along Ratchadamnoen to the Democracy Monument, often stopping for rallies at the sports field and Sanam Luang. This spatial progression evokes an important discursive narrative: the bo-tree signifies the sacred Buddhist bodhi tree and establishes spiritual legitimacy; the 'dome' building signifies the intellectual authority of Thammasat University and the law of Thamma; Sanam Luang signifies the royal 'grounding' of Thai nationhood and the mediation of the spirit of place; and Ratchadamnoen and the monument signify modernity and democracy. Thus there is a spatial narrative which connects dharma, thamma, King, earth and nation in the march to modernity and democracy.

In 1976 one of the former military leaders who had launched the killings in 1973 was permitted to return to Thailand as a monk. This was a cover for his return to power and protests escalated again at Thammasat and Sanam Luang.

On this occasion, however, the students were portrayed in the press as anti-monarchist and communist (Anderson 1998). On 7 October over 4,000 right-wing mercenaries and monarchists rallied on Sanam Luang and, supported by the police and military, they stormed the campus to engage in a frenzied killing spree. Thousands of students were arrested and many were burnt or beaten to death on Sanam Luang and hung from the Tamarind trees (Charnwit and Thamsong 1999; Wiwat 1998; Anderson 1998; Morell and Chai-anan 1981). The number of causalities may never be known and estimates range from the official figure of forty-three to over 500 (Arun 1998). There is a Thai expression that goes, 'kill the chicken to scare the monkey' (Callahan 1998); this was a new kind of orchestrated violence which also killed expressions of popular support for democracy for over a decade. There were no official cremations on Sanam Luang for these students and the unofficial ones have stained its meaning as a royal ground. The memory of students hanging from the Tamarind trees haunts the site and the trauma of these events has rendered much of what happened unthinkable and unspeakable for many Thais. Yet the memories remain, anchored by the urban spaces in which they took place. The meanings of Sanam Luang in particular – the 'ground' of royal authority, place of fertility and royal cremation – can never be quite the same.

The October events of 1973 and 1976 engendered a crisis of legitimacy for both the military and monarchy. Several attempts to deal with this were played out in urban form. Parliament House (also known as the National Assembly) was constructed in 1973 on a part of the Dusit palace several hundred metres directly behind the Throne Hall, slightly off axis, on a relatively minor street facing the zoo (Figure 7.1). Access is via a circuitous road which diverts around the Throne Hall. The design was modernist with a broad, low dome for the assembly, but its profile is barely visible from the street and it does not register on the dominant cognitive maps (nor tourist maps) of the city. The location reflected the Assembly's powerlessness, in marked contrast to the military headquarters lining the Royal Plaza (Figure 7.1).

In 1980 the entry to the Parliament building was replaced by a raised statue and forecourt, which largely conceals the entrance to the building (Figure 7.6). This was a monument to King Rama VII who abdicated in 1935 after losing power in the 1932 coup. As Thongchai (1999) argues, this monument constructs a narrative which portrays the monarch as the instigator and protector of Thai democracy; Rama VII becomes the martyr who sacrifices his power in the name of democracy. In urban spatial terms this monument completes a double-screening of parliament from the city. The building stands behind Rama VII and also behind the Throne Hall. The positioning of parliament within the city marginalizes it and frames democracy within a larger hierarchy, headed by the King.

In 1982 the Democracy Monument was officially classified by the Fine Arts Department as 'not worthy of conservation' (Vasana 1999) and there was an attempt to remove the constitution as its centrepiece, to be replaced by a statue of Rama VII. These changes were resisted, but the proposal reflects the way the

Figure 7.6
Parliament Building – the
King as protector of
democracy.

widespread love of the King in Thailand has been portrayed as a form of democracy, as if he were 'elected' (Hewison 1997). This contradictory ideal of a
'democratic monarch' has fuelled resistance to any written constitution that formally strips the King of political power. The monarch is seen by many as the real
constitution or foundation of the nation; the monarchy is portrayed as 'Thai
style' democracy (Hewison 1997: 73).

While the concept of democracy in the West is relatively stable, when
imported to Thailand it leaves one discursive field and enters another. The double
naming and slippages of meaning have enabled this contradiction of a democratic monarch to persist. Kasian (1996) has argued that in the absence of democratic institutions the popular meanings of democracy become anchored by the
constellation of urban places which have framed the struggle – Thammasat University, Sanam Luang, Ratchadamnoen and the Democracy Monument:

> As the battleground where key historical battles for democracy were waged, these
> natural or man-made physical things are popularly regarded as the concrete and hence
> stable and solid embodiment of the memory and spirit of the democratic movement . . .
> For people to whom democracy remains an abstract, amorphous and oft-thwarted
> aspiration, they give a sense of concreteness, of shape and form, or time and place, to
> their dreams of 'democracy'.
>
> (Kasian 1996: 11)

A gradual opening up of the political process in the 1980s led to elections in
1988, only to be followed by a military coup in 1991. In May 1992 the opposition
leader went on a hunger strike in the Royal Plaza, attracting protest rallies of over
100,000 people, which moved between there and Sanam Luang (Figure 7.7). This

Figure 7.7
Sanam Luang, May 1992.

hunger strike followed the use of such tactics in Tienanmen Square 3 years earlier. Fasting is a form of Buddhist merit-making, strengthening the spirit through self-control and self-denial. A hunger striker therefore claims the spiritual high-ground and highlights the contrast between military strength based on force and the inner strength of the democracy movement. The early phases of this protest had a playful sense of carnival – social norms were suspended and the chaotic traffic disrupted as people from different classes mixed in a new public space where street theatre and dance mingled with free speech, music and food vendors. The demonstrations at once constructed and occupied, as Callahan (1998: 3) puts it, 'a special space set off from the normal routine of traffic and pollution'. Ribbons were tied to trees along Ratchadamnoen like tree-shrines, rendering the entire boulevard as sacred space (Askew 1994: 155) and the confrontation was later portrayed in artwork as a dance (Callahan 1998).

A crackdown by the military and police began on 17 May and continued for several days along the length of Ratchadamnoen Avenue. A primary point of confrontation was the Paan Fa bridge where the military set up a barbed wire barricade to prevent movement into the northern stretch of the boulevard. Makeshift bridges formed of boats were constructed to get around the barricade, yet there was little strategic interest in doing so since the continued confrontation was the primary focus of media attention. While the electronic press was strongly censored, newspapers remained a reliable source of news. Ironically, the electronic censorship attracted people to participate in a spectacle which they could not see on television (Pongsudhirak 1997). The struggle over media representation had an impact in real space as newspaper photographers became military targets and the government's public relations building was burnt down.

Middle-class demonstrators also brought a new communications network in the form of mobile phones, enabling the crowd to both organize and evade police. Resistance became decentred, relying on horizontal rhizomatic networks more than vertical hierarchies for organization: 'Whenever the army dispersed a crowd in one spot another would appear elsewhere' (Callahan 1998: 86). The conjunction of modernist open spaces with permeable street structures along the central section of Ratchadamnoen was crucial in enabling this kind of resistance to persist. However, these events were not called 'Bloody May' for nothing – estimates of the total death toll range from fifty to over 100. Despite its portrayal as a middle-class uprising, the victims were found to be mostly labourers, traders and street vendors (Callahan 1998). The conflict finally concluded when the Prime Minister (General Suchinda) resigned at the King's request.

MONUMENTS AND MEMORIES

The memories of these three major phases of protest and violence have been kept alive in books, magazines, photographs and videos (Arun 1998; Charnwit and Thamsong 1999; Kwanjai 1998; Vasana 1999; Wiwat 1998). Ratchadamneon Avenue is regularly decorated with images of King and nation juxtaposed with the Democracy Monument (Figure 7.8) but until 2001 there was nothing to indicate the history of bloodshed. With broad support from the government and the King a memorial was finally opened in October 2001 on a site about 200 metres west of the Democracy Monument, where one of the government buildings was burnt down in 1973. The monument is in the form of a pyramid surmounted by a cone (Anjira 1999). There was little dispute over the site or design of the monument but considerable tension over the name: should it be called the '14 October Monument' (identifying the 1973 killings) or the 'October Monument' (including those killed on 7 October 1976)? Underlying this dispute is the different role of the King in those events. The 1976 killings remain unrecognized (Anjira 1999; Chaiwat 1998).

Figure 7.8
The face of democracy.

Political rallies along this stretch of urban space surged again in early 2006 as part of the movement to unseat the corrupt Prime Minister Thaksin. Peaceful protests of up to 100,000 people moved between the Royal Plaza, Sanam Luang and the Democracy Monument and were often focused on the right of the public to occupy public space without permission. One rally was organized to coincide with the anniversary of the fall of the Marcos regime in the Philippines, only to find that Sanam Luang was 'booked'. On at least one occasion the government suggested that permission would be given if only protesters would apply. What is at stake here is the 'right to the city' versus the right of the State to mediate access.

These rolling protests moved over time from Sanam Luang in the south-west to Government House in the north-east; people camped out on the streets in a festive atmosphere, cooling off in fountains with massages provided by a 'Dharma Army' of saffron-clad monks. With the Prime Minister looking for any excuse to call a state of emergency, protesters were careful to avoid any signs of chaos or violence. The demonstrations were marked by ambivalence: a series of rolling protests peaked in the evenings when the middle classes were off work and the disruption to traffic was minimized; they only blocked one side of Ratchadamnoen Boulevard, enabling traffic to continue to flow. This ambivalence also reflected a division in public sentiment – the protesters were middle-class while Thaksin's support base was with the rural poor for whom vote-buying was seen as a redistribution of wealth. The protests were not calling for democracy but for the boycott of a snap election that was believed to be corrupt. Eventually the King intervened again and endorsed another military coup with a promised return to democracy. An extraordinary cult of kingship has followed, saturating the major public spaces with giant billboards of the King's image and colours. At one level this is a way for the middle-class to show their support for the military coup and the ousting of Prime Minister Thaksin, yet it can also be read as an indication of a legitimation crisis. In early 2007 a Swiss citizen was imprisoned for 10 years under the 'lèse majesté' law for spraying graffiti on a public photograph of the King.

This is an unfinished story where much is at stake and many lives have been lost. It is a story of nationalism, modernity, militarism and monarchy which demonstrates a multiplicity of dimensions through which built form mediates power relations. The master narrative of the 'royal road' was appropriated as the 'people's path' to democracy. The grand modernist narrative of open space and visibility rendered the city available for a newly imagined community of democracy. The Democracy Monument, originally a legitimating image for a military dictatorship, was re-appropriated and its meaning reconstructed through political action. This case also illustrates the importance of rhizomatic practices of resistance and their complex relationships to spatial structure, information technologies and the mass media. In terms of urban design theory it shows some ways in which the city as text (as discourse, as a constellation of constructed meanings and memories) intersects with the city as a set of spatial practices (as spatial structure and 'movement economy'). The outcomes are multiple and indecisive: Ratchadamnoen remains both a Royal Road and a Path to Democracy, reflecting a constitution that remains both democratic and monarchic.

The role of urban design in political change is a particularly oblique one in the socio-political landscape of Thailand, where fluid and ambiguous meanings are common. Ratchadamnoen is far from the idealized Western space of the agora where, as Arendt (1958) puts it, 'words are not empty and deeds are not brutal'. This is a space where meanings are fluid and deeds are sometimes brutal. Yet it is a space where, in Arendt's terms again, power is actualized and new realities are created. There are some lessons here in the multiplicitous ways in which struggles for power relations are mediated by urban design. The various forms of 'power over' outlined in Chapter 1 (force, coercion, domination, manipulation, seduction and authority) are all at play but so are various forms of empowerment, emancipation and resistance. All of these are mediated, yet none are directly produced nor guaranteed by built form. Urban design structures the cognitive maps through which we imagine the body politic and the city becomes available for a politics of representation. This story echoes others from western cities where dynamic images of modernity have been deployed to herald a new social order of emancipation and progress (King 2004: Ch 1). It also echoes the way urban design can evoke the idea of a sacred 'ground' of 'soil and soul', constructing a myth connecting power to the authenticity of nature. Likewise the urban choreography of public rituals, ceremonies and symbolic displays of discipline in public space echo a universal trend.

The story is also interesting for the ways urban space becomes available for practices of resistance. For Lefebvre (1991, 1996) urban space is like a social 'mirror' through which social reality is constructed, imagined and transformed. His well-known proclamation of the 'right to the city' is not only a right to democratic participation, but also a right to the pleasures of urbanity, including the joys of resistance (Lefebvre 1991: 384). Ratchadamnoen Boulevard is a good example of what de Certeau (1985) suggest are places haunted by memory, ever available for redemption and semantic inversion. These practices of resistance have largely relied upon an avoidance of chaos and violence for their success; they are often more like the reciprocity of the 'dance' than a struggle between opposite forces (Pile 1997). These are often rhizomatic practices where meanings and identities are camouflaged, where the maximum effect can be produced by the minimum of conflict.

To understand such a relationship of urban space to democracy requires an eye for the nuances of place experience, for its representational narratives and for those practices which are enabled and constrained within the urban spatial structure and its constellation of monuments. The city can be considered a field wherein the meanings of monuments, spaces, traffic jams and behaviour interweave; where ideologies and power relations are inscribed at once in urban iconography and in everyday life. This is also a field where virtual and actual intersect. Public space plays a role in weakening state and military control of electronic media. The ideological control of television only works to the degree that people believe that it represents a realistic window on a real world. Political spectacle in public space has a very large market. Finally we see here a series of global connections between actions in public space from the fall of Marcos in the Phillipines in 1986 to the Tienanmen protests of 1989 and the Bangkok protests of 1992. It is apparent in all of these cases that the political meanings of urban space are strongly culturally situated.

Part III

Global Types

Chapter 8: Tall Storeys

The Corporate Tower

It is only shallow people who do not judge by appearances.

Oscar Wilde (quoted in office tower advertisement)

The corporate office tower dominates the skyline of most modern cities – a global building type for the command functions of increasingly global corporations. Expressing the Zeitgeist of the twentieth century, such buildings have long captured a certain element of the public imagination. Early skyscrapers, such as the Woolworth and Chrysler buildings in New York, were full of the romance of reaching for the sky. They were also urbane buildings which sat easily within the city and its vital street life, and not tall by today's standards. We no longer use the term 'skyscraper' so much – the romance of distance has faded. They are now the common buildings of corporate culture, a kind of corporate vernacular, and the allure has faded for a range of reasons.

Tall buildings are a response to market pressure for more rentable space on a given site area, yet there are physical limits to this increase in site efficiency. As a long, thin building serviced entirely from one end, the tower loses efficiency with height as banks of elevators progressively consume the volume. Despite these functional limits corporate towers proliferate, primarily because of their role in the symbolic discourse of corporate culture, their market becomes increasingly based in symbolic capital – the capital value attributable to a symbolic or aesthetic 'aura' (Bourdieu 1977). The building image takes on renewed economic importance as a primary generator of symbolic capital. As capital has become increasingly concerned with the production of signs and images rather than use value (Baudrillard 1981; Ewen 1988) so the tower grows taller based on the political economy of the sign. To the extent that serviced floor space is a standardized product, symbolic capital and locational advantage (also largely symbolic) are what gives one office building a market advantage over another.

My initial window into corporate culture is the advertising of corporate towers in Melbourne during the boom of 1989–1991.[1] This advertising is the field of discourse which frames the decision to lease, on which profit is based. It is expensive, market sensitive and therefore likely to reflect the primary values of those at whom it is directed – the corporate elite. The advertising is a primary circuit of symbolic capital. This particular range of discourse reflects the field of symbolic capital of that era but also provides insight into what has and has not changed since then. The aim of the discourse analysis is a decoding of the myths of advertising as ideology, to articulate the experience and subjectivity of corporate culture.[2] The advertising portrays an ideal rather than a reality; it distorts as it mythologizes. Distortions are also indications of the ideals and values that may be driving the image-making process. I shall not discuss the intentions of the architects, nor the experiences of the users. This is not because these intentions and experiences are less important, but in order to focus on the source of profit – the decision to lease. While the particular images are now somewhat dated they offer a particular cross-sectional view of meanings of this building type; while the forms of symbolic capital evolve many of the meanings persist. I shall also bypass the issue of the extent to which this was a local or global discourse, although clearly the global economy of the late twentieth century was marked by a high flexibility of capital investment, and a struggle between cities both for this investment and for position in the hierarchy of world cities (King 2004).

DISTINCTION

The successful corporate tower offers a distinctive image to which lessees are invited to link their corporate image. This quest is for an image of the building as figure against a background which can be achieved in a variety of ways. One of these is the distinction of the work of art, authentically created by the individual genius. One series of advertisements presented the building as a 'masterpiece' created in turn by Van Gogh, Seurat, Michelangelo, Rembrandt, Toulouse-Lautrec and Leonardo da Vinci. In a series of mock interviews these artists extolled the virtues of the building as they posed with it represented in their particular style (Figure 8.1). The building stands alone against the sky with the artist engaged in the creative act. Michelangelo is immersed in a pile of marble rubble as he chisels out the final window details:

> very occasionally a work of art achieves a level of excellence that earns it the title of masterpiece. A sculpture by Michelangelo for instance that by its form and balance surpasses all others. A new sculptural masterpiece is now taking shape.

Leonardo is shown at the drawing board with a feather quill in hand, counterposed against a modern drafting machine. The aesthetic 'aura' masks the facts of social, political and economic process as it constructs an authenticity linked to notions of genius and authority. This is a surface that signifies a false depth while effacing its own spatial and temporal depth. Of course, no-one believes that the

Figure 8.1
Genius and distinction.

building was actually produced in this manner (the real building is steel and glass) but the production of the aura does not rely on such belief.

Distinction is also achieved through a quest for uniqueness of form, whether viewed in the city skyline or in relation to neighbouring buildings. The ideal tower is a landmark in the literal sense of leaving a mark on the land. The buildings are variously described as: 'One of the most significant landmarks in this city' and a 'unique identity when viewed in the city skyline'. The common metaphor is to 'strike': 'a striking new profile on the cityscape', says one, and another 'has a striking sculptural roof, it stamps authority'. Views of the building on the skyline often erase the neighbouring high-rise buildings, reduce them in size or show them in a ghost-like outline to diminish their presence (Figure 8.2).

The quest for visual distinction is also pursued through materials. High-tech images of reflective glass where buildings 'Reflect your corporate image' gave way during the 1980s to polished façades of granite and reconstructed stone. One building, it was argued, will 'dominate with its superb detailed stone exterior' and another 'stands out in a forest of concrete'. The discourse of distinction embodies metaphors of strength and stature, drawing on what Tafuri (1979) calls the 'metaphysics of quantity'; the metonym is spelled out in one advertising campaign as: 'Capital prominence. Business dominance.' One building 'towers over the competition', while another is 'designed to dominate'. The terms 'stature', 'status', 'stability', 'establishment' and 'estate' all share the root *sta* (to stand). The masculinity of this figure against the ground of urban space is underlined by a counter example where a low-rise office development using a courtyard typology was advertised with a female image and the promise that the building 'will seduce you'.

Figure 8.2
Standing alone.

This discourse reveals a corporate community wherein architectural image is of fundamental importance. Collectively these meanings lead to a city where every building wants to be different, to claim identity and authenticity. These forces are likely to lead to an increasingly diverse skyline of new images forever seeking distinction. And they are also likely to lead to a taller skyline where today's landmarks are lost in the crowd or to whatever new range of images claims their meanings.

A further theme in the aura of the ideal corporate tower is a sense of time-lessness. One building incorporates a 'timeless façade of richly ornamented granite'. Stone is an important signifier of permanence and nature, for authentic values that do not change. The brochures show jewel-like samples of reconstituted stone in rustic, quasi-natural form. One tower was described as 'crystal cut', a metaphor attributed to the architect (Kisho Kurokawa). The ideal tower refers both back and forward in time, it is 'designed for the future, but with echoes of an elegant past'. One building is 'designed to span three centuries'; the developers are shown posing with photographs of the Taj Mahal and St Peter's Basilica. Toulouse-Lautrec's 'masterpiece' is labelled *Qualité éternelle d'une œuvre*. The language is targeted at an educated executive taste, portraying an architecture that escapes fashion by achieving standards of eternal quality. Thus, an investment in the sym-bolic capital that the building embodies will not become devalued.

Location within the city also generates symbolic capital: places embody power. The centre of the older financial district was sold as:

> Australia's most powerful business address: . . . In every country there is a street which is home to the most powerful and successful businesses. Wall Street in New York, Threadneedle Street in London. And Collins Street in Melbourne . . . That 300 metre corridor of power . . . the address has a long history of power and success dating back to the 1890s.

Developments in another district used its history and the military metaphor of the 'high ground' to weave a myth of art, science and politics that will enhance the symbolic capital of the place:

> Over the decades great artists, great doctors, great political figures have all resided on the High Ground . . . This is the High Ground . . . There are other parts of Collins Street, but naturally the High Ground dominates them all.

The use of capitals in the text is a common tactic in the weaving of myth, signify-ing that the language connotes far more than it denotes. One building 'has all the credentials you would expect of The Finest Address'.

The corporate neighbourhood is an important form of amenity and sym-bolic capital. The brochures have maps showing nearby companies, hotels and centres of governance, as well as spreads of photos showing street life, restaur-ants, shops, heritage streetscapes, luxury cars, elegant women and nightlife. The ideal office tower is conceived as in harmony with this context; it contributes to the urban character and preserves the qualities of the past. One building is 'dis-tinctly Melbourne with details of the façade, tower and lobby related to the traditional forms' while another is 'inspired by the classic features typical of Collins Street'. These connotations of harmony are sustained by streetscape illus-trations which are distorted to produce views from across the street which would be quite impossible with the human eye (Figure 8.3). A project that was forced to conserve an historic tree claims the design shows 'respect for those things that may not have monetary value but are priceless because of their beauty and

Figure 8.3
Harmony and history.

historical significance . . . working in harmony with nature'. This naturalization of the image, the myth of the enhancement of the city and the connections with context, both temporal and spatial, sustains an ideology of the inevitability of these buildings, of the continued progress of the city skyline ever onwards and upwards. The city is being rebuilt in the name of a 'sense of place', nature and respect for the past. I shall return to these contradictions later.

PROMENADE AND PROSPECT

> The first impression your clients, business associates and suppliers get of your company occurs when they enter the foyer of your building.

The symbolic importance of the foyer is evident in the ubiquity with which it is illustrated and described. In contrast to the static images of the exterior here the text adopts a narrative form describing the experience of entry: 'through a high stone portico into a soaring atrium foyer rising three levels above the floor. In this spacious and airy environment, you'll glance up to dramatic structural ribbing defining the edge of the space'.

The foyer is a major site for architectural innovation in spatial grandeur, with the aim to 'entrance' through impression management: 'the foyer and fore-court area are an architectural achievement in sheer grandeur'. The foyer is a stage set for the drama of 'entering'; we are offered 'the impression of a grand hall and the ultimate experience of space'. Illustrations commonly show overhead spotlights and the play of light on the stone surfaces creates an evanescent effect. One foyer is flanked by 'Juliet balconies'.

The prevailing materials in the foyer are marble and smooth stone; slippery surfaces enriched with artworks frame large volumes of space. The vertical dimension lends the building symbolic value as it lays claim to that awe-filled crick in the neck of the grand public and religious buildings of the past. 'One will be immediately uplifted by its size, yet welcomed by the warmth of its colours and textures. A true work of art.' The use of the qualifier 'yet' in this text reveals that the 'uplift' is not entirely commensurate with the 'welcome'. The foyer is both a welcome celebrated with art and architectural display and also a kind of intimidation. The lavish graphics share a shiny coldness and a severe order with echoes here of the marble halls and slippery surfaces of Versailles and Berlin (Figure 8.4). The foyers are populated by people in business dress, walking through or engaged in greetings. This is not a place to linger, nor for the casually dressed. The foyers are a showcase in techniques of place celebration, but it is 'place' reduced to image of both behaviour and architecture. In the foyer, the triumph of the surface reaches a peak as a spectacle of art, space and light, and the symbolic choreography of corporate discipline.

The view available from the corporate tower is a primary selling point and the valued views are of two types. First are the long views of nature and land-scape: the parks, gardens, lakes, river, bay, beaches and mountains. Second are the panoramic views of the city and its dominant institutions. The view, as

Figure 8.4
Slippery surfaces.

advertised, is never onto a streetscape with people and city life. It is the city in the abstract, from above and at a distance – the surface, not the life. The view directly into nearby office buildings never intrudes on the advertising. The implication is that one is always looking out from the tallest building in the neighbourhood and never into other tall buildings. Thus there is a premium on edge positions with views that cannot be built out: 'the views you lease now will be there forever'. The demand for a long view means that the symbolic capital of a building is linked not only to its site but also to the tower as a building type with a service core surrounded by a rim of rentable space.

The meaning of the view has several components. One is simply aesthetic sustenance, linked to both pleasure and health. One city panorama is captioned 'Consider this as part of your corporate health plan'. The view is an important part of the behaviour setting for corporate decision-making; executives are often shown gazing out while talking or thinking. And the view is a status symbol that is believed to impress visitors, a component in the discourse of corporate negotiation: 'Impress people with your point of view'. To have a view is to be seen to have a vision, and the views are widely described as 'commanding'. The 'interview' with 'Toulouse-Lautrec' uses a cruel humour (for those in the know) to spell out what most of the advertising hints at: 'Drink in that sort of view and you understand what it is to feel stature. Makes you feel ten foot tall'. A literal connection is established between the tall building, tall people and the feeling of power. The use of humour in such advertising establishes a distancing effect from such desires; it enables potent meanings (big buildings for little men) to be flagged without literal endorsement. The dominance of the building as a landmark on the skyline is meshed with the feeling of power engendered by the commanding view from the corner office.

Figure 8.5
Four scenes from the
corporate tower.

The view, however, is not for everyone. Some of the brochures offer indicative interior layouts and images which may be interpreted for the meanings and social hierarchies they indicate. There are four primary work settings which form these plans: the executive office, the reception area, the board room and the open-plan work stations. Figure 8.5 shows these settings clearly and, with the exception of the work stations, they are widely illustrated elsewhere in the advertising. The executive office shows a male executive conferring with other men over an old style wooden desk. In the background is a fireplace and mantel with family portraits, all flooded with natural light. This is a highly personalized and masculine domain where solid conservative images of nature, home and family prevail. The reception area, by contrast, is designed in glossy corporate fashion, is served exclusively by young women and has no windows. This is a mini version of the foyer, a tightly controlled image complete with dramatic lighting, flooring patterns and flowers. The board room is described as a 'dramatic high tech board room with expansive views of the central city'. Two male figures are facing out while they study a report. The final setting is the open planned windowless work stations, which are identical and computerized. This setting is referred to in the text as 'the engine room', a nautical metaphor which relegates productivity to the windowless bilge of the dynamic corporate ship. The flexibility of this interior space is the dominant advertising theme.

Analysis of the indicative plans shows that only about 40 per cent of work stations receive natural light and views.[3] While there are more egalitarian exceptions, the ideal tower is organized in general terms with an executive (male) rim surrounding a core of production. It must be added to this that the consumption of floor space (and therefore of view) per executive is often several times that of the production worker and that the latter will spend a greater proportion of the working day at the work station. If a view and natural light are healthy, then the male head of the corporate body appears to get a disproportionate benefit.

Clearly the most highly valued place on any floor is the corner office, for the double views, the 'light on two sides' and the symbolic prestige that flows from these. During this boom of the early 1990s the trend was towards the design of corrugated façades that produce extra corner offices; one tower had 'up to twelve corner offices per floor' (Figure 8.2). This trend can be linked in part to the fact that corporate headquarters are increasingly the command and control functions of larger conglomerates wherein much of the productive 'engine room' function has been decanted to suburban 'back' offices. This has produced an increase in the proportion of executive occupation of the corporate tower, and an increased demand for the prestige positions. However, there are two interesting contradictions in the corrugated façade. The first is that all of the external offices lose their privacy as they can be observed from corner to corner across the façade and from adjacent floors. There is no more view being produced; the 'extra' view is back into other offices. The second contradiction is that the extra corner offices have to share the same amount of status; more corners equals less meaning per corner. The general principle here is that the quest for symbolic capital is a zero-sum game.

The final advertising theme concerns a cluster of myths constructed around the technology of the building. The brochures were replete with claims about the intelligence of the building and photographs of satellite dishes, micro chips and fibre-optic cables. It is tempting to interpret this advertising as simply good building services, but it too has a powerful mythological component; it is selling a future. The buildings are 'Wired for Tomorrow's Needs', they 'Communicate to the Future'. In his mock interview 'Seurat' claims: 'I never start a picture unless I know exactly where I'm going . . . I see Bourke Place like a giant printed circuit.' The advertising posits a future which will bring rapid change in information technology and service space has been allocated to cope with this change. This belief in constant progress inside the building contrasts with the belief in the 'timeless' façade.

The ideal tower not only shelters but also connects; it is a node of the global village in an information economy. While selling this global information access, the buildings are also selling total secrecy. Information as commodity is protected by secure communications rooms on each floor, connected to rooftop satellite dishes. Corporate operations are protected by 24-hour security whereby behaviour is monitored on closed circuit television. Lessees are offered an environment of total information control and global access in total secrecy. With its commanding views and high levels of both spatial and informational privacy, the corporate office tower is a prime example of the prospect/refuge effect (Appleton 1975).

DOMINANT CONTEXTUALISM

To immerse oneself in this advertising is to become aware of a range of contra-dictions in the production of such a built environment. The ideal and the reality are logically and necessarily at odds with each other. Tall stories are woven around tall storeys. The first contradiction is that of 'dominant contextualism'. The ideal tower achieves symbolic capital through its distinctiveness as a land-mark that dominates its surrounds. Yet it also gains symbolically from being seen as in harmony with this context. The references to context cannot proceed beyond rhetoric without distorted images (Figures 8.2 and 8.3). The quest for dominance leads to a fragmentation of the city because, as Clarke (1989: 56) argues, 'symbolic capital must distinguish itself . . . It must define its edges to protect itself as a symbol and to protect itself as investment . . . As such it cannot be "infill" within the urban continuum'. The formal result of this contradiction is generally a podium on the street frontage with the tower set back behind. The symbolic spectacle of the foyer often claims the entire street frontage and the first few floors of the building – it separates the inhabitants from the street and inhibits any contribution to street life. At other times the podium becomes a thinly disguised parking garage. The rhetoric of contextualism is a cover for a radical separation between life within the building and the life of the street.

To sell the locational advantages, the advertising shows photographs of human scaled streetscapes, sunshine, trees, street life and traditional buildings. This is the 'character' of the neighbourhood which lends the location symbolic capital yet which will be eventually destroyed by the addition of tall buildings. City districts with an attractive sense of place then attract their own destruction at the hands of the corporate tower, a process not dissimilar to what Jacobs (1965) long ago called the self-destruction of urban diversity. Each new tower in a given district contributes to the collective decline in symbolic meaning until such time as the place has been transformed, its symbolic capital consumed.

The quest for locational advantage and the 'powerful address' leads to a clustering of towers. However, as this clustering occurs, the dominant landmark status and the commanding views are lost in the cluster. The quest for domi-nance and view leads to both an increase in height and dispersal. The capital value of the building is enhanced by the view, yet every new building blocks everyone else's view and lowers capital value. Corporate culture seeks to inhabit tall buildings in lower rise districts. The towers grow ever upwards and spread outwards. The quest for height, left unchecked, has no limit since every new tower devalues both the view and the dominance of adjacent towers and fuels the quest for both height and dispersal. Symbolic capital is not so much created as it is moved around from one temporary landmark to another.

The contradiction of 'dominant contextualism' is more than a gesture to the forces of urban conservation. It is linked to another contradictory image of 'dynamic stability' – the aggressive corporation with roots in the conservative past. The dynamic height of the tower juxtaposed on a solid conservative base is the source rather than the limit of its meaning. It is the perceived resolution of this contradiction in the signifier of 'stable dynamism' that maximizes symbolic capital (Harvey 1989: 288). A final contradiction is that of 'timeless fashion' – the tower is forever chasing an image of timelessness which is paradoxically subject to accelerating cycles of fashion. The appetite for distinction leads to increased turnover of imagery and renders buildings quickly obsolete. Signifiers of timelessness go in and out of fashion.

A complex set of dialectics are at work in the semiotics of the corporate tower. The quest for symbolic capital must ride a shifting tide of public opinion as the signifiers of success and domination become those of failure. This is not a new story but its cycles have accelerated. When banks collapsed in the 1930s the solid neo-classical imagery of their buildings was undermined. One such building in Melbourne had a fine neo-classical façade removed at that time to renew its symbolic capital.[4] The replacement façade appears in Figure 8.3 where it has been preserved as a contextual entry to a new building behind – which is paradoxically claimed to be 'as timeless and enduring as the buildings which formerly graced the site'.

The use of design to address the contradictions of corporate culture reached new heights in the early 1990s when a tower in Sydney was developed as headquarters for a major corporation. Upon its completion the firm was bankrupt and its chief executive was in prison.[5] The building was then renamed and advertised as reminiscent of 'buildings designed at a time when business empires were founded on rock-solid principles of ethics and integrity'. Where this meaning market will take us is not clear, but design will continue to mirror a swiftly changing economy and symbolic market in the imagery of money. In the world of modern finance, 'money is water' writes Barna (1992: 8–9), which helps to explain the mirrored glass and polished surfaces. Since the boom of the early 1990s reflected in this advertising we have seen the development of fluid and crystalline buildings which capture the mythologies of the natural, sustainable and flexible. Yet corporate imagery also remains based in older discourses of domination and timelessness. What really persists are the contradictions of dominant contextualism and dynamic stability.

WORLD'S TALLEST

The quest for height in Melbourne reached a peak in the late 1990s with an ultimately unsuccessful attempt to build the world's tallest building. The proposed

'Grollo Tower' was named after the recently deceased patriarch of a large construction company. For his son, Bruno Grollo, this was to be a building for a global stage: 'To do something for Melbourne that did what the pyramids did for Egypt, or the Collosseum did for Rome, or the Opera House and Harbour Bridge did for Sydney'.[6] The proposal was submitted in 1997 as a bid for the docklands redevelopment on the edge of the city grid. The design for a single building on a 13 hectare site showed a slender and elegant obelisk, a stretched pyramid rising from parkland (Figure 8.7). The occupied space was to be a mix of corporate offices, hotel and luxury residential; the lowest floor was to begin 50 metres above the ground and the top part of the pyramid was a giant light beacon to be known as the Melbourne Torch.

There was a great deal of public and press fascination with the tower, much of which lay in some sensitive questions of its deeper layers of meaning. The links to the pyramidal tombs of the pharoahs and to timeless qualities all suggested its beginnings as a memorial to the family patriarch. There were suggestions of a quest for legitimacy with tax-fraud and conspiracy charges pending against the developer. Many of the deeper meanings were best articulated in cartoons, which focused on the symbolic construction of political and sexual identities. This was all clearly linked to the broader quest for identity, power and legitimacy in which architecture has long had its roots. The question was not whether the tower partook in such symbolism, but the scale at which it did so.

Figure 8.6
Grollo Tower proposal.

Public opinion was roughly evenly divided on whether this was a bold move onto the global stage or an embarrassing and damaging project both globally and locally. The developers responded to the various criticisms of the tower and a new vision was released with the site around the base transformed – no longer an isolated object but rising from a new urban precinct with a multicultural food market, festival centre and heritage museum in a neighbourhood of 'cobbled streets' and 'multicultural trading mews'. The 'world's tallest' narrative was played down in an attempt to resolve the dominant contextualism contradiction. The Grollo Tower was finally approved after a 5 year saga but then collapsed over the lack of a government subsidy.

In an interesting twist the tower proposal proved highly useful for the state as a form of political camouflage to capture debate and deflect attention from broader planning issues. Every time a new planning proposal was released the tower proposal was included as a possibility – a striking image guaranteed to consume the attentions of the mass media. The government had a motive for keeping the project alive despite its lack of economic viability. The postscript to this story is that the proposal was briefly revived again in 2003 with the identical design to be constructed on a new site in Dubai, until it was replaced by an even taller building – the Burj Dubai at over 800 metres.[7]

This quest for the world's tallest has been well critiqued by King (2004), who argues that this renewed global quest for height reflects a mix of forces, including the desire for images of modernity, progress and reform in developing nations, constructions of national and cultural identity as well as corporate identity. Interestingly, the demand for higher densities and office space are not among them. The height of the world's tallest inhabited buildings rose rapidly through the early twentieth century; the mantle was held successively by the Woolworth, Chrysler, Empire State and World Trade Centre Buildings until it was claimed and held for over 20 years by the Sears Tower at 443 metres. Pinnacles on more recent towers in Asia have only marginally increased this height. There are fundamental reasons for this flattening out. While density and profit rises with height, these gains have limits since every tall building is effectively a cul-de-sac in the urban fabric which becomes progressively less efficient with height. As the height of the building increases, the space required to get people and services in and out rises exponentially in relation to the useful floor area. Banks of elevators consume more and more of the building volume; and with ever-increasing trip times more elevators per floor are required. The question is not whether, but at what height, this becomes economically (and ecologically) unviable. Taller buildings become enclaves, disconnected from the life of urban networks. Their circulation structures are fundamentally tree-like rather than networked. As the tower grows taller it loses ready access to the dense urban networks that give the city its economic and social life.

In the case of the Grollo Tower proposal, nearly 30 per cent of the height of the tower was to be void – 50 metres at the base and 111 metres of light beacon on top. The project was to occupy a 13 hectare site with a floor area ratio of about 1.25, lower than most of the central city and an underdevelopment of the site's potential. Much of the ground space was to be designed around the imperative of getting massive volumes of vehicles in and out of the underground car park in peak periods. The project was essentially anti-urban and would have left a 13 hectare hole in the dense urban networks of central Melbourne.

There are also powerful economic reasons for the limits to corporate towers. The economic life of cities relies on the co-location of a high density and diversity of people with good access to face-to-face contact in urban space (Jacobs 1965). The information economy thrives in diverse parts of cities with a creative 'buzz' and where new chance encounters are enabled (Storper 2004; Florida 2005). In parallel with the way globalization both evens out and intensifies place experience, cheap telecommunications both reduce and intensify the economic value of face-to-face interaction. Knowledge creation, creative invention, linkages between firms and with customers are all nourished more by open spatial networks than by tree-like spatial enclaves. High-rise buildings are suited to compartmentalized organizations and institutions with high levels of social capital within compartments that do not rely on ad hoc interconnection. The generic spatial structure of the very tall building is diagrammed in Figure 8.7. The foyer and car park control all entry and exit to and from the building; they also separate an executive class with private parking from visitors and others who use the foyer. It is this syntax that enables the investment of symbolic capital in the foyer since it services such a vast range of interior spaces. The structure is shallow in the sense that every floor can be reached within three segments of the street. However, it is also highly fanned or tree-like; moving between floors is often more difficult than getting to the street and as the building gets taller separate

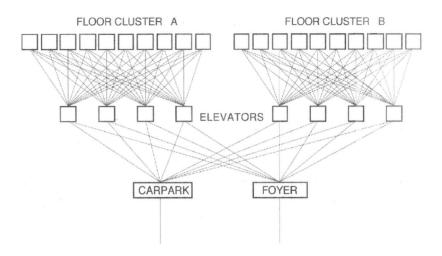

Figure 8.7
Spatial structure of the tower.

clusters of elevators servicing separate clusters of floors accentuate the tree-structure. While the building is generally branded with a particular corporate identity through naming rights, this identity is not apparent in the foyer or elevators which are often shared with many other corporations. Thus the semi-public spaces of the tower interior become what Augé (1996) terms 'non-places', places of comfort and privilege where specific identifications are resisted in favour of an anonymous corporate choreography. The syntax of the tower is a highly sophisticated way of generating maximum access to the street with minimum connection between compartments. The material construction of the large tower is also generally tree-like rather than networked. The structure depends on the stability of a narrow shaft, the vulnerability of which was radically demonstrated on 11 September 2001. While the stems of the World Trade Centre melted, the Pentagon (a networked building type) was not even fully evacuated and continued to function.

There are also environmental limits to this quest for height. While higher densities in general generate sustainability through high levels of walkability and public transport, the new tower typology does not contribute to, and detracts from, this urban ecology. The major contribution of tall buildings to sustainability is made in the first ten storeys. Beyond these limits it is very difficult to protect solar rights unless the diverse small-grain fabric of the city is completely abandoned. If solar is to be the key energy source of the future then it follows that property rights will incorporate solar rights that need to be protected from overshadowing.

The landmark status of tall buildings generates considerable symbolic capital which offsets the inefficiencies that increase with height. The Petronas Towers in Kuala Lumpur, which claimed the mantle of world's tallest for a few years, are effectively public buildings with a giant State subsidy. The architect (Cesar Pelli) was able to fold together the symbolism of nation, Islam and the corporation (King 2004). A second major tactic for offsetting the reduced efficiencies is to reduce the lettable floor area along with demand for elevators, parking and so on. The paradox is that the less habitable space, the higher you can go; and the higher you go the less dense you become.

CREATIVE DESTRUCTION

So what kind of city are these forces of capital creating? First, I want to acknowledge again the positive side to the character of the high-rise city. This is well-expressed by Moholy-Nagy's description of New York in the 1930s:

> This is what made it so fantastic – these buildings, the skyscrapers of New York.
> Obelisks, menhirs, megaliths – every shape, historic and prehistoric . . . There was no
> detail. Night came and even the sharp edged contours melted. A million lights
> perforated the huge masses – switching, flickering – a light modulation dissolving the
> solid form . . . I got drunk – from seeing.
>
> (Moholy-Nagy 1969: 141–143, quoted in Ewen 1988: 166)

This is the evanescent vision of the high-rise city, the play of light on surface with 'no detail'. We can recognize in it the vision of the city that is reproduced in the advertising, in the glossy images and the distant views. This is the place experience of image consumption and even of inebriation. It is a particularly exciting kind of urban place experience which is strongly linked to the experience of the sublime – the encounter with immensity. It is the urban equivalent of being overwhelmed by nature, and it is reminiscent of Benjamin's celebration of the emancipatory capacity of urban poetics. This intoxicating effect of the high-rise city is one kind of vital urban experience but it is not automatically produced by an unregulated market. The sublime experience of the high-rise city requires the clustering of towers; it is paradoxically created and accentuated by height limits which prevent dispersal.

There is a deep paradox in that the most urban of buildings has become a profoundly anti-urban building type. The contradictions embodied in the corporate tower can be seen as manifestations of 'creative destruction', the 'perpetual struggle in which capital builds a physical landscape appropriate to its own condition at a particular moment in time, only to have to destroy it . . . at a subsequent point in time' (Harvey 1985: 25). The New York of the 1930s has been transformed and 50 years later Huxtable wrote:

> As bulk and density increase, avenues darken and close in; shadows lengthen and downdrafts multiply; winter sun becomes a fleeting penetration of cold canyons at midday, leaving neither warmth nor cheer . . . Art becomes worthless in a city brutalized by over development.
>
> (Huxtable 1984: 105)

The anti-urban character of the larger towers is also linked to increased parking requirements. Large towers require huge sites where much of the street frontage is dominated by several storeys of parking garage with gaping holes for entry and exit. These black holes and blank walls are highly damaging to urban street life and attempts to ameliorate their effects are generally superficial. Life inside the building becomes severed from the city since there are no windows on the street and many occupants drive in and out without ever setting foot in public space. The paradox is that as we go higher, urban street life becomes less dense and less diverse. Mega-towers are not the next phase of a vital city; they are anti-urban monoliths which kill urban life.

The scale, the grand foyer and the plinth of parking garage have produced a fundamentally different building type from that which captured the imagination earlier in the twentieth century. While the form of such towers may still inspire admiration from a distance and the views may be spectacular from within, their proliferation has become a form of place destruction in which architects and planners are deeply implicated. The advertising discourse reveals a predatory character – the market preys upon vital and attractive urban places and destroys their value. Corporate towers spread, weed-like, across the landscape. They are not natural, necessary, or inevitable and they are not produced out of ignorance. Much of their prevalence can be attributed to the rational pursuit of symbolic capital. They are the popular buildings of a patriarchal and predatory corporate culture. While towers have tree-like structures, their operations in the market are rhizomatic in a manner that displaces other rhizomatic networks.

So what are the prospects for planning control and for architectural innovation? While my discussion on the advertising does not broach the intentions of the architects, this is not to suggest that they are always or only the mute agents of developers, creating mythology for a fee. It is rather because their stories are told regularly in magazines and coffee table books and scarcely deserve repeating. To critique such discourse is a larger task and the stories of symbolic capital are rarely told there. Architecture magazines tend to treat the economy as somehow neutral with respect to good architecture, which is concerned solely with the autonomous creativity of architecture as art. Yet as Zukin (1991: 161) has pointed out, these magazines and picture books are crucially important symbolic circuits which establish the cultural capital of architects and therefore the symbolic capital of their buildings. Small wonder that lavish coffee-table monographs are often funded by both the subject architects and their clients. The use of well-known architects builds corporate credibility, but requires architects to have an identifiable 'signature'.[8]

It is the cultural and not the technical capacities of architects which make them indispensable to this market – using cultural capital to produce symbolic capital. This produces an uneasy relationship between developers and architects. While developers deploy the mythology of timelessness and authenticity to sell the building, they have their attention firmly on the bottom line and are often disdainful of the cultural elitism and presumed autonomy of architects. Architects, on the other hand, are disdainful of the economic determinism of corporate culture, seeing themselves as reconciling public and private interest in autonomous works of art. Each sees the other as self-interested – whether for profit or reputation. But this is a marriage of convenience which works for each (Barna 1992), hence the joint funding of coffee-table monographs. With the increased turnover and value of building image, the architect's work as producer of symbolic capital becomes more valuable than ever. The market for new images requires imagination and architects are the imaginative agents of urban development. Control over the production of taste is a form of control over symbolic capital (Knox 1982). To the extent that symbolic capital is socially produced, the 'taste' for tall buildings is manipulable.

On the other hand, so long as the quest for market domination is played on a field of urban imagery, so long as profits 'rise' and 'fall', it is difficult to imagine a corporate architecture which does not engage vertical metaphors in some manner. Architecture will always have its roots in the quest for identity and immortality – it has the paradoxical ability to simultaneously signify progress and construct illusions of immortality, of holding back time. And the urge to produce a timeless vertical erection cannot be divorced from the phallic. Much of the best architecture engages a certain aesthetic of sexuality which I would not want to eradicate. But the tall tower syndrome can also be construed as a variation on the schoolyard game of 'mine's bigger than yours'. There is some hope in the idea that the quest for height is a nouveau riche phenomenon where meanings begin to invert and size becomes a signifier of inadequacy.

While it is naive to expect individual architects to refuse to service the dreams of their clients, it is in the collective interest of both the architecture profession and the community to support height limits and renounce these periodic orgies of place destruction. The short-term gains for the few undermine the longer-term legitimacy of the profession. A city wherein good architecture is possible and contributes to urban vitality, where recurring architectural commissions are distributed around the profession on merit, is a city with strong height controls. Professional ethics requires that design imagination is to be placed in the service of the larger community, to develop urban visions that capture the public imagination for a better urban future.

Chapter 9: Inverted City

The Shopping Mall

The Beverly Centre is a three-level shopping mall sitting on a five-storey parking lot, at a major intersection in West Hollywood, Los Angeles. At street level is the Planet Hollywood restaurant with its iconic advertising image of a car entering the street wall. A constantly changing digital sign documents the world's rising population and its declining acreage of rainforest for an audience primarily sitting in traffic (Figure 9.1). Across the globe, closer to both the population and the rainforest, is a city which is similar in more than size. Blok M Plaza in downtown Jakarta is a close cousin of the Beverly Centre and employs its urban wall to support a giant video screen flashing images to the passing, though often jammed, traffic (Figure 9.2). Los Angeles has a reputation for privileging wheels over feet, and for pioneering sequestered zones of safety in a dangerous urban public realm (Davis 1991; Flusty 1997). The main streets of Jakarta present one of the worst pedestrian environments in urban history. Only the poor walk anywhere, and to do so they must negotiate tiny strips of sidewalk which are often blocked. Yet through the portals of either of these malls one experiences an inversion of urban spatial experience. The difficulties and tensions of public space are eased as one enters a protected realm of consumption and spectacle. The enclosed retail environment of the private shopping mall was the most popular and successful new building type of the second half of the twentieth century. It is in many ways the quintessential building type of the age, embodying new and evolving forms of subjectivity, representation and spatial practice.

ARCADE AND MALL

The term 'mall' derives from the game of 'Pall Mall', popular with the French bourgeoisie in the seventeenth century. A small ball was hit with a 'mall' or mallet, along a strip of grass which was fenced and lined with trees. Protected from traffic, this strip soon became a popular place for promenading (Kostof 1991: 251). Its formal qualities were consistent with those of the political vista

Figure 9.1
Beverly Centre, Los
Angeles.

Figure 9.2
Blok M Plaza, Jakarta.

and led to its use for military parades and to the naming of spaces of centralized power in London and Washington as 'malls', while also retaining the meaning of a protected promenade.

As a place for shopping, the modern mall has its sources in the nineteenth-century urban arcades. Milan's Galleria Vittorio of 1867 is the prototype, a series of 'galleries' which radiate from a central domed space in a cruciform plan. These early arcades were located near the '100 per cent locations' of maximum pedestrian traffic in the city. They created new means of access, adding to the permeability of the urban structure by providing private shortcuts. Thus they gained their economic life through the capacity to redirect existing pedestrian flows off the city streets. This connection of economic vitality to urban permeability was theorized much later by Jacobs (1965) in her famous study of American cities.

Walter Benjamin became interested in the small Parisian arcades of the early nineteenth century as the harbinger of a fundamentally new kind of space. This was an interior dream world of luxury commerce made possible by new technologies of glass, steel and gas lighting.[1] In contrast to most theorists of his time, Benjamin saw modernity not as enlightenment or demystification but as a new mythology. Archaic collective myths steeped in ideas of the eternal were being replaced by a collective dream world of mass culture – the fleeting and dynamic myth of the commodity. In the arcades he saw a new integration in the production of space, architecture, commodity and subjectivity. The arcades caught the collective imagination, but curiously without the social solidarity of the public street and square (Buck-Morss 1989: 261). Thus emerged a spatial milieu which was social but not communal, a zone of 'public life' that privileged the individual over the group. The arcades privatized the public imagination.

Benjamin linked the development of the arcades with the figure of the flâneur – the nineteenth-century stroller on the streets, promenading to see and be seen. The flâneur combined conspicuous consumption with urban voyeurism and consumption of street life as spectacle. The 'enclosure' of this spectacle also had a strongly gendered dimension. The nineteenth-century city was seen as labyrinthine, impure and dangerous – not a place for women (Wilson 1991). The development of the arcades coincided with the gendered 'separation of spheres' which marginalized women to the suburbs. The arcade constructed a protected place for women in the city, both as consumers and as subjects of the male gaze (Rendell 2002). Thus the economic advantage of the arcade came as a conjunction of innovations in urban spatial structure and the enclosure of a place with new forms of social relations and subjectivity.

A related source for the mall was the department store, which paralleled the development of the arcades. The department store removed the obligation on the consumer to be shopping *for* something in particular. Instead, it surrounded the consumer with a world of possible goods and removed the counter as a boundary between the two. As Ferguson (1992: 30) points out, 'The department store is ideally a building which absorbs and swallows the shopper'. The consumer is not so much servicing a need as exploring a world. In this context the purchase is not predetermined; desires and identities are constructed in the shopping experience. The arcade was at once a short-cut in the urban structure, a refuge from the noise, dust and weather, a zone of urban voyeurism and a dream world of mass consumption. The private shopping mall was a development of both the structural and representational effects of both arcade and department store. I shall deal with the spatial structure first.

SYNTACTIC INVERSION

The building type we now know as the mall emerged in the 1950s with the discovery that pedestrian densities could be created artificially in the car-based suburbs through a coupling of the arcade with the department store as a 'magnet' or 'anchor'. This structural invention is generally attributed to Victor Gruen at Southdale Mall, Minneapolis in 1956.[2] Gruen was a modernist community planner who was nostalgic for the urbanism of his native Vienna. He saw the US suburbs as lacking a 'heart' for face-to-face communication and community life (Hardwick 2004). His key innovation was the structural marriage of the department store and the arcade – the so-called 'dumb-bell' plan. A large 'anchor' store at either end was joined by an arcade (the 'handle') lined with a string of smaller shops. The essential innovation, however, was the syntax and not the plan. The principle was that the 'anchors' act as 'magnets' to draw customers past the smaller shops, increasing the density of pedestrian traffic and ensuring that there are no economic dead ends. While this spatial structure is named after its early 'dumb-bell' plans, the governing syntax was the lineal link from car park to magnet with the mall as control space and the two magnets generating a fan structure as in Figure 9.3.

Thus the new mall structure generated high pedestrian densities with high rental value. This added value lay in the potential to seduce the passing consumer into impulse consumption. This is the time-honoured function of the shop window, yet the capacity of the architecture to transfer the attention of the consumer was new and was attributed to the architect as the 'Gruen Transfer' (Crawford 1992). The spatial syntax of the 'dumb-bell' structure ensures that the magnet stores which hold the power of attraction are located as the deepest cells of the structure, such that entry to them passes first through the mall spaces and past the specialty shops. Yet it is in the interest of both the consumer and the anchor store to give direct access from the parking lot to the anchor store, permitting the consumer to engage in convenience shopping and avoid the mall entirely. This of course undermines the viability of the smaller stores, which rely on passing traffic and impulse purchasing. Thus the structure of the mall is fundamentally coercive in that it manipulates consumers into long pathways to

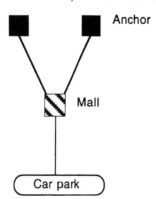

Figure 9.3
Shopping mall genotype.

maximize impulse consumption. The shortcut of the urban arcade becomes a detour in the suburban mall.

While the dumb-bell principle remains pervasive it is rarely built in its pure form. The manipulation of consumers through long pathways is in contradiction with the need to attract them with convenience. Direct entry is sometimes given to anchor stores and the structure has been elaborated over the decades into multiple levels and multiple 'dumb-bells', often in diagonal and cruciform plans. Furthermore, a large range of hybrid malls has developed, based on the realization that anything which attracts people can have a mall inserted between the entrance and the attraction. Thus we have a proliferation of malls grafted onto waterfronts, museums, airports, theme parks, movie studios, casinos, hotels and historic attractions (Kowinski 1985; Sudjic 1993). A good deal of attention has focused on mega-malls like West Edmonton Mall and the Mall of America, where the mall itself becomes a regional attraction (Karasov and Martin 1993; Shields 1989). My concern, however, is with the more generic type and its more pervasive effects on everyday life.

Figure 9.4 shows a spatial analysis of three typical suburban malls. Chadstone and Forest Hills in Melbourne, Australia, were developed in the 1960s and

Figure 9.4
Three typical malls: spatial structure.

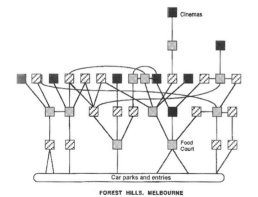

FOREST HILLS, MELBOURNE

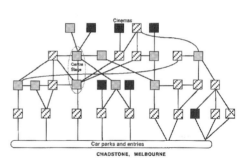

CHADSTONE, MELBOURNE

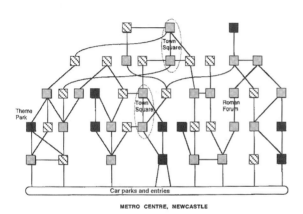

METRO CENTRE, NEWCASTLE

KEY

■ Anchors
▨ Courts
▨ Malls

Specialty stores are omitted for clarity

141 □

expanded in the 1980s with about 200 specialty stores on two or three levels. Each has from six to eight anchor stores including supermarkets, cinemas and department stores. The Metro Centre near Newcastle, England, is a larger mall with a children's theme park, two 'town squares' and themed shopping zones ('Roman Forum' and 'Mediterranean Village').[3] The spatial analysis treats the car parks as a base, with the various internal courts and mall sections as segments of the structure. Smaller shops lining the malls and courts are omitted from the diagrams for clarity. While there is a certain arbitrariness about this segmentation method, it reveals the remnants of the generic dumb-bell structure within complex multilevel structures of this kind. The mall segments and courts are located at an average of about two segments deep from the car park.

While the anchor stores have a higher average depth than the mall segments, as the mall grows larger the simple dumb-bell structure is dissipated. Attractions such as the fun park and food hall become directly accessible from the car park and the sheer size of the mall becomes an attractor in itself. While these structures are deeper and vastly more complex than the original dumb-bell, the manipulative control over the pathway from the car park to the anchor stores remains evident. These common and complex malls can be construed as a series of interlacing dumb-bell structures which sometimes accede to direct connections with anchors while maintaining a primarily internal orientation.

Once one penetrates to a depth of two or three segments, this structure becomes highly permeable or 'ringy'. There are many alternate paths for circulation throughout these levels, but the parking lot is never part of a ring. The most shallow segments, where one enters from the car park, have a primarily lineal syntax. These locations are generally marginal to the dominant modes of economic life and encounter within the mall. While car parks may connect with each other, their use is governed by the lineal connection to the closest entrance to the mall.

The ringy heart at a depth of two to three segments is the most significant structural development since the dumb-bell. It combines the dumb-bell with high levels of permeability. There is a strong connection here with Jacobs' (1965) insight that urban ringiness or permeability is strongly linked to urban street life. The staged events and spectacles, which are the major 'adjacent attractions' of the mall, are usually located at these levels. Thus the mall structure uses the drawing power of its anchors to artificially generate a certain vitality and permeable sense of urban encounter at its heart. This is one primary sense in which the mall is the 'city inverted'. Urban public life has been 'recreated' in private space. The open encounter of the permeable street network has been enclosed under conditions of controlled encounter. And, ironically, the urban impermeability generated by large lump developments like the mall is inverted once inside it.

The structure of the mall determines rental values within it, and unlike the city where rental values are a function of competition, the mall is a highly controlled market. The variety of shops is determined by a formularized 'mix' to maximize profit for mall management. The anchor stores or magnets get the cheapest rental space because they are the attractors. The shallow shops close to the car park entrances are the cheapest of the small shops since people rarely pass except when entering or exiting. These shallow marginal locations are used for convenience outlets such as photo shops, dry cleaners and banks. They are also used for low-profit specialty stores which attract a particular rather than a general clientele – carpets, furniture, fabric, do-it-yourself, pets and optics. In this function they operate as minor attractors for specific customers. Peak rents are charged in the ringy heart, the primary zone of impulse purchasing where the 'mix' favours jewellery, gifts, clothes and accessories. This zone constitutes a structural separation between the low rent conveniences of the entry zones and the anchors. By combining a large range of shops in one location and then making the attractors difficult to get to, the mall creates high levels of convenience and inconvenience simultaneously. Free parking and one stop shopping in a safe environment are meshed with controlled and enforced window shopping.

The lessons learnt from Jacobs' critique of urban functional mix are also apparent in the design of the mall. She noted the ways in which a free property market squeezed out marginal uses in a process she termed the 'self-destruction of diversity' (Jacobs 1965). Districts with a vital urban mix tend to attract high rent functions which displace low rent uses and destroy the diversity which attracted high rents and vitality in the first place. The mall seeks to address this problem with a formularized mix of anchors, specialty shops and small stalls, coupled with differential rent fixing. Banks are not permitted to deaden the vital pedestrian frontage at the heart of the mall as they can do in the city.

While the mall is designed to resemble the vital diversity of the urban realm, there is little freedom of enterprise within it. The range and variety of goods on offer is a product of strong policy and control over shop proprietors. Restrictive leases ensure control over opening hours, shopfront design and product placement. Management have access to financial records, often receiving a share of the turnover. Enterprises which do not fit the formula are excluded from the successful mall. Small business comes under the control of big business. Formularized chain stores (big business with small outlets) are the only small stores which can hold their own in this league. Genuine diversity is eliminated.

Such totalizing control within the mall renders the market somewhat opaque. There is little of the 'transparency' that Lynch (1981) theorizes as a primary value of urban form. There are no closing down sales; one cannot read the signs of success or failure. The semiotics of urban space come under the control of mall marketing as vacant shops are swiftly filled and shopfront designs are regularly renovated. Advertising is strictly controlled to avoid saturation of the visual field. There is only so much space in the semantic field and it is managed to maximize consumption. While there is little of the free market within the mall, there is fierce competition with other malls and with public shopping districts. This competition is often framed in terms of the scale of the centre and the range of stores it can offer. Thus malls grow ever larger and more complex in the urge to outgrow each other. But this competition is also one of design and semantics as malls seek to differentiate themselves as places within the suburban landscape.

The mall structure embodies a central contradiction between convenience and manipulation. The mall attracts consumers with greater convenience than other malls or shopping centres. Yet this imperative to attract is coupled with the imperative to manipulate consumers past as many shops as possible. To this end paths through the mall are often bent on the basis that if consumers can see the long distance they will not walk it (Garreau 1991).

SEMANTIC INVERSION

The spatial opposition between the mall and its context is also semantic; to enter the mall is to undergo a set of semantic inversions. The mall constitutes a safe and predictable realm within a world rendered dangerous by both crime and cars. It also holds a strong attraction in terms of shelter from the prevailing weather. It contrasts with its context as cool when the weather is hot, warm when cold, dry when wet and calm when windy (Crawford 1992). There is no mall weather. While malls first became popular in cold climates, they have a similar advantage in hot and humid climates and are very popular in Southeast Asia. The mall is a clean and highly designed place in contrast to a sometimes derelict context. It embodies the signifiers of class – terrazzo paving, brass and glass – and there are no signs of poverty. The mall creates a purified environment, not only physically and climatically, but also socially. The mall offers at least the illusion of a vital public life and harmonious community. These meanings are congruent with those of 'home' – a stable and sheltered sense of enclosure which gains its meaning from the inside/outside dialectic (Dovey 1985b). The mall establishes its meaning in opposition to the perceived dereliction, danger, placelessness and alienation of the public realm. Indeed, the more the public places of our cities decline in quality and safety, the greater the relative advantage of the private mall.

The mall establishes a place that is semantically and structurally severed from the city which sustains it. Such oppositions are often starkly apparent in the entry transition from the car park to the mall. The car park is a continuous, rationally gridded surface with long sight lines, abstract codes for orientation and minimal design expression. Undercover car parks have low ceiling heights, often with poor light and air quality. This world inverts on the threshold between the car park and the mall. On one side the subject is conceived and constructed as rational, destination oriented and asocial, with aesthetic judgements somehow suspended. Beyond the threshold, the world reverses and brightens as the senses are pampered and seduced with a massive investment in design.

This inversion is akin to Bourdieu's (1973, 1977) notion of the *habitus* as a 'world reversed', where the rules and the game can shift on a threshold. In this case one enters a kind of theatre. Shopping is no longer a functional task, it moves to front stage and becomes a form of lifestyle (Shields 1992). As in the

Figure 9.5
'Rome', Metro Centre,
Newcastle.

department store, one is consumed by the mall which combines entertainment with consumption. As in a theatre, there is an element of hyperreality, a suspension of disbelief strongly influenced by the theme park. It is a heterotopic environment where far-flung and exotic places come together in a collage of simulations. In a kind of 'reverse tourism', the mall brings the world to us. Its fantasy themes are often drawn from film and television – from ancient history (Figure 9.5) to a high-tech future – any time or place that catches the imagination can be simulated in the mall (Gottdiener 1995).

But if this is theatre, it is a theatre of life – the world as stage, on which our role is to consume. The function of fantasy in the mall is the stimulation of consumption (Gottdiener 1995: 289). Court and plaza segments of the mall are designed as 'adjacent attractions' – fountains, events and displays which relieve shopping fatigue and revive the shopper for another round (Crawford 1992). Yet its effects rely on the fact that it is a 'liminal' space, it lies between categories – theatre/life; entertainment/consumption; public/private (Zukin 1991). Our consumption of the micro-climate and spectacle melds into our consumption of commodities as part of our immersion in the 'sense of place'. The mall is a place of fluid identity where the suspension of disbelief becomes reflexive. It is a place where we 'watch the world go round' (Ferguson 1992), but this is a world where we lose our 'selves' in both space and time. There are no clocks within the mall and views to the surrounding landscape are rare. Entrances are 'one-way portals' (Clarke 1989) which read as entry from the exterior but not as 'exit' from the interior.

The mall is the most pervasive everyday example of what Jameson (1984) named postmodern 'hyperspace' – a disorienting world of fragmented surfaces and superficial reflections coupled with a highly eclectic collage of architectural styles. The deliberately decentring effects of 'deconstructive' architectural style, with clashing grids and glass floors, are easily incorporated into the mall. This is a form of design which confounds our capacities for cognitive mapping (Jameson 1988). In his seminal work on urban imagination Lynch (1969) established a language for speaking about the image of the city, the ways we make sense of the public world through cognitive imagery. While his work was weak on issues of meaning, the categories of landmarks, nodes, districts, paths and edges have persisted. The mall both utilizes and confounds such imagery. It seeks to establish the malls as landmarks in the urban landscape. But the orientation to an urban landscape is then displaced and replaced with a reorientation to a new set of co-ordinates – primarily the nodes, landmarks, plazas, attractions and the connecting paths between them. Thus the mall has no cognitive edges – the interior is a seamless web of continuous façades.

Shields (1989: 155) suggests that this disorientation in space and time 'wreaks havoc with our cultural sense of collective identity, with the spatial metaphors which mediate and represent the relationship between communities and individuals, and with linear notions of historicity as progress'. The mall uses a 'sense of place' to dismantle a 'sense of history'. The temporal orientation to a particular history is replaced with a collage of places and times. 'Mall sickness' is the label some give to a vague sense of anxiety, the loss of the sense of time and memory of what you wanted to buy (Kowinski 1985). This 'zombie' effect is not unlike that which can be induced by too much television. And, like television, the mall can induce both excitement and docility simultaneously.

PSEUDO-COMMUNITY

The control over spatial structure and representation is coupled with strong controls over behaviour, enforced by surveillance cameras and security staff. The mall is a highly purified and controlling place where anything different to the norm of the happy consumer is subtly excluded. The mall constructs an ideal 'community' with no poverty, division or eccentricities. It has a permanently festive atmosphere geared to spending with abandon, but without the genuine abandon of the public carnival or the tensions of political protest. These are Foucauldian regimes of 'normalization' whereby potential disruptions to the designed effect are recognized and evicted. Variations from the neatly dressed and normally behaved consumer are suspect. Shabby clothes, sitting on the floor or even sitting for long in one place can all lead to exclusion. These prohibitions are, in some contexts, made quite explicit, including clothes 'likely to create a disturbance' or any 'expressive activity without the written permission of the management'.[4] As everyday practice, however, these forms of control are generally invisible; the 'rules' are embodied in the *habitus* of the mall. The subtle exclusion of difference melts into the exclusion of overt politics – leafleting, picketing, demonstrating and lobbying. Limited forms of managed politicking are permitted in malls, where they function as forms of legitimation, reassurances that this is a genuine public space while sources of disruptive conflict remain repressed.

Indeed, shopping malls have become ideal places for politicians to meet and mix with 'the people' during election campaigns. The mall offers a collection of 'normal' folk in a bright yet passive mood, in a context where any genuine conflict will be avoided. The exclusion of politics has political uses since it delivers a guaranteed 'community' of docile subjects.

The pseudo-public space of the mall constructs what Habermas (1989) has construed as a distorted speech situation, a situation which generates the illusion of free speech. The mall is framed as unstructured encounter yet with instrumental imperatives. This is a spatial manifestation of the system colonizing the lifeworld of 'public space'. It is far from Arendt's ideal of a space where words and deeds are joined, where power is defined in the capacity to reach agreement and to act in concert (Arendt 1986). While its signifiers are heterotopic, the mall embodies the utopian desire for a purified community of social harmony, abundance and classlessness. Yet the mall needs the illusion of genuine public life – community organization, politics and festivity. It claims the meanings of public space without the politics; the ideal consumer will see it in one way and use it in another. A schism is introduced between the place as text and as lifeworld. While it is owned and controlled privately, it claims the meanings of public space often down to the use of street signs and the 'town square'.

Shields (1992: 9) points out that leisure and legitimation share the same Latin root *lex*: 'law'. In this sense the mall is a zone of legitimized pleasure linked to Bakhtin's (1984) notion of the carnival as a spectacle of urban transgression and inversion, where social codes and hierarchies are suspended. The carnival constructs a place and time of fantasy, intoxication and exaggeration wherein emotions may be unleashed (Featherstone 1991: 22). The mall aims for an almost permanent yet benign festive effect – exuberant spending without behavioural abandon. The proliferation of banners in malls is part of this construction of permanent carnival. A series of banners at the Metro Centre (Figure 9.6) features various staff members of the mall and constructs short narratives weaving together their roles as consumer and worker: 'Nikki works for Marks and Spencer selling kitchen ware and buys impulsively, mostly sparkling jewellery'. This forges a community of interest between shopper and staff, discouraging shoplifting and encouraging spending.

The mall embodies the contradiction of a 'private community'. As a space of private control coupled with public meanings, it relies upon the illusion of public space. Thus the mall needs public buildings, politics and community life to sustain this illusion and the mall as a building type is gradually opening up to 'public' functions – churches, police stations, museums, libraries, social services and medical facilities (Shields 1989). Cities are negotiating and paying for the inclusion of public facilities within the private space of malls and it remains to be seen just where this will lead. Thus far such public facilities tend to occupy marginal locations within the mall structure so as not to disrupt the representational effects nor consume vital retail frontage.

The mall seeks to legitimize itself as public and communal, yet this mostly leads to gestures of legitimation which are framed within private space. A

NIKKI works for
Marks & Spencer
selling kitchen ware
and buys impulsively,
mostly sparkling
jewellery.

Figure 9.6
Metro Centre, Newcastle:
community of
consumption.

good example is the proliferation of car raffles, where gleaming luxury cars are parked in the mall and raffled for the benefit of 'charity'. The cars serve also as adjacent attractions and community legitimators. They are seductive 'wish images' which also represent the public interest idea of charity and goodwill. Yet unlike real charity raffles, these are highly instrumentalized, with strings of identical cars (but only one real prize) on display throughout a string of malls. This ensures a swift turnover of both raffle draws and 'adjacent attractions'. The mall generates an illusion of civic life and a mis-recognition of community (Shields 1989). As Gottdiener (1995: 289) puts it, the mall is 'instrumental rationality disguised as social communion . . . Urban ambience is harnessed to the profit motives of privately controlled space'. This illusion is not only representational but also constructed through structural inversion. This 'enclosure' of the 'urban' that one finds in the typical mall generates a curious new category of space. As Hillier and Hansen (1984) have shown, one of the key differences between interior and exterior space is that building interiors are far more deterministic of behaviour and encounter, with greater capacities for social control and reproduction. By contrast, the free flow of everyday life in exterior urban space renders social encounter more probabilistic than deterministic. From this viewpoint the mall constructs a new kind of interior space with high levels of social control, while maintaining the illusion of public space and free encounter.

Lest this argument sounds too totalizing, the mall is too complex to be reduced to a mechanistic function of the imperatives of the market. Practices of resistance within the mall would seem to refute such instrumentalizing, as Shields argues:

> its carnivalesque appropriation as a site for *flânerie* by its users . . . redeems the
> authenticity of the mall, which is pushed into the background of users' authentic
> meeting and interaction . . . one finds individual reversals, destabilizations, and
> interventions in a continuous play for the freedom of this space made by users who
> must not be 'written off' as passive consumers.

> (Shields 1989: 161)

Fiske (1989: 37) shows evidence of this among adolescents, who use the behavioural code of the mall as a foil for confrontation. They deploy guerrilla tactics for disrupting its regimes and creating a spectacle for their own consumption. They drink alcohol from soft drink cans under the nose of security guards, and the inverse – acting inebriated to goad security guards into action. Following the work of de Certeau, Fiske celebrates such forms of resistance and points out the paradox that 'power can achieve its ends only by offering up its underbelly to the attacker' (Fiske 1989: 41). The carefully contrived representational effects of the mall, its exclusion of difference, make it vulnerable. The production of a carnival atmosphere encourages carnivalesque behaviour. The more the mall deploys the signifiers of democratic public space, the more it encourages democratic public use. Malls are meeting the adolescent challenge with restructuring – locating game arcades, cinemas and food halls in a manner that will separate them from the heart of the mall. Thus the logic of the 'dumb-bell' structure is undermined as magnets become accessible directly from the car park and teenage behaviour is subtly spilled to the car park and street, where they become a public rather than private problem. These defensive strategies show a certain power of the mall subject to resist the mall's seduction and to alter the manner in which its manipulations are exercised. However, these forms of resistance are rarely more than trivial; my suburban high school was full of such resistances, creatively testing the boundaries of disciplinary regimes. To suggest that it redeems the mall is to trivialize the practices of power and the more general constructions of docile urban life. Practices of behavioural control in the mall are highly sophisticated, as Langman (1992: 48) argues: 'the control is not so much through surveillance as the organization of spatial settings and the allocation of fantasy and pleasure'. The mall operates like a drug rather than a prison – teenage resistance may be no more than an early phase of addiction.

Sennett (1973, 1974, 1994) has long argued that a diverse urban public realm is crucial for the constructions of identity that occur during adolescence and for the forms of tolerance that characterize truly 'civil' urban life. It is in diverse urban encounter with difference that we grow up and become fully civilized. For Sennett, the fear of difference leads to a stunting of identity and a retreat to the ideal of a purified community. He notes the rise of individualism in public space in the nineteenth century with the emergence of the right to not be spoken to on the street, linked to the rise of the urban *flâneur* (Sennett 1994: 324). This links in turn to the retreat to the suburbs and the urban marginalization of women (Wilson 1991). From this view the mall can be seen as part of a larger imperative to reduce uncertainty and to neutralize the potency of urban space. The greater tragedy of the mall is not so much the manipulation as the loss of opportunity – it offers neither the challenge nor the inspiration of genuine urban life.

There are also clues to this question of resistance in a return to the work of Benjamin, who saw a revolutionary energy at the heart of the collective dreaming of commodity culture (Buck-Morss 1989; Gilloch 1996). He believed that the ludic dimension of creative imagination in childhood play becomes repressed by forces of social order, and that these repressed fantasies were exploited in the seductions of the arcades. Benjamin suggested that the creative connection between perception and action that characterizes childhood play also characterizes revolutionary consciousness in adults (Buck-Morss 1989: 263). This repressed ludic dimension embodies a liberating energy of resistance, a rejection of given meanings and creation of new meaning. The repression of the ludic embodies an acceptance of 'correct' meanings and a repression of action – look but don't touch. Yet for Benjamin it is possible to see the dream *as* a dream through a dialectic of awakening. Arcades and malls as 'dream worlds' harbour a utopian wish for an ideal society of harmony and abundance. For Benjamin such 'wish-images' have a political potential which can be awakened by each new generation, bringing the old symbols back to life (Buck-Morss 1989: 275).

From this view the danger of urban life is part of its vitality, linked to the aesthetic of the sublime (Savage 1995). Benjamin saw that urban experience offered an aesthetic realm which resisted the loss of the 'aura' that characterizes twentieth century art. Unlike the fine arts, the urban spectacle is experienced in distraction, which lends it an added potential to trigger dreams and memories. While the ludic dimension thrives in the mall, this is an expropriation of the urban. The mall polarizes the city, it offers a place of ersatz pleasure without danger within an urban context that increasingly offers the danger without the pleasure. The high hopes of the early shopping malls were understandable. The damage to street life and community from cars was apparent and the dangers of privatization were not. The utopian ideals of remaking community life were pervasive and there are some who celebrate a limited success. For Kowinski (1985):

> The malls responded with what the city no longer had: clean, safe, human-scaled
> environments where people could walk and see other people . . . They didn't lock out
> the kitsch and kin of human tastes and interaction; they enclosed them in a protective
> embrace. They didn't embody visions of the ideal; they fulfilled pedestrian fantasies.
>
> (Kowinski 1985: 272–273)

This portrayal of the enclosure as protection rather than manipulation, the spectacle as fulfilment rather than seduction, shows the ideological success of the mall. Its advantages over its urban context lead us to rationalize away what has been lost. It is often suggested that the mall has a democratizing effect in bringing a taste of luxury to socially disadvantaged areas. But Gruen's dream of community life has not been realized. He became disillusioned with these forms of 'community' and disowned the mall idea long before he died in 1980 (Kowinski 1985). His original Southdale Mall has been through a series of renovations and additions since 1956 yet remains recognizeably different, primarily because of the generous 'plaza' at its heart, and because the public artwork and clock have been protected as heritage. It is infused with the same tensions over behaviour that are common at least throughout North America. Photographs are prohibited, as are youths under 16 without 'parental escorts' on Friday and Saturday nights.[5]

URBAN MALAISE

The story of the shopping mall has been presented thus far in terms of the standard regional variety that prevailed throughout most of the late twentieth century. Regional malls of this type have developed in a range of different ways but have generally been losing customers since the 1990s for a range of reasons – consumer resistance due to mall sickness and lack of variety; accelerating competition between malls and with the public city. One result has been what are known as 'dead malls' where one or more of the anchors become vacant and the mall goes into economic decline. In some cases this is little more than a private version of a low-rent shopping strip. In other cases entire malls or parts of them become derelict.[6] One wing of the Forest Hill mall in Melbourne, documented earlier, has since become dead. Dead malls become available for marginal functions and anchor tenancies have become educational institutions. In complete dereliction, dead malls take on a ghostly, uncanny quality and have become sites for movie making and photography. A new semantic inversion takes place as striated spaces become smoother and the place gains a level of transparency and authenticity that stands as an inversion of its original qualities. In the US the decline of the traditional mall has become a major urban phenomenon as the market deterritorializes the city and creates opportunities for new forms of redevelopment (Hayden 2004: 66; Egan 2000).

Malls that succeed often do so by growing larger and larger until forced to abandon the structural type of the regional mall. The Mall of America, in suburban Minneapolis, is widely cited as the largest in the world, with 40 per cent of its customers travelling from outside the region.[7] The spatial structure is that of a large theme park encircled by the shopping mall, which is structured as a chain of four dumb-bells. All of this sits within and on a giant car park encircled by a constellation of tourist hotels. This is of course a quite different building type – the anchor stores are accessed directly from the carpark and the labyrinthine shopping network is missing. The shopping mall has become the entrance to the theme park; the scale ensures that local customers need to drive from one side to the other.

Such mega-malls have a limited future because they service the local population poorly. Phase II of the Mall of America will supplement the current mall with what is commonly called a 'lifestyle center'.[8] These are private mixed-use developments focused on shopping and leisure but incorporating office, hotel and residential uses (Blum 2005). Here shopping becomes integrated with a lifestyle of leisure and pleasure; the desire to shop replaces the desire for particular goods. The transfer of attention from the planned purchase to the impulse purchase is complete and the structural innovation of the dumb-bell becomes somewhat obsolete. Cinemas, supermarkets or department stores may be part of such a mall but their role in attracting and manipulating customers is smaller. The focus of attraction moves to the social life and contrived 'sense of place' of plazas and streetscapes. One thing that does not change, indeed becomes more central, is the displacement of the public realm. Lifestyle malls replicate traditional public streets – often open to the sky with curbside parking and a greater level of integration with the public context. The model is often the traditional village with a market place and community life – the word 'mall' becomes erased from the discourse lest it remind customers of the enclosed and privatized places they have tired of. Another thing that does not change is the reliance on private transport. In its focus on the quality, diversity and authenticity of a walkable 'public' realm, on the efficiencies of mixed use and increased residential density, the lifestyle mall begins to become indistinguishable from a privatized version of the new urbanist village.

A rather different development of the mall is found in the central city of Minneapolis, where a private pedestrian network of skyways has grown incrementally and now comprises a complete alternative to public space. Every major block of the central city grid is linked to a network that is in turn linked to a range of parking lots and garages on the edge of downtown (Figure 9.7). The most common spatial structure is that a small multi-level mall is formed around an atrium within each city block and connected at first floor level with an overpass to each adjacent block. Here the role of the anchor tenant is largely subsumed by the corporate towers for which these malls form a base.

The skyway network developed incrementally over several decades, driven largely by the temperature differential between inside and outside. In winter the skyway is a giant comfort zone, yet the damage to public life lasts all year round.

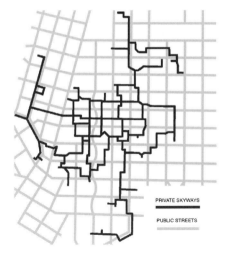

Figure 9.7
Minneapolis skyways.

Figure 9.8
'City Center Minneapolis'.

The private appropriation of the public realm is reflected in the name of the pro-motional newspaper formerly known as the *Skyway News* but changed in 2005 to *The Downtown Journal*. 'City Center' is typical of the mall atria, connected primarily to the skyway with a ground level entry from the street grid (Figure 9.8). The brochure says that: 'If for any reason City Center fails to meet your expectations we would like to know immediately . . . Thank you for choosing City Center!' These private 'Centers' compete with each other; the competition between public and private space is largely resolved with most major shopfronts having moved inside and up along with the pedestrian traffic. Outside 'City Center', a group of homeless men gather in the cold. Laws against discrimination mean they can usually come into the warmth and occupy the public seating, so long as they perform the role of the normalized urban subject, remaining upright and awake under the constant gaze of private security. The advertising brochures are not for them.

While the mall in its different variations comprises a cluster of global types, there are local variations which remain relatively unresearched (King 2004). Such variations tend to be responses to culture, climate, density and perceptions of dereliction or danger in public space. The mall operates through both a structural separation from public space and a seductive interior world that replaces it; in general terms the separation is a global constant while the forms of seduction may differ. Having said this, the interior of new malls is often almost indistin-guishable in the east and west. Bangkok's newest mall, the Siam Paragon which opened in 2005, is notable for the almost complete absence of any signage in Thai script. It is the contrast of this orderly, wealthy and global interior to the local chaos that attracts its global subjects; an internalized world of freedom that

Figure 9.9
Siam Paragon, Bangkok.

transcends the places of everyday life (Figure 9.9). The proliferation of malls in Southeast Asia is a product of a mix of potent factors – heat and humidity, social division, public danger and dereliction, and a political context that often mixes enthusiasm for privatization with corruption. Another global constant of the large shopping mall is that the scale of urban impact ensures that it is always dependent on political support for such development.

The seductions and manipulations of the mall are not totalizing, but neither are they easily resisted. They are coupled with enough genuine convenience and spectacle to attract shoppers. I want to end by addressing some questions most often raised by students. If people enjoy the mall more than public space why should their choices not prevail? Can the mall be redeemed while remaining private? Does the mall not redeem itself as it reconnects with the public city, turns itself inside out and admits greater and greater diversity? As the mall becomes better and better at replicating public space, does it become pedantic to insist on public ownership and authentic public space? These are important questions and in my mind the answers depend on others: to what extent is the mall implicated in the decline of public space and to what degree is it mis-recognized as public space? To what extent is the mall linked to the decline of democracy?

One of the oldest lessons of urban ecology is that shopping develops on main streets and nodes because that is where the passing trade is. The desire of people for products, and that of shops for publicity, means that shopping is a centralized activity that lives off traffic. Public shopping in this sense is largely rhizomatic – traffic in goods and people intersect within a richly interconnected spatial structure. New enterprises and products are invented as older ones go out of business or are remaindered. The public market is a machine where the buildings, streets, stalls, goods and people work together to produce social and economic encounter. Its fuel is traffic. From the earliest cities, this traffic has always included people, goods and ideas. The shopping mall was initially developed in order to exclude cars from this mix but it also excluded the traffic in ideas.

As malls grow and proliferate they also affiliate with one another, with housing and office developments and with private transport networks. A key issue is the scale of privatization: is the mall part of a larger structure of privatization that enables a privileged class to avoid all use of public space? To what extent does the mall remain a *cul de sac* within a public circulation network and to what extent does it become a node within a private city? As this occurs a vicious cycle ensues whereby the decline in safety, design quality, convenience and access in public space becomes the key stimulant for new mall development, which in turn enables a further withdrawal from public space and further decline. The more car-ridden and dangerous public space becomes and the more we design it accordingly, then the greater the relative advantage of the private malls. The success of the mall generates a powerful lobby against good urban design.

Such issues are not unconnected to those of state tyranny. Kusno (2000) has shown how the legitimacy of the Suharto regime in Jakarta was sustained by a campaign of deliberately provoking middle-class fear of public space. By the time of his fall in 1998 the middle-class had largely retreated to a private network of shopping malls, housing enclaves and toll roads at a safe distance from an impoverished underclass. It was not altogether surprising that the malls were targeted and burnt during the uprising. The greater tragedy is that the spatial separation of classes remains and the task of rebuilding democracy is more difficult.

Much more is at stake in this debate than safety, design quality and convenience; public space is where the 'public' comes into being and where public interests are invented and decided through collective action. The private shopping mall temporarily strips its subjects of the rights of citizenship. The docile community of the mall becomes the model of the social 'we'; the private space of the mall becomes misrecognized as public. The 'main street' as an ecology of people and products has been stripped of ideas along with the desire for them. The proliferation of private malls and their hybrids is an invasion of public space by private interest. They are slowly but surely turning our cities outside-in – capturing the meanings of the urban, the vital and the fantastic, in a manipulative and seductive manner. There are, however, many things to be learnt from the mall and primary among them is the importance of a vital and imaginative public realm. The mall captures remnants of the urban imagination and shows our public efforts of urban design to have become unnecessarily restrained and paralyzed. If highly imaginative and expensive forms of urban design are viable within the mall, then why not in the public realm? The tragedy of the mall is not that it operates on our imagination, but that it does so in the private interest.

Chapter 10: Domestic Desires

House and Enclave

> There is something irresistible about space for it brings with it a feeling of freedom and real contentment. It opens the door to endless possibilities.
>
> (Model house advertisement)

> Most people, at some point in life, dream of living in paradise. An oasis of great beauty, abundant luxuries and countless things to do. A place where friendships thrive, and adventure beckons . . . A community where dreams take flight . . . Boundaries not included.
>
> (Gated community advertisement)

The suburban dream home of North America and Australia is packaged for consumption in the form of 'model homes' or 'display houses' advertised in the property supplements of weekend newspapers. Maps lead to display 'villages' where full-scale models are available for perusal (Figure 10.1). The model 'home' (it is never called a 'house') is furnished to the last detail and the advertising text spells out the narrative:

> you are walking through the front door into a room that soars upwards into light filled space. You are standing on the upstairs balcony looking down into that same room, past the staircase and past every feeling you've ever had of there not being enough. You know only the joy of openness . . . Someone should shout 'lights, cameras, action' as you sweep down the staircase for, in this home, you entertain in a manner people talk about for a long time.

Model houses are a primary marketing tool for suburban housing. They offer a phenomenology of the future, an ideal world which we are enticed to consume. The 'model home' is a mirror which at once reflects and reproduces a suburban dream world. And it is a mirror in which we might read the suburban condition and some of the cultural values that drive it. The experience of 'home'

Figure 10.1
Laguna Niguel, southern
California: detached
dreaming.

is the most primary of spatial meanings and ideologies, founded upon a series of linked dialectic oppositions – home/journey; familiar/strange; inside/outside; safety/danger; order/chaos; private/public; and identity/community (Dovey 1985b, 2005c).[1] These dialectics are at once universal and socially constructed. The experience of home is based in childhood when the *habitus* of the first house establishes a spatial and cultural order, a vision/division of the world (Bourdieu 1977). It becomes an anchoring point for ontological security as its meaning is established through the dialectic of home and journey. The ideal home is a place of safety in a world of danger; a place where a certain taken-for-granted order prevails within a context of chaotic differences. The experience of home constructs an inside/outside dialectic where a private spatial enclosure is protected from the public gaze. And the house as a spatial base inevitably mediates, constructs and reflects one's social identity in a community. The home is a construction of ontological spatial order. To speak of the experience of home in such universal terms is also problematic. The 'home' is too often where the horror is; its 'sanctity' deployed as a cover for violence and sexual exploitation. But one will not understand the social constructions of domestic space if one ignores its ontological roots. The discourse of house and home presses some very deep and conservative buttons – that indeed is its prime engagement with mediations of power.

What follows is an interpretation of advertising discourse for display houses and communities in Australia and California.[2] The interpretation is based on newspaper advertisements, visits to display houses and analysis of the brochures.

The method here is similar to that for the corporate tower, mixing discourse analysis with spatial analysis to understand and articulate the experience with which the dweller is asked to identify. The advertising evokes the ideal rather than the lived. The models represent an apotheosis of the dream, where suburban mythology surfaces in a manner that makes it available for interpretation – as text, as spatial program and as place.

It is important to note that these are both relatively wealthy states with high levels of house ownership (over 70 per cent in Australia) and where such tenure is hinged to constructions of class identity. Both societies have low levels of public housing (6 per cent in Australia), which is stained with a low symbolic status. In both cases the context for suburban planning is market driven. California is wealthier and with a higher level of car ownership and a lower investment in public transport. While these mass-produced detached houses are a very substantial piece of the market, they are but one piece. Specifically excluded are all forms of rental, custom designed and attached urban house types.

GENOTYPE

Saunders and Williams (1988) have argued that the house has a central role in the reproduction of social life. Their metaphors are mechanistic and deterministic but provocative; the house is a 'social factory', the 'engine room' of society. It is the setting which makes interaction meaningful and predictable, linking intimate emotional and sexual life to economic and political life. It both reflects and reproduces the social world of gender, age and class relations. Such a view evokes both Giddens' (1984) notion of the constitution of society through the spatial punctuation of situations and locales, as well as Bourdieu's idea of the house as a structuring structure (Bourdieu 1977; Donley-Reid 1990).

With this in mind I want to consider how domestic space is programmed, based on the naming of segments in the advertising. The names are framings of places which may or may not be enclosed and are often clustered into zones within the house. The plan is thus a signifier of both the semantics and the syntax of domestic space. It is not assumed that each segment is necessarily used in one particular way, only that the houses are sold in this manner. Such analysis reveals the model houses to incorporate about ten to twenty-five segments. While the individual plans show a myriad of variations, there are suburban genotypes which have evolved over the years with remarkable consistency. Until the 1960s the primary genotype split domestic space into rooms divided according to living, cooking and sleeping zones (Dovey 1994). These zones were the primary divisions of domestic space which mediate relations between inhabitants and visitors, and between different generations and genders within the house. This mid-century model mixed adults and children in the same hallway and bathroom, same-sex children in the same bedroom. The formal living area was at the front and the major site of domestic order. In the latter part of the twentieth century this evolved into four primary clusters of space as follows:

- a *formal living zone*: incorporating living, dining, entrance, stairway and den or study;
- an *informal living zone*: incorporating the kitchen, nook (meals area), family, games and terrace (deck or outdoor living space);
- a *master suite*: incorporating master bedroom, bathroom, dressing and perhaps a 'retreat' and deck or court;
- a *minor bedroom zone*: incorporating children's and guest bedrooms, bathrooms and recreation areas.

An example of this 1990s genotype is shown in the plans and spatial analyses in Figures 10.2–10.5. This is a genotype in the loose sense that similar clusters and syntactic relations between them can be detected in the vast majority of detached house models of this period. However, some of the individual spatial segments may not be present and there is some variation in the relations between them. The primary structural relation between these zones is that formal living was always shallower than informal living, with the entrance to the latter through the former. A major variation between genotypes here involved an increasing separation between adult and child zones during the 1980s and 1990s, often with the master suite adjacent to the entrance (Figures 10.4–10.5).[3]

The formal living zone was an area of formal display, the remnant of the parlour, a place for ritualized talk – the dinner party and pre-dinner drinks. Yet the primary function of this zone was symbolic display as an entrance promenade, conspicuously framing the pathway of guests from the entry to the new informal zone. The visibility of the formal zone from the point of entry and the entry pathway is a key. In downmarket models dining and living areas were often little more than alcoves hung off the entrance pathway. In upmarket models they became ostentatious: 'I feel so proud when I have people over. The high windows and ceilings in the living and dining rooms create a wonderful impression.'

The formal living zone often had an extra room adjacent, variously labelled 'den', 'guest' or 'study' (Figure 10.2). It was often furnished with masculine signifiers of the dark wooden desk and heroic biographies, less often with a couch and flowers. This room generally had double doors opening onto the formal entrance area to display the more intimate pursuits of the owners. When the master bedroom suite adjoined the formal living zone it was also placed on display through double doors for a similar glimpse of intimacy. The formal living cluster framed the entrance to the house, celebrating the major pathway from the front door to the new 'heart'. This is a domestic parallel of the diplomatic promenade or the corporate foyer – highly ritualized and awe-inspiring with high symbolic value and low use value.

The informal living zone developed from the kitchen – traditionally a multi-functional place of cooking, eating, conversation and informal activity. I have explored the development of this zone in Australia from the 1960s to the 1990s (Dovey 1994) where it ballooned to outstrip the formal living zone in area.

Figure 10.2
The 'Da Vinci': northern
California (late 1990s).

Lower Level   Upper Level

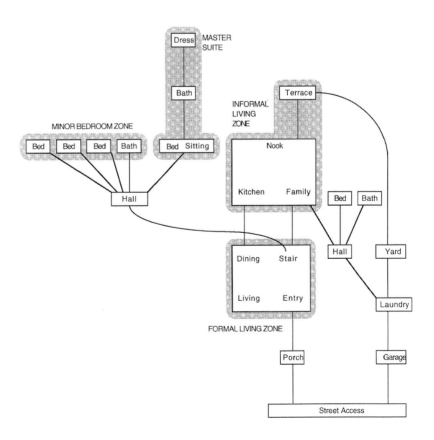

Figure 10.3
The 'Da Vinci': spatial
analysis.

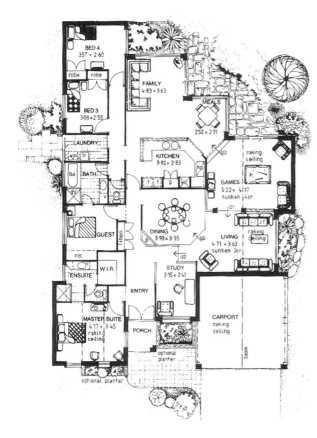

Figure 10.4
'The Chenin': Western
Australia (mid-1990s).

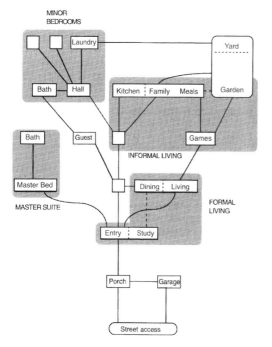

Figure 10.5
'The Chenin': spatial
analysis.

Its expansion to encompass the 'meals area' and family room opening onto a patio was a means of accommodating snacks, television and informal everyday life. The informal living area became the primary site of domestic reproduction; one advertisement proclaimed the virtues of 'total visual control of your children's play areas, both inside and out'. This panoptic function was enhanced by *sunken* family, meals or games areas – there were no sunken kitchens. The female voice still predominated: 'This kitchen and family room layout really brings the family together. We gather here and share the events of the day while I'm fixing dinner.'

During the 1980s and 1990s the informal zone took the position of the 'heart' of the house and its carefully crafted 'informality' became the primary setting for social performance. Many expensive design features, such as cathedral ceilings, bars and fireplaces, were moved from the formal to the informal zone while new retreats ('games', 'leisure' and 'media') emerged to cope with the everyday. The informal zone incorporated an outdoor living area and placed it on display: 'It's comforting to walk into a big space and see your garden through a wall of glass . . . what's outside can now be appreciated from within'. In this new inside/outside relation the backyard was formalized as a place of display and the interior was naturalized with the light and views: 'it brings the garden inside without soiling the carpet'. The backyard was transformed from a place of production into one of consumption as vegetable garden and solar clothes dryer were displaced by swimming pools, electric clothes dryers and designer landscapes.

The 'master suite' was second only to the informal heart in its progressive expansion and segmentation into en suite bathroom, dressing rooms, retreat and courtyard or deck. The bathroom grew to reflect a cult of grooming as the parents' retreat was advertised in terms of escape from children: 'absence does, after all, make the heart grow fonder'; a place to relax in the spa and 'wonder how the other half lives'. One model is described as the 'peace plan' wherein the warring generations retreat to opposite ends of the house. Another was sold on the basis that parents need not see the children at all: 'If it didn't have an intercom you'd spend days looking for the children'. Family relationships were to be improved by distance. Children's bedrooms were represented as small individual territories where gender stereotypes persisted – girls' rooms with doll's houses and cushioned window seats; boys' rooms with outdoor equipment and 'mess' fixed to the bed.

With the new millennium the genotype continues to change. Most notably the formal living zone is withering away or morphing into a grand entry promenade. Formal dining and living areas have largely migrated to the new heart where the 'great room' has become the new centre, opening onto kitchen and dining (or 'nook', 'morning room') and patio. The patio has become more strongly incorporated into the house plan, often framed or covered as an 'outdoor room'. The leisure areas of home theatre, games and rumpus areas are becoming separated to become the heart of a new children's zone where the mess can be contained away from the new heart. Some rooms are extended to become the 'super great room' or 'super games room'. In the burgeoning housing market for empty-nesters the discourse of 'bedroom' and 'family' room disappears – there is only a 'master suite' and another for 'guests'. A typical genotype of this kind has four primary zones: a main entry sequence (for guests) leading to the living zone, and two bedroom suites (separating owners from guests). The entry sequence is increasingly elaborated with a string of segments variously labelled: 'porch', 'entry', 'courtyard', 'gallery', 'foyer', 'turret' and 'entry tower'. Their purpose is to celebrate the act of entering and to bring the subject to a panoptic point near the geographic centre of the house where the spread of segments is revealed. Some patio functions are being imported into enclosed entry courtyards at the front or centre of the house, with outdoor fireplace and entertaining areas. This empty-nester genotype operates as an assemblage that primarily mediates contact between owners and guests.

STATUS AND AUTHENTICITY

Adams long ago argued that the hinging of class identity to house type, tenure and location is particularly pronounced in immigrant cultures with high social mobility: 'In an immigrant society like the U.S., a society that lacks a visible and established class or caste structure, other markers are introduced to establish and maintain social order and to communicate its meanings' (Adams 1984: 520). Model houses are powerful mediators of class relations through the differentiation between models which are marketed as rungs on the social ladder. The bottom rung marks the establishment of a new identity as home-owner and escape from a life of renting and 'money down the drain'. Down-market models tend to shrink the genotype and shed its features while maintaining its structure. Another cost-saving tactic is to abandon design quality in favour of quantity – the full dream is framed within a large box wherein segments are named rather than designed. Eating nooks and entries may be shrunk until they are merely named on the plan rather than spatially accommodated.

As one climbs this social ladder, the house signifies the social values of the class immediately above the subject: 'Invite your boss to dinner, he'll feel right at home'. The dream becomes a progressively elaborate lure which remains one rung higher as one climbs in social status. The house as a symbolic package both establishes status and communicates it to others through the 'impact it will make on all future visitors'. The house is at once a stepping stone 'for the family that's going places' and a reward for all the sacrifices: 'we designed it because you've made it'. Towards the top of the market the narrative of the house as a mirror of the self is spelled out in detail:

> You know about success. . . . It's reflected in everything that surrounds you. Like the home you choose to live in. A home that makes a statement in every one of its striking lines. A statement about you . . . A reflection of success.

Yet at the top of the market the 'statement' of success begins to invert as it tries to differentiate itself from the crass signifiers of the nouveau riche – 'understatement' becomes part of the statement:

> You know you're successful but you don't care who else does. The goals you set are for your own benefit. You have nothing to prove. And like everything you do, everything you have, your home is a reflection of this.

There are other contradictions. While the models are designed to be popular, we are told: 'Mr and Mrs Average will hate them'. Everyone is above average yet remains at least one rung below the dream. The satisfaction of desire and the production of envy are conflated in a market where distinction and difference are mass produced. The models are replicated by the thousand, yet marketed as the unique creations of a craft industry that will display the owner's taste and artistry. The 'Da Vinci' (Figure 10.2) is sold with images of paint palettes, brushes and tubes, suggesting that 'Home building, like great art, is the result of masterful attention to detail'.

The quest for authenticity has led to a proliferation of 'archetypal' imagery. In one model 'an exciting entry whisks you past a stately column' – the column is an 'optional item', the load it carries is symbolic. The spiral stair is often a pivotal point in the house as it sweeps upwards around the *axis mundi* of an indoor tree, towards a skylight. Fireplaces proliferate, generating vertical elements on the elevation (Figure 10.1) and signifiers of intimacy and gathering within. Yet these fires lose their function for heating and gathering as they are grafted onto various domestic segments including courtyards, bedrooms and bathrooms (Figure 10.2). The apotheosis of the archetypal fetish is the bathroom where one can bathe simultaneously in sunlight, firelight and water; framed by stately columns, marble hearth and coffered ceiling; and gaze across the landscape from the prospect/refuge of a bay window. This claim to essential and unchanging meanings gives elements such as fire a privilege in the market. But in order to be marketed they must be packaged as discourse. Fire presses a sensitive button – the conflated symbolism of 'heat', 'heart', 'hearth' and 'home'; a centre of gathering, light, life and passion. The columns, chimneys and spiral stairs are linked to a vertical/horizontal dialectic but likewise reduced to text – the optional 'stately column'.

This reduction of archetypes to text proliferates in response to a burgeoning quest for 'authenticity' which cannot be realized through the consumption of images (Dovey 1985a). While the proliferation of archetypal imagery holds the promise of a deeper dwelling experience, the imperatives of economic exchange contradict any resolution. Exchange value is served not by the satisfaction of desire but the ongoing production of envy. Four fireplaces, a marble spa-bath and a spiral stair can never be enough or consumption would cease.

NAMING

Each model home has a name which I have interpreted and clustered according to the various provinces of meaning that they evoke (Figure 10.6). The most common and consistent theme is for names that are linked to images of nature (Glenvale, Brentwood). These names evoke a place with a view of the natural landscape (Parkview) or are associated with water (Meadowbrook), trees (Laurel) or flowers (Primrose). The dream of suburbia is an escape from the city to a life enveloped in 'nature'. Another theme is for names with a British ancestry such as the Ascot and Mayfair, capturing connotations of tradition, class, privilege and heritage. Mediterranean names such as the Riviera and Monaco have long been fashionable and are linked in turn to others of Spanish (Granada), French (Provence) and Italian (Tusconnade) sources. All of these indicate an exotic imagery – the ideal home is found in other places and other times. There are also regional names linked to the distinctive histories and geographies of California (Malibu) and Australia (James Cook).

  Names which signify power (Dominion, Statesman) are popular, along with those evoking progress (Vogue, Precedent) and self-image (Esteem, Karisma). Some houses are named after artists (Van Gogh), films (Casablanca), stars (Aurora) or gemstones (Onyx) – linking the quest for a timeless authenticity with drama, dreams, art and glamour. The names are not easily categorized; indeed their powers of seduction are increased when they capture two or more

Figure 10.6
Provinces of meaning.

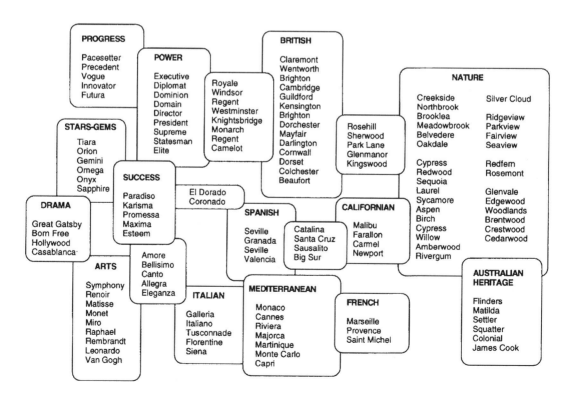

of these provinces of meaning in one name. Thus, Windsor and Westminster manage to evoke both British heritage and power, and Camelot adds a touch of Hollywood as well. Sherwood and Park Lane span images of nature and British heritage.

The strongest general province of meaning indicated by the model names is the highly conservative clustering of names related to heritage. The ideal home is new in comforts and features but with time-tested meanings that will not date. Most models come with a choice of styles that are applied as surface. If the popular housing market is a guide, nostalgia is a pervasive spirit of the age, but this is more than a superficial sentiment. Forty and Moss (1980) have suggested that historical styles enable residents to reconcile contradictions between stability and change. The pseudo-historical offers a static home base for those who see more than enough change in public life. The nostalgic imagery in the models is often coupled with modern ideals of progress and freedom. The ideal house is rooted in the permanence and tradition of the past, yet modern in its outlook to the future.

> Tradition appeals to you. No one can deny the inspiration we draw from styles of less hurried times . . . But there is a lot to be said for the modern outlook and its emphasis on freedom. There is freedom in space.

These contradictory ideals are linked through the prospect of an escape from the present. The suburban home embodies an escape not only from the city but also from the broader problems of everyday life. Saunders and Williams (1988) have argued that the home carries an increasing load of aspirations as it internalizes social problems. The new segmentation of the model houses often claims to resolve problems between generations and between genders. The model house promises a model family where the children spend more time at home yet appear less often. The home is a retreat where life 'is not so rushed and crowded all the time'. The games room is called upon to solve marital disputes: 'the family that plays together stays together'. The dwelling experience is increasingly packaged to meet a desire for 'freedom'. But it is a strangely involuted freedom that is identified with interior space: the model house 'opens the door to endless possibilities'. This door to freedom opens inwards, an enclosed freedom of escape from a difficult public lifeworld.

SANCTUARY

'Clos du Lac' is a small, gated community formed in the late 1990s in northern California where eighty-seven model houses surround artificial lakes (Figure 10.7). As one descends past the gate, through vineyards and olive trees, one retreats in both space and time:

> In the tradition of southern France, the spirit of Clos du Lac is the spirit of another time. It was a time when family estates were passed from generation to generation, along

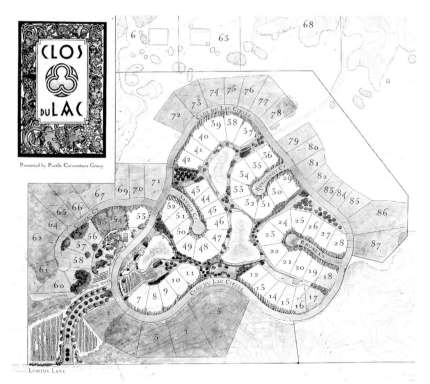

Figure 10.7
'Clos Du Lac': northern
California
(advertisement).

with the vineyards and olive groves producing wine and oil bearing the family name. It was a time made possible by the impeccable, rock-solid workmanship and design skills of Provençal artisans. Clos du Lac marks the return of that time. The spirit of fine design and construction lives again . . . – it's all part of the authentic Clos du Lac experience . . . As you stroll through Clos du Lac . . . repeat to yourself, 'This is not a Fantasy'.

The street syntax is formed of a large loop plus smaller courts. The enclosure of backyard fences has been abolished in favour of a communal village effect which 'laces' the 'community' together with walkways through olives and vines. Thus, while the perimeter is accessible only through one set of electronic gates, the interior is highly ringy. The models are in French vernacular style yet generally follow the genotype outlined earlier. There are rough-hewn ceiling beams and 'hand-carved "keystones" over each window and door'. One room is furnished as an artist's studio with appropriately creative mess fixed to the floor. Like good wine and art, your home will 'improve with age'. This is a world into which one retreats in both space and time. 'Siena' is a gated and guarded compound in southern California complete with a communal swimming pool, 'Tuscan tower' and clubhouse (Figure 10.8). Cameray Pointe nearby is marketed to young singles with the swimming pool as a site offering 'camaraderie with neighbors'.

Gated residential developments have become the most prevalent form of new residential development globally and there is now a very substantial

Figure 10.8
'Siena': southern
California.

literature on them that I cannot explore here.[4] There are many variations in the history, context, form and scale of such developments yet there are some generalizations that can be made. What they all have in common is a secured zone of privately owned urban space and the exclusion of non-residents. Blakely and Snyder (1997) suggest three primary motivations – to construct and protect the amenity of a certain lifestyle; as class-based elite compounds; and as security against crime. Economic and social exclusion is often based either formally or informally on age, class or ethnicity. While they are generally marketed as commodified 'community' there may or may not be high levels of social capital or 'community' within the gates. Such developments are neither new nor modern; they represent a return to the use of force as a mediation of social relations, modeled on the medieval gated city, the ghetto and the colonial compound. Private ownership, security and exclusion are the defining characteristics while privileged communities of class, age and ethnicity are highly prevalent.

These trends are mixed in most gated enclaves as places of privilege protected against a larger society conceived as a threat. They proliferate under conditions of social inequity, crime and an impoverished public environment in the US, Latin America, South Africa, Southeast Asia, China and the Middle East; there are relatively few in Europe, Japan, Canada and Australasia. The gated residential development is a global type yet always mediated locally in different contexts with different forms and uses that produce local/global hybrids (King 2004: 125). The types and images of houses and communities are coupled in both the advertising discourse and in the global flows of images and meanings. This expansion of what King (2004: 103–105) terms 'globurbs' and 'ethnoburbs' is linked to the global spread of market economies and the local mediation of wide economic and social divisions.

Gated enclaves comprise a significant proportion of what are known in the US as Common Interest Developments (CIDs) where residents buy into a set of covenants controlling behaviour and built form. Everyday streetlife becomes subject to a corporate image and choreography as basketball nets, clothes lines, political signage, cheap fences and recreational vehicles are proscribed. Some communities have rules against entering by the back door, gathering in the street and kissing in the driveway (McKenzie 1994). CIDs render the city less transparent in the sense that one can read the rules but not the individual desires and interests of the residents. It is a paradox that totalitarian forms of social control are voluntarily adopted by the most privileged citizens of the most individualistic of states. The advertising narratives in the US are those of freedom rather than fear – the focus is not on walls and gates but on an enclosed escape from the public lifeworld:

> When people escape the ordinary, personal growth can happen at an amazing rate . . . you will have every opportunity to enhance your wellness, your motivation, even your excitement about life itself . . . This is your new beginning.
>
> (Gated community advertisement)

The enclave is a place for personal growth and new becomings: 'a place where losing yourself and finding yourself often happen simultaneously'. Community as commodity offers escape from a life of servitude to others, where one cannot be authentic to one's 'self'. This is a larger scale variant on the idealized freedom of the house interior. Residents are referred to as 'members' who belong to a community as a 'club' rather than a society: 'Live in a place where people care about one another'. This idea of the gated community as a 'club' has been the key argument of those who defend gated developments:

> Cities naturally fragment into many small publics, each of which may be thought of as a collective consumption club. The club realm may, therefore, be a more useful – and theoretically more powerful – idea than the public realm.
>
> (Webster 2002: 397)

The theoretical tactic here is to shift the discourse away from the private/public debate and the discourse of 'community' onto the idea of the 'proprietary residential development' and the 'club'. The social fragmentation that is the key market condition for gated developments is treated as 'natural' and the retreat from the public realm is framed in terms of propriety and consumption rather than citizenship. This valorization of the market as the ground of social formation is a familiar theme that reflects the confusion of free markets and consumer choice with democracy and freedom.

The gated community thrives on an economic mix of market forces and local government opportunism. Residents are attracted by the fact that property values are protected against the wrong kinds of people moving in and the wrong kinds of development happening next door. Local governments are attracted because of increased property taxes while the infrastructure and maintenance costs of low-density sprawl are shifted to the private sector. CIDs are insulated from forces for change and from public planning because the common interests have been set by developers and there is little scope for change – a form of sanctuary from government interference and democratic planning. Despite equal voting rights among residents (excluding renters), the 'constitution' of the 'community' is not debatable – management displaces politics (McKenzie 1994).[5] Gated communities drain the capital, the commitment and the skills of the affluent. They enable the elite to bypass public institutions and thereby undermine the market for them. In the end this leads to a quest for tax rebates for enclave residents who do not wish to fund amenities they do not use. Responsibility for the city is abandoned in what Reich (1992: 270) has termed the 'secession of the successful' – a secession both from public space and from collective tax responsibilities. Gated enclaves undercut the conditions necessary to a vigorous democracy; indeed they offer the illusion of democracy coupled with secession from it.

Structurally and semiotically the enclave has similarities to the mall. Both are walled compounds which establish their meaning in the opposition between inside and outside. Both benefit from the deterioration of the public environment and establish a simulation of an ideal community within. Both enforce totalizing codes of behaviour in order to construct such ideal imagery and to protect it as economic and symbolic capital. The mall, model and enclave can integrate in the emerging gated communities of up to 6,000 hectares and more which are beginning to emerge, especially in Southeast Asia (Leisch 2002).

Gated communities are often defended on the basis that they are nothing more than the apartment building writ large, with a few amenities added to the foyer. However, the horizontal scale of the compound is also a key issue. The impermeability of gated compounds makes them anti-urban in their spatial structure. The apartment building or complex may enclose common space yet still remain integrated with the urban life that flows around it. As they spread horizontally, gated communities obstruct the flow and accessibility of public space. Such compounds are often attracted to adjacent public amenities such as beaches, which they then 'capture' for exclusive use since access is not possible through the enclave. Children outside the walls have no access to those within and vice versa; integrated open space plans cannot be implemented. Like the mall and the very tall building, the walled compound is a *cul de sac* in the urban fabric; but the scale is more damaging because it inhibits the development of richly interconnected urban networks. It is very difficult to define a scale beyond which such developments damage the public interest in this way; I suggest it is generally about a hectare in urban areas, depending on adjacent amenities. The horizontal scale is largely driven by the persistence of the detached house type or 'villa' which now embodies a global ideology that transcends cultural difference (Ackerman 1990; King 2004: 112). The figure of the detached house within the 'ground' of nature operates as a sign of family values and privileged class position.

Finally, the gated enclave reinforces and reproduces social fragmentation, ideological control and social engineering. This is a particular issue for children who have not chosen such a lifeworld and have a right to grow up in a public community. Through the eradication of difference the enclave breeds ignorance, intolerance and homogeneity among its citizens. Ultimately it renders social division invisible, producing and reproducing a generation stunted in their abilities to deal with a diverse and problematic world. It may be important to note that many informal and squatter settlements at the extreme lower end of the economic scale have a very similar structure to the gated community. While there may be no purpose built walls or gates, such communities are often hidden behind dense streetwalls with strictly controlled entry points and informal protocols for strangers who wish to enter (Figure 10.9). Here security is at stake in a quite different sense, as security from State-initiated demolition and eviction. The power of the community to survive relies to some degree on their invisibility. The

Figure 10.9
Gateway to an
informal settlement,
Manila 2005.

gated enclave is the inside/outside dialectic being played out at a grand scale. It is an effect of social division that has the effect of making social division seem to disappear. Enclave developments are but an extreme of the more pervasive retreat from urban difference – a spatial retreat behind walls and a temporal retreat into styles of the past. The gated community is a perversion of community and a reversion to archaic practices of power in space. While it constructs a seductive world of freedom it is ultimately based on the use of force to exclude difference.

HOME AS PARADOX

'Home' and 'community' are tantalizing concepts that forever slip our intellectual grasp. Tantalus of Greek myth was accused by the gods of acquiring knowledge humans should not have; he was punished by being forced to stand up to his neck in water with fruit hanging above. Every time he tried to eat or drink, the fruit blew away or the water level sank. To be 'tantalized' is to see what we desire only to have it vanish when we seek it – flows of desire are stimulated then thwarted. Bauman uses this story as a window onto the desire for an experience of 'community'. The quest for 'community' tantalizes, suggests Bauman, because the experience cannot survive the moment of self-consciousness.

> Once it starts to praise its unique valour, wax lyrical about its a pristine beauty and stick on nearby fences wordy manifestos calling its members to appreciate its wonders and telling all the others to admire them or shut up – one can be sure the community is no more . . . a community speaking of itself is a contradiction in terms.
>
> (Bauman 2001: 12)

From this view the quest for 'community' is an after effect of vulnerability and loss. The quest creates what Bauman terms 'peg communities', commodified 'homes' as places for hanging provisional identities. The advertising of houses and enclaves stimulates desires that tantalize but remain unfulfilled. Both home and community are the 'doxa' of everyday life which become something else ('para-dox') when we turn them into products (Dovey 2005c). The concept of 'home' has been wrongly conflated with the idea of 'essence'. The quest for deeply rooted territorial meanings embodies the premise of a closure of meaning and identity as somehow fixed and immutable. The paradox is that the idea of home as a quest for essential, deep and unchanging meaning has a paralysing effect on identity formation. Alternatively the experience of 'home' can be approached dialectically, as the product of conflict, contradiction and the play of difference – the tantalizing ambiguities of home are linked to its authenticities.

The fundamental dialectic here is the inside/outside dialectic, embodied in the way that built form mediates the penetrations of 'otherness' into our lives; keeping 'difference' and 'dis-ease' at bay. The inside/outside dialectic becomes ordered along the lines of closed/open, safety/danger, home/journey, familiar/strange, self/other and private/public. The work of Deleuze and Guattari is interesting in this regard, while generally privileging the journey or the 'line of flight' over stable modes of dwelling, their interest is in identity formation, in 'becoming' rather than 'being'. Within this conception the experience of 'home' is like a 'refrain':

> home does not preexist: it was necessary to draw a circle around that uncertain and fragile center, to organize a limited space. . . The forces of chaos are kept outside as much as possible . . . Finally one opens the circle a crack, opens it all the way, lets someone in, calls someone, or else goes out oneself, launches forth. One opens the circle not on the side where the old forces of chaos press against it but in another region, one created by the circle itself . . . One ventures from home on the thread of a tune . . .
>
> (Deleuze and Guattari 1988: 311)

This passage outlines a process of establishing the sense of home that keeps the forces of chaos at bay. Yet this circle finally cracks open in a way 'created by the circle itself'. This is the dialectic of inside and outside, of home and journey, of identity and difference. Without a secure ontological centre there is no journey, no acceptance of difference. From a different perspective Giddens (1990: 92) argues the importance of 'ontological security' in identity formation. The home is a protective cocoon, a way of seeing as much as an enclosure, which brackets out aspects of our world which would otherwise engulf us and cause paralysis of the will (Giddens 1991: 40). Yet this experience of home is infused to its core with local/global tensions. This is not a loss of 'home', but it is the end of the closed local home-place where singular identities are linked to semantic and spatial enclosure (Giddens 1990: 108). The creation of mock-historic 'homes' based on a retreat to a false history, a synthetic 'past' of the harmonious community, is not so much a creation of home as it is a nostalgic symptom of homelessness. In this context Franck suggests that the suburban sanctuary is a 'double cocoon' around both house and community where we construct a life-world disconnected from the moral dimensions of life (Franck 1997). Both house and neighbourhood reflect and respond to global conditions and discourses about a world full of 'terror'. Just as the boundaries of the nation state are reinforced to stop the global flows of refugees and economic migrants, to protect the security and purity of the home culture, so the gated enclave stops the internal mixing of classes and ages that comprise a healthy sense of place and community. The concept of 'home' as unselfconscious experience, as everyday practice and as ontological security also has a strong congruence with Bourdieu's notion of the *habitus*:

> The agent engaged in practice knows the world . . . without objectifying distance, takes it for granted, precisely because he is caught up in it, bound up with it; he inhabits it like a garment (*un habit*) or a familiar habitat. He feels at home in the world because the world is also in him, in the form of habitus . . .
>
> (Bourdieu 2000: 142–143)

The *habitus* as home is an ideological formation, the 'doxa' of everyday life where practices of power are driven underground in a kind of 'silent complicity'. The desire for home and community is often driven by an essentialist desire to stabilize identity and exclude difference. Yet it does not follow that this quest can be conflated with such exclusion. The dialectic is always two sided – constructions of home are equally a product of homelessness and the unhomely. There is no home without the journey. While a critique such as this can lead to a reinforcement of the idea that these houses and communities are cultural and architectural wastelands, this is not my intention, nor my view. These places frame real and interesting lives and enable forms of agency and resistance, about which I have said little. The model houses and enclaves are symptoms of a certain homesickness; they reflect a legitimate desire for ontological security. The meanings of house, home and community are not ultimately serviced by this retreat from the urban. Starved of its other, the home becomes a fetish, a fantasy, even a prison. While my task here has been to articulate some meanings of suburban life as they surface in the advertising, the larger task is to keep alive the various dialectics of private/public, inside/outside, familiar/strange, security/danger and identity/difference. We need to design new ways of putting roots in place which resist the totalizing retreat in space or time and the paralyzing view that freedom is found in enclosure.

Part IV

Localities

Chapter 11: A Sign for the 21st Century

Euralille

> Architects suffer from the gap that has grown between their mythical role and the actual situations in which they work.
>
> Rem Koolhaas (quoted in Doutriaux 1992)

Euralille is a new quarter of the city of Lille in northern France, conceived and constructed during the 1990s as a *Grand Projéct* based on Lille's new role as a hub in the northern European high speed rail network. The urban design of the project was directed by Rem Koolhaas, with a vision for a new kind of urban life and aesthetic, geared to new sensibilities of globalization, time–space compression and virtual space.[1] Euralille was conceived as a generic city of transition and movement, infused with the desire for freedom from the fixity of place and local identity. It is a mixed-use development driven by a return to the emancipatory desires of modernity and a neo-Corbusian spirit. Directed by one of the most programmatically innovative and skilled designers of the age, Euralille is also something of a test for the quest to redeem the banality and manipulations of the major project types of late twentieth century globalization – the shopping mall and corporate tower. The project is described in the advertising brochure as 'A Sign for the 21st Century' and there is much we might learn from it in terms of spatial structure, globalization and privatization.

Lille was chosen in 1987 as the major node of the northern European high speed train network. Largely shaped formally and socially by a series of historic seiges, Lille is now the centre of a conurbation which extends into Belgium and a rail hub connecting London, Amsterdam and Paris. This is an area of high unemployment with a large migrant population. The old city is largely intact with a high quality and vitality of public space and some superb public buildings. The Euralille project is a new quarter of the city created around the new high-speed transport node. The objectives, according to the publicity, were:

to erect a powerful architectural symbol of Lille's entry into the 21st century, thereby asserting the will to raise it to rank among the major European metropolitan areas. In the same move it would consolidate a lively, bustling city centre and develop an international-scale tertiary quarter . . .[2]

A semi-public development company was formed (OMA) and Rem Koolhaas was appointed in 1989 as chief architect and planner.[3] Master planning was controlled by the public sector, but kept at arm's length from public debate (Newman and Thornley 1997). The program was to develop up to 1 million square metres of new construction on about 12 hectares of land. The total cost was 5.3 billion francs, about 70 per cent of which was private investment, mostly from the banking industry.

GENERIC CITY

I want to begin with a brief account of the urban design theories which drive Euralille, primarily from the compendium 'S,M,L,XL' (OMA *et al.* 1995). For Koolhaas, the city of the future is not about the specifics of place and region, but is rather the 'generic city' of space and globalization. In a globalizing world of informational economies, virtual realities and space–time compression, urban place identity dissipates. Koolhaas sees this as a form of liberation from the constraints of 'place', 'region' and 'character'. From this view, the quest for identity in place is a fetish for 'essences', a quest which imprisons us. He is more interested in the urban periphery than the city centre, which he sees as locked into a straitjacket of tradition. He picks up on the 'flexible accumulation' strategies of corporate culture; the waves of capital investment which wash through cities are to be 'surfed' to generate new architecture and urban form. The new 'generic city' is to be construed much like an airport: 'If it gets too small it just expands. If it gets old it just self-destructs and renews . . . Like a Hollywood studio lot, it can produce a new identity every Monday morning' (Koolhaas 1995: 1250). This urban vision is clearly linked to changes in experience brought about by new technologies. Drawing on Virilio (1986) he argues:

> the representation of the contemporary city is . . . no longer determined by a ceremonial opening of gates, by a ritual of processions and parades, nor by a succession of streets and avenues. From now on urban architecture must deal with the advent of a 'technological space-time'. The access protocol of telematics replaces that of the doorway. . . . the interface man/machine replaces the facades of buildings and the surfaces of ground on which they stand.
>
> (Koolhaas 1995: 1162)

As people vacate real space for cyberspace the public realm becomes primarily a space of transition. Architecture in turn becomes increasingly vertical: 'The skyscraper looks as if it will be the final, definitive typology' (Koolhaas 1995: 1253). For Koolhaas, the traditional street is dead; the new thrills of urban space are not social but visual. They couple an aesthetic of urban anomie, the very absence of identity and place, with the joys of movement and speed: 'Pure speed revives the heart, sweeping boredom away' (Koolhaas 1995: 1164).

This is in many ways a revival of the Corbusian claim for a liberating urban vision – the generic city is to be more democratic and permissive than its alternatives: 'through its very permissiveness, the Generic City resists the dictatorial' (Koolhaas 1995: 1255). The political dimension in Koolhaas' thought is rarely overt but it paradoxically incorporates a disdain for urban sociology with a determinism we haven't heard since Le Corbusier:

> In the generic city, people are not only more beautiful than their peers, they are also reputed to be more even-tempered, less anxious about work, less hostile, more pleasant – proof, in other words that there is a connection between architecture and behavior, that the city can make better people . . .

> (Koolhaas 1995: 1262–1263)

I will return to some of these claims, many of which I would suggest are provocative rhetoric rather than urban design theory. However, they are ideas with enormous global influence and with clear effects on the design of this project.

LINES OF FLIGHT

For Koolhaas, Euralille is not so much a new quarter of the old city as a new city. It has landed in, rather than being spawned by, Lille. Euralille will eventually have a population of about 50 million within 90 minutes of travel. For Koolhaas this:

> would redefine the idea of 'address' . . . Lille itself would be an accidental appendix – almost a décor . . . What is important about this place is not where it *is* but where it *leads*, and how quickly. We imagined a series of skyscrapers straddling the station, towers that would suggest not a *place* but a distance in *time* from various cities. The address would be defined as '70 minutes from London', '50 minutes from Paris', '18 minutes from Brussels'.

> (OMA *et al.* 1995: 1170)

The vision is that the Japanese will locate corporate headquarters here; that the English will commute to London; that concerts will draw customers from across Europe.

The project lies just outside the old city walls of Lille, on the site of its former fortifications, between the old and new railway stations. The shape and culture of the city was forged through a series of sieges when this site was a kind of 'free fire zone' on the ramparts (Slessor 1991). Its history is that of a dangerous engagement with global forces, ready made for experiments like Euralille. The local station, Gare Lille Flandres, is the largest in France outside Paris. It butts into the old city, terminated by a neo-classical edifice which then fronts a busy urban space lined with a diverse mix of cafés, bars, restaurants, stores, housing and hotels. The new TGV station is about 400 metres away. The two train lines form a triangular site between the old and new (local and global) stations.

Within this triangle nine buildings are linked into one contiguous V-shaped plan with a large number of architects other than Koolhaas/OMA involved. The relationship between the architecture and urban design was a close collaboration: 'we defined levels, sections, relationships, interfaces – but not architecture. No project is our project' (OMA *et al.* 1995: 1184). A quest for aesthetic diversity was pursued through the appointment of a variety of architects, at times in deliberate contradiction.[4] The V-shaped plan opens towards the north into a large park. The first phase of the project was completed in 1995 (Figure 11.1).[5]

The eastern wing of the project comprises the new TGV station with two corporate towers above. The new station (designed by Jean-Marie Duthilleul) consists of 400 metres of highly accessible and visible platform on several levels, surmounted by a continuous 'aerofoil' roof section. The station opens on one side with a huge window to the public open space which is central to the project – here the main shopping centre becomes visible from the platforms and trains become visible as a public spectacle. The space above the station was conceived as a 'corridor of skyscrapers' that would straddle the 50 metre span across the station with architects challenged to produce seductive images (Doutriaux 1992). The aesthetic vision was overtly married to the imperatives of corporate profit: 'the clients calculated the additional cost of building over the tracks – between 8 and 10% – and decided it was an acceptable investment in pure symbolism' (OMA *et al.* 1995: 1170). This production of symbolic capital was a key component of the investment strategy and the publicity highlights the 'distinctive symbolism' and the importance of 'signature' architecture. It was not always possible to meet this challenge since the market demanded cheap rent; an early design by Richard Rogers was abandoned and by the millennium only two towers had been built.

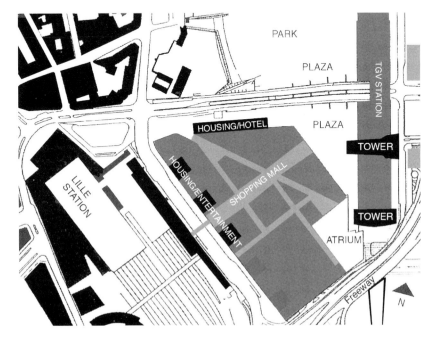

Figure 11.1
Euralille.

Figure 11.2
Lines of flight – train and tower.

The twenty-storey tower, designed by Christian de Portzamparc, is dramatically raised on two large stumps (Figure 11.2). The tower shaft slopes outwards as it rises, creating a dynamic image: 'soaring up into the metropolitan skies,' as the publicity puts it, 'like a symbol of revival'.[6] The architect describes it as 'an object ready for takeoff' (Doutriaux 1992). The way this building straddles the fast trainline and projects an image of a line of flight reflects the desire to produce an architecture of vectors and movement rather than stable points of order. For the locals, however, the building's most immediate metaphor is that of a 'ski-boot' (Buchanan 1995), since the tower shaft and 'heel' is entirely on one side of the station with a 'toe' stepping across the tracks. This shape emerged in the attempt to reduce the cost of the span – the internal area above the railway line is largely a concealed void. The tower thus has two entrances – one to the station and car park (from the 'heel'), the other to the public plaza (from the 'toe'). The building generates an illusion of straddling the railway, an architecture of flight rather than of stasis. By 2007 the tower had lost its major tenant (Credit Lyonnais) and one entry was closed and derelict. The second tower (designed by Claude Vasconi) is more the conventionally named and designed World Trade Centre with adjacent low-rise atrium office development. While early proposals were for a string of towers along the train line by the millennium, this has not eventuated and much of the existing commercial space was vacant.

REDEEMING THE MALL

The largest building in the development, designed primarily by Jean Nouvel, consists of an internal shopping mall of two levels over 4 hectares with five smaller buildings interlocking around its edges. The main building is formed of a single inclined roof surface covered with a semi-transparent surface of metallic grille (Figure 11.3). The vast roof surface slopes gently up towards the old city, perforated by towers at its margins. At the corner closest to the old train station, the

Figure 11.3
Shopping mall and plaza.

Figure 11.4
Shopping mall entrance.

building bulk is carved out to form a giant entrance space, over which the roof continues as a portico (Figure 11.4). This is the most visually engaging part of the project and the most urban. It shows a fine collaboration between Koolhaas and Nouvel as urban designer and architect – the jutting roof form captures the sense of speed and movement of the new at the point where it meets the old city. It is well-scaled and often busy with traffic to and from the mall – primarily a place of transition.

Nouvel was faced with producing a large commercial space at low cost and the building is unashamedly made available for advertising – a play on the dual seductions of technology and commodity. As Nouvel puts it: 'The image I see in my mind's eye is that of the sponsorized object, like a racing car' (Doutriaux 1992: 145). The urban tactic of inserting a range of other buildings into the edges of the mall succeeds in avoiding the blank anti-urban walls which malls generally produce on street façades. The double-storey shopping mall is comprised of 130 small shops, seven larger stores and one major 'anchor'. The whole project sits on a 3,000 car parking garage which offers free parking with purchases.

Koolhaas views the shopping mall as the inevitable displacement of the street: 'the Roman forum is to the Greek agora what the shopping mall is to the high street . . . the street is dead' (Koolhaas 1995: 1252). The claim here is to have urbanized the mall:

> To make the centre truly urban, it had to offer more than the amorphous undifferentiated space – deliberate maze – of the typical shopping center. Nouvel organized it through public axes that cut through the commercial substance to connect the city to the station.
>
> (OMA et al. 1995: 1198)

While these axes are aligned with and connected to public space, they are not 'public' and they are not used as thoroughfares – indeed one of the entries is locked. The pedestrian traffic within the mall is almost entirely generated by traffic to and from the car park and the old city, with the anchor store as the single attraction. In other words, the mall works like any other private mall as a cul-de-sac rather than a thoroughfare in the urban fabric. Its market is local rather than global – traffic to and from the TGV station and the corporate zone are minimal.

There are other similarities with the standard type; the mall interior has private security guards, stationed at all the entry points and nodes – teenage exhuberance is under tight control and photography is prohibited. The mall is a two-storey galleria style, with a few variations from the formula – there are no palm trees and it is not a theme park. The shops sit under a vast 'starry night' of lights under the roof surface. On its north-eastern edge the mall opens a wall of glass to face the open space and new train station. The mall is designed with some good intentions but the result scarcely redeems the global formula which constructs an anti-urban private world, wherein a pseudo-public street life is enacted under the gaze of private police.

On the south-eastern boundary of Euralille where it faces the old railway station across the street, a new streetwall is formed of a series of three towers (originally intended as a row of five) which are dovetailed into the bulk of the mall. On its lower floors this façade opens onto broad and springy walkways of galvanized steel, cantilevered over the street (Figure 11.5). The fifteen-storey towers consist of serviced apartments, student housing and professional offices. Behind each of them a generous courtyard has been scooped out above the mall. The spaces surrounding these courtyards were proposed for various uses,

Figure 11.5
Elevated walkways.

including a 1,500 seat concert hall, production space for contemporary music, a bar and a school. All of these spaces are accessed only from the external walkways.

This tactic of splicing different functions together is a highly innovative move, but it has not worked. Some spaces are derelict, escalators have been turned off and part of the walkway has been fenced off. This is largely a problem of spatial structure. This entire section of the development is several levels higher and many segments removed from the active public spaces of the city. It is a cul-de-sac designed to look like a network. The upper walkways are potentially very exciting, with views of the old city from the new, but they are largely deserted. Concerns for text and image seem to have displaced those of program, space and urban structure. On the tops of the towers, the intention was that: 'enormous blocks of neon will emit commercial, artistic and ideological messages to the city' (OMA *et al.* 1995: 1198). The plant and equipment has been screened with semi-transparent billboards for this purpose and they advertise the shopping mall. The glass façade of Nouvel's building lining the walkway is etched with holographic scenes – supermarket trolleys, cinematic action and crowds – but there is little audience.

GLOBAL SPACE

Between the mall and the new train station is a large plaza of about 1.5 hectares that opens to adjacent parkland (Figures 11.3–11.6). A new elevated roadway slices across the top of this open space, connecting the old city and train station with the upper level of the new train station. The prevailing idea for this plaza was to tilt the surface of the earth down towards the side of the new train

Figure 11.6
The global gaze.

station as a theatre for the spectacle of speed as the trains shoot through behind a 400 metre long and 15 metre high 'window' which forms the side of the station. This is in many ways the centrepiece of the vision of a fast new world of transparency and global travel. A broad reflecting pond lines this huge window where images of speed and movement were to be reflected; however, the pond is empty. The shopping mall lines this open space with cafes (some of which are vacant). The elevated roadway, called 'Avenue Le Corbusier', is a wafer-thin ribbon of road which flies above the plaza and cuts through the roof of the new station. Supported on flexible mounts and low steel arches, it trembles when vehicles drive across.

The major pedestrian life of both the plaza and the viaduct above comes from a steady stream of people towing or carrying luggage to make the 400 metre connection between the two train stations. The other substantial use of the plaza is that it has been appropriated to some degree by local teenagers hanging out in small groups. The edges of the plaza are not utilized for anything beyond a few tables and chairs attached to a fast food outlet. Teenagers who claim them without paying are moved along. The idea of 'active edges' may have become a cliché in urban design theory (Bentley *et al.* 1985), but the penalty for ignoring it is precisely the deadly emptiness we see here, redeemed only by the aesthetic spectacle of global subjects on the move (Figure 11.7). A key driving idea seems to be the two-way gaze between the mall and train station – the cafe crowd inside the mall gazes at the fast trains, whose global travellers gaze at the city of the future. The reality is that the mall and plaza have little life and the giant window onto the trains is filthy. A homeless man lives in a niche under the 'ski-boot' and uses the dry reflecting pond for soccer practice.

The publicity suggests that the plaza is a kind of event space: 'a big amphitheatre with a floor packed with technical equipment to host all kinds of activities and events'.[7] One can imagine certain events with the drawing power to bring this place alive but it is difficult to experience the reality without a sense

Figure 11.7
Avenue Le Corbusier and plaza.

of dismay at how little has been learnt. This is another attempt to redeem the modernist dream of liberation expressed in vast horizontal spaces signifying speed and visibility. It succeeds visually and fails socially in the same ways it did for Le Corbusier. And as in its antecedents there is a certain melding of political and aesthetic ideology. A statue of François Mitterand, the father of the *Grand Projects*, steps forward into the plaza.

The account of this project which appears in 'S,M,L,XL' contains almost no mention of this public open space, and elsewhere Koolhaas recognizes some shortcomings in this regard: 'I'm discovering the spatial dimension in architecture more and more . . . In our approach there is a little distrust for spatial questions and a relative incapacity to talk about them openly' (Doutriaux 1992: 147). There was client pressure to render this open space more livable. Some of the cartoon-like images used by OMA to communicate the scheme during the design process show the plaza with market stalls but there is no evidence of such local use (Doutriaux 1992: 119–123).

MULTIPLICITY AND COMPLICITY

It is not easy to bring rigorous critique to this project – Koolhaas' ideas are slip-pery; his imagery is seductive; and he would most likely reject many of the urban design values that drive this critique. In pointing out shortcomings I am in no way trying to pour scorn upon the attempts at innovation – programmatic or formal. The city becomes a much more exciting place when the imagination is given room to explore new visions, and it becomes a richer place when its programs are audaciously taken apart and re-configured. Koolhaas holds out the promise of an urbanism which embodies a 'multipli-city' of images, identities, functions and behaviours.

Early in this project Koolhaas described the task at Euralille as 'to try and imagine a fragment of the city that might escape from the violent criticism . . . against modern architecture, for its incapacity to inscribe sufficiently contrasted rich and complex programs in simple modern forms' (Doutriaux 1992: 97). This implied critique of modernity is now 30 years old but its deepest strains remain relevant – the Jacobs (1965) critique of the monofunctionality and impermeability of modernist planning; Alexander's (1965) opposition to the city-as-tree; Sennett's (1973) argument that unstructured encounter with difference in civic space is vital to civilized human development. At a philosophical level, this older critique can also be linked to that of Deleuze (1993), who utilizes the metaphor of the 'rhizome' for forms of life which operate in a fragmented or 'nomadic' rather than hierarchic manner, growing roots and shoots in the interstices of some larger order. It is not surprising to see Koolhaas (1996) quoting Deleuze in his work. Euralille, however, does not have such multiplicitous forms of life. Indeed there are parts which are decidedly tree-like – the corporate towers are private enclaves; the mall and atrium are under tight panoptic control. There is a strongly controlled aesthetic and with half a dozen designers responsible for about 12 hectares there is less visual diversity than one would find in the traditional city.

Koolhaas wishes to resist notions of fixed urban identity, yet urban designs embody enormous invested capital – material and symbolic. For better or worse, built form fixes a certain kind of image and locks in certain forms of urban life. Euralille captures the prevailing narrative myths of globalization, virtuality and transparency very well indeed – the expanding tower; the soaring roof portico where the new city meets the old; the train flashing past – these are urban visions of the first order and they may become the urban heritage of the next century. But they are clearly not temporary, fluid or lacking in 'identity' or ego. These are images connected to their designers as 'signature' architects. Koolhaas recognizes the problems of the 'star system, with its frantic quest for individual identity . . . an obsession with the signature' and argues that at Euralille there has been 'a relative renouncement of the ego' (Doutriaux 1992: 147). Yet the idea of 'signature' architecture permeates the publicity used to sell the project and was necessary to get it built. The idea of an aesthetically authenticated architecture is the source of the symbolic capital. The expanding tower has a great deal of such capital and unlike its cousins in other financial districts, this capital is protected through the generous spacing of towers along the 'corridor'. There is no evidence for a diminished fetish for identity.

At Euralille the denial of local place identity and its replacement with the global space of transition has become a kind of ideology. The understandings of globalization that permeate the project are primitive and superficial, a form of social theory reduced to urban imagery. Koolhaas refers to the community within 90 minutes of Lille as a 'virtual community' (OMA et al., 1995; Buchanan 1995). Yet 'virtual space' is surely the spatial experience produced by telepresence and cyberspace, not fast trains (Rheingold 1993; Mitchell 2000). Without the persistent desire for face-to-face communication the market for fast trains would not exist. Koolhaas draws upon the new experiences of telepresence and cyberspace as forms of representation in 'real' space. Nothing wrong with this, but the idea of virtuality and globalization can congeal into gimmickry.

A range of video screens are set in the concrete wall of the 'Le Corbusier Viaduct', where the publicity suggests we will find a continuous display of real-time images from around the world. But with few passing pedestrians the global screens are empty and gathering local dust. By contrast, in the markets of old Lille one finds a global order of a different kind – a rich mix of Arabs, Indo-chinese, French, Africans and others trading everything from carpets to herbs. A 'call box' shop offers rates per minute to call home – for people without private telephones let alone virtual cities or very fast trains. Here the global and local are spliced together. The street as market place and community has not died, it has been transformed as virtual communities co-exist with face-to-face communication (Featherstone 1993; Hannerz 1996; Harvey 1993). One of the mistakes at Euralille seems to be in treating the global and local as exclusive; a distinction most apparent in the steady flow of 'glocal' traffic between the two train stations.

There is a key focus in this project on pathways of movement, yet so many walkways have been closed due to lack of traffic that the network has produced a series of derelict cul-de-sacs. There is a slippage we are familiar with in certain kinds of discourse wherein practices of disciplinary control and privatization are subsumed under the rhetoric of a revitalization of public life. Such rhetoric effaces distinctions between private and public space along with those between culture and commerce. According to the publicity: 'Euralille's public areas are more than just thoroughfares . . . Artists can perform . . . in the walkways of the shopping centre . . . You may come face to face with a clown on your way out of a shop'.[8] This is the familiar face of the private masquerading as public; commerce as carnival; consumption as culture.

Recall the claim that in the 'generic city' people will be 'more even-tempered, less anxious about work, less hostile, more pleasant' (Koolhaas 1995: 1262–1263). Teenagers in the plaza do not seem free of anxiety and a small police station has been inserted into the edge of the plaza with full surveillance over it. Is there a parallel here with the way Le Corbusier's vision of liberation through high-rise public housing became complicit with forms of social control and state legitimation? While Koolhaas is expert at 'surfing' the waves of corporate capital, these are also waves of privatization and social control. All urban designers have to deal with such forces and a good many succumb to the rhetoric that the pseudo-public realm is acceptable as urban public space. Koolhaas joins them when he argues:

> The most important coherence is not formal but programmatic – a continuous
> pedestrian trajectory: a viaduct leads to the station; the station is conceived as a public
> arcade; a diagonal axis that connects the city to the end of the new station runs through
> Nouvel's commercial center. The towers become part of this urban network.
>
> (OMA *et al.* 1995: 1184)

Note that any distinction between public and private space and behavioural control is blurred here; the reality is that much of this network is private and the towers are extraneous to it.

Sitting in the mall watching the global trains reminds me of Ferguson's depiction of the shopping mall atrium as a place for 'watching the world go round' (Ferguson 1992). She suggests such new spaces of consumption are linked to the construction of new forms of identity wherein: 'the self, as an integrated unity is cast aside ... Now we consume, not as an act of self-completion, but as a means of preventing the illusion of selfhood taking root in us' (Ferguson 1992: 35). This loss of 'self' in the transitory fluidity of urban life is evident in this project (Figure 11.7), yet it is scarcely immune to the manipulations of the shopping mall. There is a sense in which the spectacle of the very fast train has become what mall developers call an 'adjacency attraction'.

Euralille is a bold attempt at a fundamentally different kind of urbanism, but in several significant ways it does not work in its own terms. Many of its ideals have congealed into ideologies, the fetish for 'place identity' has been countered by a fetish for the virtual and global. The idea that place and identity disappear into the fluidity, transparency and virtuality of the global flies in the face of the theory and reality. The achievements of the project tend to be formal rather than social – privileging the image over everyday urban life and the significations of the global over its local impact. The second stage of the project has not developed as planned; there has been minimal global investment and no corridor of skyscrapers. The 'wave' that Koolhaas has 'surfed' here has passed. There is also evidence that the project has contributed to social polarization within the Lille region (Moulaert et al. 2001). This project brings a high quality of design expression to the shopping mall and corporate tower – but these are old projects in a new garb. One is reminded of Benjamin's claim that modernity is often the 'ever-the-same' dressed up as the 'ever-new' (Gilloch 1996). There is a sense in which Euralille has become what Debord long ago called the 'society of the spectacle' where 'All that once was directly lived becomes mere representation' (Debord 1994: 12–14). The global is reduced to an image for the meaning market. The Euralille aesthetic captures the Zeitgeist of the millennium; it is, as its publicity claims, 'A Sign for the 21st Century' – a signpost to a future. But it is infected with some familiar practices of power from the twentieth century, and in these ways it leads us to a future that is locked in the past.

Chapter 12: Rust and Irony

Rottnest Island

> There is no place that is not haunted by many different spirits hidden there in silence . . .
> Haunted places are the only ones people can live in – and this inverts the schema of the
> panopticon.
>
> de Certeau (1984: 108)

Places are experienced in states of distraction. We read them and act within them while pursuing the agendas of everyday life. To 'understand' places one must 'stand under' them. This requires an attention to how we each construct places through action and in memory. This chapter, then, is a turn from theory towards the personal – how might theories of power and built form change the ways we understand and 'excavate' places in our own lives? It is a rather personal account of Rottnest Island, off the coast of Perth, Western Australia. And it is a turn towards questions of liberation, exploring the ironies of a place of incarceration becoming a place of emancipation and then exclusion. Rottnest is a place of semantic inversions, haunted by intangible and buried meanings. The tactics for excavating and articulating them are necessarily oblique.

The Rottnest Island ferry left at 9 a.m. With bicycles lashed into a small mountain on the deck we set off down river and across to the island. Entering the open sea in a south-west breeze the ferry would roll nauseatingly. Clutching paint-encrusted rails with sheets of spray lashing my face, I tried with mixed success to vomit over the edge. 'The best thing is to have a good breakfast,' said the man collecting fares, as mine disappeared into the Indian Ocean. My memories of Rottnest Island are laced with small ironies such as these. The seasickness was tempered by the powerful attraction of the island growing larger on the horizon. For me at least, Rottnest offered an intangible sense of freedom. And this is the larger irony since the place was originally developed as an Aboriginal prison.[1]

Rottnest was an uninhabited island marked by a proliferation of small marsupials when it was named 'rat-nest' by Dutch explorers in the seventeenth century. The prison was developed from 1838, within a decade of British invasion and settlement of the mainland Swan River Colony, as a means of dealing with Aboriginal prisoners. The island became the colony of a colony and offered the chance for some spatial latitude within its larger confines. Every Sunday the prisoners were set loose and encouraged to hunt for their own food.

All of the early buildings were built of local limestone by the prisoners, mostly to the design of Superintendent Henry Vincent. Those that remain include a large collection of cottages lining the top of a grand sea-wall. After an early prison burnt down, the main prison was built in 1864 – at the top of a small hill with a single entry facing down towards the bay (Figure 12.1). It forms an octagon of about 50 metres diameter comprising a continuous ring of cells and support rooms facing a courtyard, known as the Quod (slang for prison). There was formerly a well in the centre, now a small octagonal pavillion.

Vincent's design shows the influence of Bentham's panopticon prison (Evans 1982). While the Quod lacks the transparent visibility and the central guard tower, it can be construed in Foucault's (1979) terms as a panoptic technology for the disciplining of heterogeneous behaviour through surveillance. Vincent had previously been the gaoler at Fremantle prison on the mainland, where Bentham's ideas of reform through surveillance had been influential. Figure 12.2 shows the prisoners lined up in three rows – sitting, bending and standing respectively – on display to a white audience with all the bodily discipline of a sporting team poster. They are flanked by guards, contained within the encircling structure of the prison, under the lamp of British civilization – and framed within the photograph for display. Treatment of the prisoners by Vincent was brutal and he was eventually removed from his position. Up to five prisoners slept in each 6 square metre cell, conditions that led to influenza and measles epidemics that killed a third of all inmates in some years during the 1860s. All Aboriginal prisoners who died were buried in unmarked graves in a cypress forest to the north-west of the Quod, enclosed by a cobblestone wall (Watson 1998: 138; Green and Moon 1997).

Other buildings which date from the nineteenth century include a range of agricultural buildings and a summer house for the governor of the colony. The island's penal role continued and was expanded in 1881 to include a boys' reformatory adjacent to the prison. The prison was closed in 1901 and, in the face of powerful pressure to privatize, the island was declared a public reserve in 1917. It was then developed as an inexpensive public holiday resort. The prison and adjacent reformatory became a hostel and the governor's house became a hotel. Most of the old cottages were let to holidaymakers. During World War II large sections of the island were appropriated for military purposes. Two 9 inch guns with a 30 kilometre range and a 360 degree arc were built on the hills in the centre of the island with panoptic views of the sea lanes approaching Fremantle harbour.

Over the years of my childhood and adolescence I stayed in a variety of places. The first was a tiny and dark former prison cell in the Quod. The enclosed

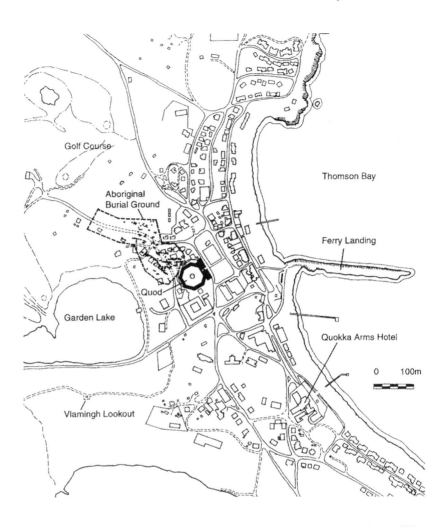

Figure 12.1
Rottnest Island
settlement plan.

Figure 12.2
Aboriginal prisoners in
the Quod, c.1883.

Figure 12.3
Thomson's Bay and
sea-wall.

prison yard, where I first learned to ride a bike, was alive with children. Another time we stayed in cottage F, on top of the sea-wall, where I struggled to haul suitcases up the broad set of steps from the ferry (Figure 12.3). Cottage F began its life as part of the superintendent's house. I recall a minuscule bedroom, a skewed and sloping passage and an almost circular semi-detached kitchen. I sensed none of the history, but the strange forms left a delightful and indelible memory. All of the old buildings were built of limestone and rendered with a lime whitewash with rusty nails added to reduce the glare; this has given all of the older settlement a distinctive 'rust' colour.

I also stayed in a two-roomed weatherboard bungalow, built between the wars. The large verandah was semi-enclosed with wooden lattice which we wove with newspaper and plastic to keep out the worst of the August weather. The bungalows were scattered throughout the settlement, painted in a motley range of faded pastels. They were but one step up from the bathing sheds upon which they were modeled – tiny and cold with no bathroom. But these holidays would never have been possible without them. I later stayed in a newly built brick 'pheasant cottage' with a bathroom and suburban feel. Confronted with the familiar, I began to realize what a different kind of place Rottnest was and the architecture was but one piece of it.[2]

Rottnest was a liberating place for parents because children would disappear safely for most of the day – adolescents for half the night as well. The movie hall was a large shed filled with deck chairs, canvas stretched almost to the floor, often under the extra stress of teenage passion. Kids outside threw pebbles onto the corrugated iron roof, pitched near the ridge so that they rolled noisily to the eaves. The film in the projection box caught fire once and it seemed like part of the show. Afterwards came a walk to the haunted house, inland from the settlement beyond the salt lakes. The journey was lit by the western lighthouse with an arc of light sweeping regularly across the lakes as we walked across the narrow causeway. Behind some trees on the bank of the lake was an abandoned wooden house, haunted indeed by teenagers hiding in the trees, roof and dark rooms.

In the centre of the island on Oliver's Hill were the 9 inch guns from World War II – the guard without the prison, keeping the exogenous population out rather than the indigenous population in. We discovered a hole in the bricked-up entrance to an underground armaments complex. We crawled through and felt our way along a pitch-dark broad tunnel which opened into a large rectangular chamber with niches in the walls and the floor. An opening in one wall led to a narrower tunnel just wide enough for two people to pass if they turned side-ways. It twisted and then climbed into the hill. The underground complex seemed dangerous but this forbidden, unknown and unclaimed world was far too interesting to ignore. We returned with a torch and followed the tunnel up some steps until it forked into a small complex of chambers and tunnels under one of the guns. In subsequent visits we became more daring – walking through from one end to the other without a light, not knowing what or who we would bump into. The haunted tunnel, like the haunted house, became a self-fulfilling prophecy.

The guns were connected by railway to a small military base called Kingstown. The barracks lined a quadrangle on three sides with a tower in the centre. Officers occupied detached houses facing in a circle at a slightly higher elevation and higher still were the commanding officers. While the base remained under army control, abandoned military buildings were scattered nearby. One year some friends squatted in the attic of one of these buildings. We could hear planes taking off a few metres overhead as we played cards and drank cheap brandy. Nearby were gun turrets and concrete bunkers covered in rusty metal camouflage. I found a small piece of brass with no decipherable use, took it home and kept it polished for many years. It spoke of a military world which I held in disdain, but detached from its context the shining solid brass also came to represent the appropriation of abandoned form and space that Rottnest offered. As I became old enough I camped with friends on the open camp-grounds north-west of the Quod. This was a broad swathe of tents and camp-fires, a noisy mix of alcohol and teenage passion. It was also the Aboriginal cemetery, its enclosing stone wall long erased and a road constructed through the middle.

To endorse all of these experiences would be both irresponsible and some-what contradictory. They were dangerous at times and adult endorsement would drain them of meaning. But, they were some of the most exciting and significant experiences of my adolescence. Forty years later I still find Rottnest indelibly stained with these memories. While some of the recent changes are lamentable, I am grateful for the continuity of form that has been preserved, and which enables this persistence of memory. The movie hall has been painted with a seemingly endless supply of 'rust' coloured paint. The haunted house is a private

Figure 12.4
Guns and tourism.

dwelling. The army barracks has become an Environmental Education Centre and the nearby collection of camouflaged bunkers is packaged as a 'heritage trail'. Out on Oliver's Hill a volunteer guide leads tours of the gun emplacement and the tunnel complex beneath it (Figure 12.4). The empty chamber, which I once explored in the pitch black, is lined with photographs explaining how the live artillery shells were prepared and protected. When I mentioned to the guide how I had explored the tunnels as a child he said: 'Yeah, we all did.' Not far away is another gun and another underground complex which remains closed to public access, yet perhaps still open to the adolescent imagination.

The cottages constructed by the prisoners have been restored and the bungalows mostly survive. The newer architecture of Rottnest follows the precedents of the past, in most part, without the pretensions of kitsch and fakery, just as the forms of nineteenth-century Rottnest were borrowed with little thought and some adaptation from elsewhere. The more recent settlements are formed in rows of simple cottages directly onto a sea-wall, a model developed from prototypes at the old settlement.[3] Many of the dwellings are without freshwater showers, a tactic that preserves fresh water (which is in short supply) and keeps the rental almost affordable.

The former reformatory and prison, however, has been privatized, moved upmarket, developed, extended and renamed 'The Lodge' – an enclave for 'house guests only'. The Quod – site of Aboriginal incarceration, campfires, floggings and executions – is largely bereft of life (Figure 12.5). A social hierarchy has emerged on the island and it is signified spatially – from the campground at the bottom, through the bungalows, to the cottages and then the Lodge. Despite the changes, social egalitarianism remains important to Rottnest as a place. When the prison closed, there was a proposal to sell off private lots on the island and it is clear where that would have led. There was a struggle to ensure that it became a public reserve and it has been a successful case of public development in the public interest. Furthermore, Rottnest offers lessons in public amenity planning, as a working example of what can be achieved without cars. There are no car parks, service stations, drunk drivers or dangerous streets; there is little traffic noise and no carbon monoxide pumped in children's faces. A bicycle gives five-minute access to beaches, shops, recreation, medical aid, ferries and pub. Children of 7 years get the kind of spatial access they won't otherwise get until 17. Rottnest shows how safe, quiet, healthy and efficient the bicycle is in the absence of cars.

The sense of relaxation and even liberation on the island is palpable and, I would contend, widely experienced. Rottnest resists, to some extent, the excesses of industrialization and capitalism. The absence of cars and private property is linked to the relaxation of the regimes and hierarchies of everyday life. While the food prices are often outrageous, the best things on Rottnest are still free – the beaches, the landscape, the architecture, the sense of 'place'. In a world where the concept of 'place' is increasingly packaged for consumption, this former colony of a colony seems to have a certain resistance. The island satisfies a quest for places that are not simply products of the market. It has not (yet) become reduced to what Lefebvre (1991: 361) calls 'that "world of the image" which is the enemy of the imagination'. Rottnest Island is a place of bodily pleasure, where codes of dress and behaviour are relaxed. In my imagination at least it is a place of liberation, the very antithesis of its beginnings as a prison.

These experiences are nourished also by the built setting, its layers of meaning and successive appropriations. There is a potential liberation, especially for the young, in the leftover places described earlier. Imagination thrives in the margins and cracks left abandoned or unfilled by the regimes of power, capital and image. This authentic appropriation of place contrasts with the passive contemplation of formal imagery and the consumption of preconceived meaning. These appropriations generate a haunted landscape of hidden meanings, which, as de Certeau argues, can insinuate themselves into the very structures of surveillance and discipline. The older penal and military developments on Rottnest are such transparent symbols of those regimes that they become ironically untied from those meanings, without losing them. Meaning becomes mutable through reappropriation. 'Like words,' argues de Certeau (1985: 131), 'places are articulated by a thousand usages.'

This quality has some characteristics of the French notion of *terrain vague* as popularized by Solâ-Morales and others. This term refers to places of uncertain use and meaning, the meaning of 'vague' carries connotations of both 'vacant' and 'unstable' or 'blurred'. *Terrain vague* is a kind of semantic vacuum which presents as availability, empty yet full of possibility. As Solâ-Morales (1997) puts it: 'The relationship between the absence of use, of activity, and the sense of freedom, of expectancy, is fundamental to understanding the evocative potential of the city's terrains vagues.' It can also be useful to think of such experience in terms of Deleuze and Guatarri's (1988) distinction of smooth/

striated space. Many of my experiences on Rottnest, such as the armaments tunnels and the haunted house, were in spaces that had been strictly controlled and striated at one time and then abandoned. They were in a sense 'smooth' or at least without stricture; yet it is the remnants of 'striation' that lend these places potency. They are places that have been territorialized, abandoned and now reterritorialized. It is the moment between territorializations that creates the possibility.

With all of this in mind, there are signs of deterioration on Rottnest Island. The most obvious is the proliferation of the distinctive rust colour, now a copy of the rusty nails original, marketed by a local paint company as 'Rottnest Orange'. Houses, temporary buildings and toilet blocks, whether steel, brick or timber, have all turned to 'rust'. As in a military camp, there is little choice being exercised under this regime. The rust colour is an important part of the Rottnest heritage but, like authentic rust, it was the product of the vagaries of time, not purity of intention.

The formal language of much of the newer architecture also lacks the richness and variety of the originals. Indeed the architectural history of the island is more varied than the current ideology. This lifeworld was not produced from a precious attitude and it should continue to develop without one. If 'authenticity' can mean anything in an era which tends to reduce lifeworld to text, then it stems from the imagination and not the image; authenticity is the very wellspring that brings meaning to form (Dovey 1985a). The threat to places such as Rottnest is that they will be tailored to meet certain expectations. And the island's best defence is that despite its historic importance and amenity it will never be a particularly marketable product. People who visit on a day trip are often unimpressed. When a newspaper once held a competition for 'worst travel destinations', Rottnest received a nomination. The 'Rottnest Experience' is not easily consumed; one cannot see it while trying to look at it. The place must therefore be protected against such expectations.

One of the design lessons of Rottnest is the importance of the contingencies of built form in its development. What was once a hay-store and mill (now a small museum) has an odd bulge in the plan produced by the circular motion of the horse-driven grain mill. The severe enclosure of the octagonal Quod bounded the Aboriginal prisoners within a secure colonial order. The monolithic curvilinear sea-wall, the rounded kitchen and the rusty render are all products of specific circumstances that have now passed. While the symbolic and practical functions may have gone, these colours and forms remain the hooks on which we hang our memories precisely because of this specificity which lends them their differences.

Some narrow steps penetrate the sea-wall where it curves up towards the shops, framing the lighthouse in the gap as you approach. In my memory it is flanked by large rusty anchors, monuments to sunken ships which have been forgotten. Yet they anchor memories of balmy nights flirting with the possibilities of teenage life. Such are the contingencies of place; opportunities that form enables yet no designer anticipates. Places and landscapes are the warehouses of memory, their forms and colours are the mnemonic hooks upon which we hang experience. Places anchor occasions through the contingencies of built form.

Paradoxically, Rottnest holds lessons in how little the specificities of form matter by the manner in which it has worn the changes in occupation and meaning over 170 years. The former hay-store and stables have long served well as shops. The governor's house with its ostentatious turrets makes a wonderful hotel – front garden crowded with drinkers while children spill across the old stone fence onto the beach. The guns and tunnels produced under the imperatives of war are appropriated by the teenager and then delivered back to the public in the guided tour. Forms of the old order are appropriated by the new and the cracks are filled by the spontaneous appropriations of youth.

In this regard the prison Quod, the settlement's *raison d'être*, seems not to have found its place. The former prison cells sell for the same price as an upmarket hotel room. But the Quod as enclave is almost deserted, a manicured green lawn with no bicycles or ball games allowed (Figure 12.5). The main entrance gate is locked and unused, its boundary function reversed from keeping Aboriginal prisoners in to keeping the Rottnest community out (Figure 12.6). Plans to construct a swimming pool in the Quod ran into opposition from Perth's Aboriginal community, who are keen to reclaim the honour of those who built this settlement, which they term a 'slave camp'. Their persistent efforts led to a radar survey which revealed the location of graves under the camping area to the north-west of the Quod (Figure 12.1).[4] All traces of later development including ten buildings and a major through street have been removed and the area has been reinstated as a cemetery – a small open forest without grave markings, framed but not fenced (Figure 12.7). This is now a rather poignant place, haunted by the memory of teenage camping parties and by the more general history of white colonization of Aboriginal cultures.

Figure 12.5
Interior of Quod.

Figure 12.6
Quod entrance: the inverted prison.

Figure 12.7
Aboriginal graveyard.

The former prison Quod, its front gate sealed, now faces mutely down the hill. This was an architecture produced under conditions of racial tyranny which stands in stark contrast to the hedonistic present. Laced as it is with contradictions, this 'self-built prison' is a fine form upon which to anchor the memory of the Aboriginal contribution to the island. It is ripe for Aboriginal reappropriation. This would be a final irony, since Rottnest is one of the very few parts of Australia that was uninhabited before the British invasion.

Irony, like rust, is one of time's retorts to the certainties of meaning.

Afterword

Chapter 13: Liberty and Complicity

Liberty is a practice . . . it can never be inherent in the structure of things to guarantee the exercise of freedom. The guarantee of freedom is freedom.

(Foucault 1997: 371)

There are many threads to the place/power nexus that cut across the various case studies I have explored here. The uses of enclosure recur in different forms and meanings, from the Forbidden City and bunker to the shopping mall, residential enclave and prison. Seductive significations of nature, harmony, stability, authenticity and history are common from the Chancellery to the suburban house. Images of dynamism are apparent from Berlin and Bangkok to the corporate tower and Euralille; open space as freedom from Beijing to the suburban interior. Authority and identity become 'grounded' in 'blood and soil', in the 'Royal Ground' and the suburban dream. Meanings of built form and the practices that produce them change over time and can become inverted, as in the case of the island prison, military landscape and democracy monument. The intimidating scale and slippery surfaces echo from the Berlin Chancellery to Tienanmen Square and the corporate foyer. Pathways of privilege recur from Berlin to the Imperial Axis and Royal Road, interrupted or twisted in every case by the turns of history. The production of controlled crowds and behaviour connects Berlin and Tienanmen to the residential enclave and shopping mall, along with rhizomatic practices of resistance. I have no intention of weaving a grand theory out of these threads, nor do I claim to have done little more than touch the surface of such practices. Rather I want to conclude with some questions about the prospects for designers who wish to engage in making places which embody something of the quest for equity, justice and liberty.

Two generalizations in relation to the nexus of place and power seem plausible. The first is that there is no zone of autonomy or neutrality in which to practice architecture and urban design. Such practice exists only in alliance with those who control land and resources. The imperative to build and the forms of that construction cannot be unhinged from the quest for power. The second is that the built environment does not inherently oppress or liberate; rather, people use built form in the attempt to do so. There are no styles or forms of liberty or oppression and any built form can serve interests for which it was not intended. Claims of liberation from practices of power through design are often revealed as either new practices of power or more of the same in the guise of the new.

Oppression and liberation are forms of social practice which are mediated by built form. These practices 'take place': they frame and are framed by certain spatial structures and provinces of meaning. The nature of architecture and urban design, their silent framings of everyday life, lend themselves to practices of coercion, seduction, domination and the legitimation of authority. There is no way around this nexus. Rather, designers must enter into and understand some necessary complicities and complexities. The mediations of power in built form have both positive and negative manifestations.

Power is a two-sided coin. Buildings necessarily both constrain and enable certain kinds of life and experience; they are inherently coercive in that they enforce limits to action. This coercion is a large part of what enables agency in everyday life to 'take place'. The control over access to the tutorial room or the bedroom enables freedom of debate or of sexual behaviour, which an open syntax would constrain. Designers who believe that they are engaged in an architecture of liberation by refusing to segment space are simply engaged in a different form of coercion – an 'enforced' subjection to uncontrolled encounter and a disciplinary gaze. Both open and closed spaces each enable and constrain human action. Enabling and constraining are poles of a dialectic of coercion in architecture. Architects 'manipulate' spatial behaviour – the issue is not whether but how they do so.

Inasmuch as all design of built form attempts to satisfy human desire, all successful architecture and urban design is seductive. Like all forms of art and advertising, architecture and urban design engages in imaginative play with our dreams (identity, sexuality, domination, immortality) and our fears (violence, death, difference). Dominating scale in architectural and urban form can both inspire and intimidate. The joys and delights, fears and horrors of the various experiences of place and dwelling cannot be unravelled from the seductions of place. Designers inevitably engage with human desire and fear – the issue is not whether but how they do so.

All built form has inertia, it 'fixes' a great deal of economic capital into a certain form in a certain place, stabilizing the spatial 'order'. Successful design inevitably carries authority and produces symbolic capital. Architecture is a controlling framework for 'appropriate' behaviour; as Hollier (1989: ix) puts it: 'Architecture is society's superego'. The complicities of built form with practices of power are inevitable. They are to be understood, recognized, theorized, critiqued and debated. But the attempt to avoid such complicity is often fraught with new forms of deception. Designers who believe they escape this nexus through the production of form are engaged in self-deception. As a means of opening up such issues I shall briefly discuss four well-known architectural projects of the 1980s and 1990s. They are chosen because they are each infused with a certain liberating intent, fine architectural talent, and certain complicities with practices of power that become clearer over time.

AUTHORIZING MADNESS

Parc de la Villette in Paris is the most famous and celebrated of deconstructionist projects – a 35 hectare complex of museum, park and cultural facilities primarily designed by Bernard Tschumi on the site of a former slaughterworks. Tschumi's design is an abstract layering of points, surfaces and lines which includes a series of bright red *folies* occupying the node points of an invisible grid. They are inspired by the deconstructive desire to unpack the ways that meaning is constructed; to oppose fixity of meaning; to expose underlying ideology. They are also inspired by the liberating spirit of Bolshevik 'constructivism' for which the redness is a clear reference. The *folies* have no predetermined function, they seek to undo architecture's supposed grounding in function and shelter. They are called folies to evoke the 'madness' of an architecture which defies reason, the frivolity of the traditional gazebo in the park and the idea that their meaning remains 'in play'.

In terms of Tschumi's intent this is an architecture which has severed its contaminating relations with function and authority – the language of architecture is used against itself, an assault on the idea of stable meaning (Tschumi 1987, 1988). Through the evasion of function the folies are designed to call into question an architecture which 'serves' authority in any simple manner. Yet

Figure 13.1
Parc de la Villette:
authorizing madness.

severing relations with authority is more difficult than it seems since the project relies strongly on its representation and theorization in architectural magazines, including the philosophical authority of Derrida, who argues: 'These folies destabilize meaning, the meaning of meaning . . . They revive, perhaps, an energy that was infinitely anaesthetised' (quoted in Jencks 1988: 24).

I would suggest that it is not in the simulated world of the journals but in the lived world of Paris that the work must ultimately be judged. If we explore Parc de la Villette as a lived place, we find the folies are intriguing, engaging and often quite beautiful. They are all scaled for human use with sheltered space, and many can be mounted as lookout towers. Like fragmented echoes of the Eiffel Tower they are progressive urban objects which continue the highly innovative and refined aesthetic standards of French public design. But what of their deconstructive effects – the ideological shock value? Framed and encountered as a series of sculptures in a verdant context they clearly do not disturb those who explore, climb and gaze across the landscape. Complacent expectations for park design are wonderfully displaced but the subject is scarcely 'shocked' out of old mythologies.

Despite the denial of program, the folies also service a conservative agenda, beyond the control of the architect, about which they are silent. Hollier (1989: xiv) suggests that the park is a site of cultural consumption with the function 'to appropriate and discipline proletarian expenditure' and Markus (1988) has called attention to certain hidden agendas that have not been deconstructed:

> The text which needs deconstructing is not the metaphorical one of the buildings, but the real one which designs the building as soon as it is written, without the presence of designer . . . Who is to define the function of the red cubes; whose resources for conversions or re-use will be available? How will decisions be made – by whom, for whom, in the real political world of Paris?
>
> (Markus 1988: 16)

The erasure of function and the celebration of madness and difference create an illusion of design freedom which in turn obscures a covert program. Parc de la Villette is one of the 'grand projects' of the French state, programmed to demonstrate and promote French cultural, intellectual and aesthetic authority. How better than an aesthetic showcase that one needs to read French philosophy to understand? The *folies*, however engaging as architectural forms, are not without ideological function and fixed meaning. They signify the aesthetic and intellectual supremacy, and therefore the legitimacy, of the French State. It is worth reflecting on the fact that the park was commissioned at the same time and by the same state that commissioned South Pacific nuclear tests (against huge local resistance) and the bombing of the Greenpeace ship (killing one of its crew). This does not diminish the formal design but I would suggest that any design which can so successfully capture the imagery of an architecture of emancipation, also and at the same time may be appropriated to other ends. The liber-

Figure 13.2
Loyola Law School:
deconstructing law.

ating 'energy' referred to by Derrida is precisely the 'symbolic capital' which Bourdieu argues the avant-garde have traditionally supplied in service of aesthetic authority.

DECONSTRUCTING LAW

The Loyola Law School campus in Los Angeles has been the site of a series of projects by architect Frank Gehry since the early 1980s. Gehry has long been a master of semantic inversion – the use of devalued and 'cheap' forms and materials redeemed through a sophisticated collagist architecture in a manner reminiscent of Duchamp's 'found objects' redeemed as art. On the Loyola campus Gehry has engaged in a play of the relationship of architecture with law. Building types traditionally used in the legitimation of lawful authority such as temple, column and chapel become fragments of a collage – columns without pediments raising questions about support, authority and the rule of law (Figure 13.2). As King puts it: 'All the set pieces of classicism appropriate to a law school are there, except that they all imply discontinuity, difference' (King 1996: 165). The architecture is designed to throw into doubt the legitimizing symbols of law and order for an audience of students preparing for practice in one of the most class-divided of societies.

The location of the Loyola School on the fringe of downtown in a Central American barrio has led to it being constructed somewhat like a fortress. The campus covers a whole block, with all buildings facing inwards and only one guarded entrance to the street, primarily for cars. The basic urban plan form (the spatial syntax) is that of the enclave. All of the playful imagery is focused on a framing of the central open space of the small campus. By contrast the street elevations are hard-edged and streetsmart as the project fences out the crime.

In his well-known book on Los Angeles, Davis (1991) points out a range of complicities of 'fortress building' in Gehry's Los Angeles work. Under the title of 'Frank Gehry as Dirty Harry', Davis characterizes Gehry as producing a form of 'make my day' architecture which highlights the use of playful displays of force to create beachheads of privilege in decaying landscapes, a 'recycling of the elements of a decayed and polarized urban landscape . . . into light and airy expressions of a happy lifestyle . . . combining delightful geometries with complex security systems' (Davis 1991: 81). He calls the Law School 'neo-conservative' for its refusal to engage with the local Central American community in anything more than a provocative and exclusionary manner (Davis 1991: 239).

Davis's critique of Gehry is a refreshing balance to the cheerleading which often passes for architectural criticism in the journals, but it is a partial view. Blaming architects for such complicity sets them up to take the blame for a system where it suits quite a range of interests to locate the problem in the design. One effect is to drive the best designers into 'gallery architecture' or 'boutique' practices (where many already hide), leaving the built environment to more regressive alternatives. Davis is derisive of the lack of engagement with the public realm, yet Habermas (1989) defines the 'public realm' in terms of the possibilities for communicative action. He has pointed out the historical importance and emancipatory potential of the bourgeois public realm – places which don't fit the open traditions of the agora yet which approach the ideal speech situation of democratic communicative action (Calhoun 1992). While the Loyola campus is a privileged enclave restricted to students and staff, it is also a retreat from a public lifeworld which is brutalized by crime and saturated by the penetrations of the market. Recall that Arendt defines power as the capacity for agreement in a public realm 'where words are not empty and deeds not brutal, where words are not used to veil intentions but to disclose realities, and deeds are not used to violate and destroy but to establish relations and create new realities' (Arendt 1958: 200).

The central open space of the campus is a rather pleasant place to study, chat and debate. Its collagist play of imagery and fortress-like enclosure have some parallels with the shopping mall and housing enclave. But it is the very engagement with the tensions of urban life that gives Gehry's early work much of its interest. By the 1990s he graduated beyond the social problems of the barrios to become the sculptor of museums and concert halls – safe from the overt complicities of Loyola and from critics like Davis. This is a common story for successful architects, reflecting the desire to define architecture as a pure artform operating within an austere and abstract zone of autonomy. Would the Loyola School be better architecture, or a better law school, if it were in a middle-class context representing a spurious harmony between law and community? I think not, and its complicities with power would simply be more hidden.

INCISING MEMORIES

The Vietnam Veterans Memorial in Washington, DC, designed by Maya Lin, was the result of a public competition in 1982. The site is in the Washington mall among a constellation of monuments to founding fathers of the US State. The Washington obelisk, the Lincoln temple and the Jefferson pantheon evoke a familiar narrative myth of empire from Egypt, through Greece and Rome to the White House (Vale 1992: 57–67). The new memorial is slightly off-axis between the Washington and Lincoln monuments. The program called for a memorial that was reflective and contemplative, that harmonized with its site and the surrounding monuments. It had to include the names of the 58,000 dead and make no political statement about the war.

Minimalist in style, but rich in meaning, the design is a simple V-shaped incision in the grass landscape, with the concave interior of the V cutting down to about 3 metres deep at the point (Figure 13.3). The earth walls formed by this incision are lined with polished black granite inscribed with the names of the dead. The place is structured as a single pathway along the wall into the enclo-sure, turning at the bottom, and then out. The black granite enclosing walls are aligned with the nearby Washington and Lincoln memorials. These at once cele-brate the alignment with traditions of power and democracy, yet also beg ques-tions about the relationships between the war, founding values and the history of empire. The V-shaped path can be read as a diversion from the main axis.

No narrative of the war is offered with the exception that the names are inscribed in the order in which they died, without reference to rank, company or place. The lack of an alphabetical order requires a search for names among those who died in the same year. The stone is highly polished and the surface of inscribed names becomes a mirror/screen through which we see images of our-selves and others. The inscriptions are designed for pencil rubbings, fragments of memory which disperse across the nation. The memorial is not visible from a dis-tance and it begins and ends imperceptibly, reflecting a war that was never declared and was lost slowly against a barely identifiable enemy. The semi-underground space is highly charged with emotion. The grief of veterans in battle fatigues who have largely appropriated the place mingles with that of tourists. The search for particular names echoes the larger search for meaning which the memorial engages in the general public.

While the memorial engages in a play of significations, it does so in a manner which integrates action with representation. The inscribed walls frame the semi-underground space within a grove of trees. It is a landmark which establishes its place in the cognitive map of Washington – the icon of the nation. Yet it marks the land by subtraction rather than addition. The unsettling quality is due mostly to the silences and absences – the memorial is a question rather than an answer. The inverted tetrahedral form is void rather than mass, absence rather than presence. The tomb-like form has traces of Egyptian and Greek antecedents, yet captures the 'mnemonic' quality without the 'monumental' scale. It engages the vertical/horizontal dimension by excavating, not by 'grounding' our aspirations so much as by signifying a 'loss of ground'.

These 'readings' of the memorial could indicate that its success stems from the multiplicity of significations, yet the potency of the design is experiential rather than intellectual. Indeed some of the meanings that can be gleaned are a bit glib – the V for Vietnam; an inversion of the V for 'Victory'. As text it is relatively accessible and 'readerly', yet I would suggest that it has a deconstructive dimension in that it incisively addresses issues of ideology and keeps meaning in play. It has unsettled many veterans who lobbied with some success for more literal affirmations of the war. A figurative sculpture was added nearby, followed by a large flagpole with the base inscribed 'they died for our freedom' – a single answer to displace so many questions.

The memorial takes its place in the packaged tour of American identity, framed by the larger constellation of monuments through which the nation-state affirms and legitimizes its domination. The memorial has little capacity to disturb this larger order and more recent history confirms that the lessons of Vietnam have not been learned. Yet it affirms the idea that one can design public and political monuments that touch a broad public consciousness without affirming authorized narratives.

CONSTRUCTING LAW

The Uluru/Kata Tjuta Aboriginal Cultural Centre was completed near Uluru (formerly Ayers Rock) in central Australia in 1996. It is a place of cultural exchange with the goal to enable tourists to understand the meanings of an extraordinary landscape from the viewpoint of its traditional owners. The design process was highly collaborative between the local Anangu Aboriginal community and the non-Aboriginal architect (Gregory Burgess). It incorporated the commissioning of paintings of the rock and its major 'Dreaming' story as a source of design. Many aspects of Anangu law or Tjukurpa are embodied in this story of a struggle between two snakes (Tawa 1996). The plan of the Centre is formed of two metaphoric 'snakes' framing a central open space – the likeness is a metaphoric weaving of serpentine pathways, walls and roof lines rather than literal representation (Figure 13.4). The building appears in the desert landscape as a series of undulating roofs dwarfed by the overwhelming presence of the rock. The tourist pathway through the centre begins with a tightly controlled and darkened sequence of spaces which tell stories of Anangu law. Beyond this display, pathways branch to include shops, restaurants, environmental displays, craft work and performance spaces. The view from the open space frames the enormous rock between the buildings but photographs are forbidden. The Anangu community use the centre and do not wish to be photographed.

From both tourist and professional architectural points of view this is a highly successful design which has won prizes and been broadly published in the international architectural press (Tawa 1996; Uluru-Kata Tjuta Cultural Centre

Figure 13.3
Vietnam Veterans'
Memorial: incising
memory.

Figure 13.4
Uluru/Kata Tjuta Cultural
Centre: constructing law.

1997; Underwood 1996; Findley 2005). But how successful is it for traditional owners? Based on discussions with Anangu elders and others, I suggest two different responses.[1] First, there is an appreciation of the form of the building and the manner in which the Tjukurpa stories (law) have been represented, coupled with pride in their role in this process. Stories previously 'held' in the rock are now also 'held' in the architecture. Yet the second response from the Anangu is to deflect questions away from the form of the building, refusing to adopt the privileged aesthetic gaze from which the building is judged. The community design process generated expectations of a space of genuine cultural exchange, economic development and equal recognition – yet it has largely failed to deliver. Instead there is a perception that Anangu culture has been packaged for the tourist market – Aboriginality is consumed rather than understood. There is resentment that despite the formal success of the project, in social terms it has not produced equality of recognition.

Funding for the building was based on the tourist market and the major source of visitors is package tours which funnel their subjects through the centre on half-hour cycles geared to global schedules. Such schedules always allow the necessary two hours to climb the rock, yet a major part of Tjukurpa law is that the rock is sacred and should not be climbed. Indeed the success of the cultural centre is measured by many in the declining number of climbers – in enabling visitors to see the landscape from perspectives other than that of the dominating gaze. The building services a global market wherein its meanings are not under the control of either traditional owners or architects. Postcolonial critique suggests that the voice of the native 'other' is framed and heard only within the dominant forms of discourse. The serpentine zoomorphic forms of the building identify Aboriginality with the irregular and organic in contrast with the regularity and abstraction of modern architecture. To what extent does this reinforce a reassuring stereotype – the Aboriginal as part of 'nature', as 'other' to the modern global subject? And how do we reconcile such a critique with the fact that zoomorphic forms are a broadly recurrent feature of Aboriginal agency in architecture?[2] At a time when race relations in Australia are subject to deep division and heated debate, can the building be read as a gesture of reconciliation, representing a spurious harmony?

The Uluru building attempts the opposite of the Loyola Law School – instead of deconstructing the legitimizing images of Western law, it constructs legitimizing images of Anangu law. While the design does the opposite of deconstruction (it orients, it establishes presence), it also aims to displace stereotyped ways of seeing. Visitors cannot approach the rock without the prejudices framed by the tourist industry: they come to see the 'real' thing, to photograph and to climb it. The centre attempts to supplant such preconceptions and throw stereotypes into doubt.

This is a highly complex project which meets its various meaning markets: the commercial market as a signature building for cultural tourism; the political market as a signifier of reconciliation; the architectural market as an aesthetic object. Yet it also creates a space for another way of seeing. And for the Anangu? While the project has not delivered on its illusions of reconciliation, recognition and equality, this may be a liberating lesson.

LIBERTY AND COMPLICITY

Each of these projects embodies aspects of both emancipation and complicity in the mediation of power. In each design the formal language and the creativity of the architect is fundamentally important to the constructions of meaning. Yet my purpose here is not to pass judgement on the architects. A major problem with the architectural profession lies in its focus on a fragile hierarchy of professional reputations, and within this frame the role of academic critique becomes easily reduced to that of cheerleading or booing. While these projects are scarcely bereft of the heroic quest (a struggle for power which I have not addressed in this book), architecture is too important to be side-tracked by professional jealousies.

Return again to the question of what the prospects are for a liberating architectural practice. The most plausible answer is that the answer must remain forever in play. And again, my two conclusions about how such answers are framed: there are no forms or styles of liberty; and no zone of neutrality in which to practise. As Foucault suggests, there are no guarantees, because liberty is something one 'practises'. But he adds in a rather uncharacteristic comment that architecture 'can and does produce positive effects when the liberating intentions of the architect coincide with the real practice of people in the exercise of their freedom' (Foucault 1997: 371–372). This talk of 'positive effects', 'real practice' and a coincidence of interest suggests a certain congruence between the deconstructive imperative to undercut prevailing ideologies and some kind of 'participative' design. Foucault never spelt out what this might mean, but it is surely more than a play of formal imagery and more than participative stereotypes of 'community architecture'.

Community architecture is to some degree a tautology since all architectural production takes place within communities of interest. All architectural practice is a form of what Habermas (1984) calls 'communicative action' – a task which presumes a certain transparency of representation and meaning and participative decision-making. Yet how is this to be reconciled with the creativity of architectural form-making and the differences of interest that comprise real communities? The participatory process must go beyond any 'community architecture' stereotype which suggests the simple handing over of power to client or community groups. Such practices are rarely free from manipulation, no matter how well intentioned. And the built forms which result can become banal emblems of democracy, indeed a cover for its declining practice. The idea of communicative action with a focus on the 'public interest' does not imply that a community of subjects holds a consensual view nor that they understand their own interests. It does suggest that they share a 'common interest' in the future of a place and certain rights to debate that future. The public interest does not exist pre-formed but is constructed in the design process.

So much participative design becomes infected with a regressive desire for a purity of community, a comforting consensus and closure of place experience. Engagement with the dilemmas and contradictions of an 'impure' or even 'inoperative' community is one of the key tasks of the epoch.[3] From a Deleuzian perspective such a process is based on flows of desire; the desire for a better world is a precondition for empowerment and architecture can be seen as an aggregate rather than confluence of such desires (Petrescu 2005). Good participatory processes are transformative in that they change people as well as places; designers as well as participants. They enlarge the spatial imagination and stimulate the flows of desire.[4] The prospect of such engagement is not that it will produce consensual placemaking but that it will transform people, places and practices of power – the resulting forms and identities of people and places is unpredictable by definition.

The idea of the 'public interest' affronts many architects with its implications of populism and comfortable consensus. Yet while communicative action may generate consensus, it may also expose sectional interests and contradictions. Differences of identity, ethnicity, age, class and gender can be frightening, but they are precisely the stuff of deconstruction – the exposure of sub-texts and contradictions so often hidden under false consensus. Deconstruction and communicative action are united by the imperative to enter into the difficulty of things, resisting the desire to remain above the fray, the illusion of autonomy.

The deconstructive task must lead to more than a play of formal imagery. It cannot be achieved by a retreat from function nor by a retreat into private dialect. The design of built form must proceed in the knowledge that any 'shock value' will be cashed in the 'meaning markets' of property, politics and profession. There is also a larger deconstructive task which is to unpack and reconstruct the lifeworld and its spatial programs. Such a programmatic deconstruction would entail a systematic engagement with the ways in which the lifeworld has been sliced, its functions categorized, coded, juxtaposed and omitted (Markus 1993: 317–318). Issues of program cannot be segregated from design, as Pecora argues:

> If architecture as a discipline ever hopes to cut through the various ideologies that continue to maintain its symbolic capital, its aura, it will have to take seriously the fact that architecture is embedded in the habitual utility of social relations, that it is precisely those social relations that finally give meaning to all built form.
>
> (Pecora 1991: 74–75)

The key role of designers is to join imagination to the public interest; it is to catch the public imagination with visions for a better future. There is an ancient model for such a role which Plato called the 'demiurge' – the creative spirit who shapes the visible world out of chaos. The 'demiurge' is an artisan who encounters a world which resists rational ordering; a bricoleur who engages with chance, disorder and contingency. As the etymology suggests (*demos:* people; *ergos:* worker), the 'demiurge' works for the people – creative imagination is deployed in the public interest. The 'demiurge' is a useful model for designers of buildings and cities, yet it must be divorced from Plato's ideal 'forms' and authoritarian politics. The desire to liberate through the art of design can become part of the problem. In his account of the avant-garde Miles points out the inevitable reduction of art to the aesthetic and asks:

> Perhaps this is where the flaw in the concept of an avant-garde is most clearly evident, in the desire to lead society upward, onward, in a way which retains power (and expertise) in the hands of those leading . . .

> (Miles 2004: 59)

Yet the idea that design expertise can be disavowed, rendered transparent or reduced to the technical has been one of the more damaging ideologies of participatory design – the demotion of the designer creates a vacuum that is most easily filled by the instrumental imperatives of the state or the market. Design expertise needs to encompass the social process and the knowledge base needs to incorporate critiques of power. 'Participation is not a worthy sop to our political masters,' argues Till (2005: 41), 'nor is it an excuse for mediocrity; it is not a distraction from supposedly higher values. Participation is the space in which hope is negotiated.' This turns us away from Platonic purity to the Socratic ideal of public debate. The most basic principle of democracy is that the legitimation of authority lies in the effective participation of citizens in public affairs. Such a principle predates capitalism, modernity and the industrial revolution; and it will outlive postmodernity and post-industrialism (Saul 1997). If architecture and urban design always represents and stabilizes authority, then the task of the architect or designer is to engage with the processes of authorization and legitimation.

I began this book with the suggestion that the task for designers, albeit in a small way, is to 'change the world'. The understanding of how power is mediated in built form is necessary, but ultimately not sufficient, to this task. Design practice must engage with a major antinomy of our era – the theoretical and methodological tension between deconstruction and communicative action. How can we remain open to the lessons of discursive analysis and yet redeem notions of truth, justice and democracy? We must hang on to these antinomous elements – we must refuse to refuse either. Design practices, along with education and research, may be kept in play by this tension. One cannot predict the forms that will result, nor their meanings. Differences must be permitted to speak for themselves; there can be no rules for liberating practices. The task is not to reduce design to ideology – there will remain a certain mystery in the ways the best designs play on our imagination. Designers have a leading role at a certain moment in the life of a place – fixing some forms within which life will be lived, upon which memories will be hung and meanings constructed. This must be done with imagination, rigour, courage and integrity. The task is to keep alive the liberating spirit of design without the illusion of autonomy. In the end, the complicities of built form with power rest on a tautology: places are programmed, designed and built by those with the power to do so. To practice in the light of this complicity is the primary liberating move.

Notes

Chapter 1: Power

1 There is a considerable literature in this regard and contention over definitions. In addition to specific citations, what follows garners various insights from: Airaksinen (1992); Ball (1992); Barnes (1988); Cox *et al.* (1985); Kertzer (1988); Lukes (1974, 1986); Ng (1980); Olsen and Marger (1993); Rosenbaum (1986); Wartenberg (1992); Weinstein (1972); and Wrong (1979).

Chapter 2: Program

1 See: Giddens (1979, 1981, 1984); Pred (1990); Cassell (1993).
2 Bourdieu was the French translator for Panofsky's 'Gothic Architecture and Scholasticism' (Panofsky 1967), which interprets architecture as a form of knowledge. His early structuralist account of the Berber house (Bourdieu 1973) was the base for the theory of *habitus*. See also: Bourdieu (1977, 1990b, 1993, 2000); Jenkins (1992); Robbins (1991).
3 Key sources include Foucault (1979, 1980, 1988, 1997). See also Dreyfus and Rabinow (1982); Miller (1993); Dandeker (1990); and Fraser (1989).
4 Sources for Deleuze include: Deleuze (1993; 1994); Deleuze and Guattari (1988); Colebrook (2002); Massumi (1992); Patton (2000); Rajchman (2000); Frichot (2005); and Doel (1996).
5 What follows is primarily based on Hillier and Hanson (1984). See also: Hillier (1988); Hillier *et al.* (1993); and Hillier (1996a and b).
6 This tripartite division is borrowed from Robinson (1994) as adapted from Hillier and Hanson (1984).
7 I am indebted to Tom Markus for an ongoing debate on these issues. However, I note his disagreement with this interpretation of the limits of spatial syntax.
8 I am thinking here of the early promise in work such as Altman (1975); Altman and Chemers (1980); Barker (1968); Hall (1966); Lynch (1969, 1981); Rapoport (1982).

Chapter 3: Representation

1 Sources here include Barthes (1967, 1973, 1974, 1976, 1979, 1988).
2 The responses were collectively entitled 'Eisenman (and Company) Responds' (*Progressive Architecture* 1995, February: 88–91). Notable defenders included Wigley, Koolhaas, Tschumi, Balfour, Kipnis, Bloomer, Diller, Libeskind, Krauss and Hays. See also further letters in response from Ghirardo and Peccora (*Progressive Architecture* 1995, May: 11, 13, 15, 26).
3 See: Forty (2000); Markus and Cameron (2002); Crysler (2003).

Chapter 4 Place

1 For more philosophical and geographic sources on the phenomenology of place see: Buttimer and Seamon (1980); Mugerauer (1994, 1995); Norberg-Schulz (1980, 1985); Perez-Gomez (1983); Relph (1976, 1981); Seamon (1979); Seamon and Mugerauer (1985); and Tuan (1977).

2 These terms are translated in various confusing ways such as 'at handness' versus 'on handness'; I shall retain the originals for clarity. See also Dovey (1985a: 36–38).

3 I am indebted to Tony King and Tom Markus as series editors for a stimulating challenge to some of the ideas outlined in these preceding pages. I note both their tolerance and their continuing disagreement.

4 Sources here also include Gottdiener (1985); Martins (1982); Rendell (2002); Borden (2001); Harris and Burke (1997); Soja (1989, 1991, 2000); Zukin (1995).

5 On theories of globalization see also: Sassen (2006); Featherstone et al. (2001).

6 This distinction parallels that made by Deleuze and Guattari (1988: 32–33) between extensive and intensive multiplicities.

7 Sources here include Benhabib (1992); Calhoun (1992); Forester (1985); Fraser (1989); Habermas (1971, 1984, 1989); Mayo (1985).

Chapter 5: Take Your Breath Away: Berlin

1 The communists were acquitted and a Dutchman (van der Lubbe) was executed for it. Goering, who had underground access to the building, reportedly later bragged that he had a hand in the fire (Shirer 1960: 193).

2 Sources on Hitler's attitudes to architecture include Helmer (1985); Krier (1985a); Lane (1968); Maser (1973); Speer (1970); Taylor (1974); Canetti (1979).

3 While Heidegger's well-documented Nazism has been used by critics to undermine his ontology, in my view it problematizes rather than refutes his ontology of dwelling; see: Dovey (1993).

4 Hitler had annexed Austria and part of Czechoslovakia, and his plans for Poland and the remainder of Czechoslovakia were in train as the Chancellery was completed.

5 The best sources on these plans are Helmer (1985) and Krier (1985a). There were many versions of the plan; comments here are on the most developed plans of 1938–1940.

6 Much of his time after 1941 was spent at the eastern front headquarters at Rastenburg, where he lived in a giant bunker complex (O'Donnell 1979; Speer 1970: 217).

Chapter 6: Hidden Power: Beijing

1 My account here owes a strong debt to the work of Zhu (1994, 2005). Other sources include Meyer (1991); Weng (1982); Yu (1984).

2 The English term 'eunuch' derives originally from the Latin *eunuchus*, 'keeper of the bed'; the meaning of the castrated male comes later. Their power base and name parallels that of the 'chamberlains' of the European tradition.

3 All references to the spaces of Mao's private life are from the account of his doctor, Li (1994).

4 This account of the development and meanings of Tiananmen Square owes a good deal to Wu (1991, 2005).

5 Mao's doctor describes both his pessimism about the effectiveness of the embalming and the construction of a provisional wax replica (Li 1994).

6 A great deal has been published about the sequence of events from April to June 1989. Much of it is sloppy reporting, and some of it remains in contention. This account draws especially from Brook (1992) and also from Chung (1989); Salisbury (1989); Spence (1990); Wark (1993); Wu (1991).

7 It appears that the substantial underground tunnel system from the Great Hall to the military headquarters in the western hills was not used, perhaps because this would have compromised security for Party leaders (Brook 1992).

8 Brook (1992: 151–169) has convincing arguments for this 'guestimate', which is shared by the Red Cross.

Chapter 7: Paths to Democracy: Bangkok

1 With regard to issues of Thai culture and language, my sources are all secondary.
2 Yet as Bourdieu's work on cultural production shows, this is a familiar pattern in the West where discursive fields are commonly structured in a manner that sustains the authority of those who already possess it (Bourdieu 1993).
3 To even consider the King's role in politics is insulting to some Thais since the standard view sees the King as above politics and beyond criticism (Hewison 1997). Respect for the King is enforced by 'lèse majesté' laws and self-censorship. While I regret any offence felt by Thai readers, it is not possible to properly examine issues of political legitimation in public space without examining the King's role.
4 While the King was the key agent in both initiating the development and overseeing its form, the urban design has been credited to the government architect Fariola.
5 The design of the monument is attributed to Mew Aphaiwong, whose brother was a leader of the military regime; the Italian-born sculptor Corado Feroci (also known as Bhirasri) undertook the bas reliefs.

Chapter 8: Tall Storeys: The Corporate Tower

1 The analysis involved a total sample of seventy-two brochures and advertisements marketing a total of twenty-three towers ranging from eight to fifty-six levels and from about 3,000 to 82,000 square metres of lettable space. Most were speculative developments with naming rights available. The forms of advertising ranged from a glossy hardback book to one-off newspaper advertisements.
2 See: Fairclough (1995); Rose (2001); Jhally (1977); Wernick (1983); Williamson (1978).
3 The sample here was eleven plans with 687 work-stations.
4 It was given to the University of Melbourne where it is now a protected historic façade fronting part of the architecture and planning faculty.
5 Developed by Alan Bond and the Bond Corporation, later renamed the Chifley Tower.
6 Heinrichs, P. '2001 – An Office Space Odyssey', *The Age*, 27 April, 1995. For a more extensive discussion of this project see: Dovey (2005b: Ch.11).
7 See: skyscraperpage.com accessed October 2006.
8 The developers of the building pictured in Figure 8.2 hired Philip Johnson simply to add an entrance and foyer. In his 'deconstructive' phase he added four non-functional columns, to the dismay of the local architects (Denton Corker Marshall).

Chapter 9: Inverted City: The Shopping Mall

1 This work remained in note form at the time of his death in 1940 (Benjamin 1999). I rely here on the interpretations of Buck-Morss (1989). See also: Benjamin (1992); Gilloch (1996); Gregory (1994); King (1996).
2 Gruen's first enclosed mall was Southdale in Minnesota in 1956. An earlier project with an open street of shops with a car park was designed by Graham and built in Seattle in 1950 (Rybczynski 1993) but it lacked Gruen's structural innovations. For the early history of mall design see Crawford (1992); Kowinski (1985); Hardwick (2004).
3 This analysis was undertaken in 1998.
4 Beckett, A. (1994) 'The Safe Way to Shop', *The Age* (Melbourne), 7 May: 34–38.
5 Fieldwork in Minneapolis was undertaken during two visits in 2003.
6 This is largely documented on the internet. See: www.deadmalls.com.
7 The Mall of America was completed in 1992 with 520 stores and 23 hectares of retail space. The Grand Bazaar in Istanbul has a far greater variety of shops (about 4,000), albeit in a much smaller area.
8 See: www.mallofamerica.com/about_moa_phase_II_linkto.aspx accessed January 2007.

Chapter 10: Domestic Desires: House and Enclave

1 There is a substantial literature on the meanings of home that I will not explore here. See Altman and Werner (1985); Buttimer (1980); Cooper Marcus (1995); Despres (1991); Lawrence (1991); Seamon (1979); Dovey (2005c).

2 This fieldwork was initially undertaken in the 1990s and updated in 2006. Examples are drawn from the Sacramento, Bay Area and Los Angeles areas in California, and from Melbourne and Perth in Australia. Much of the Californian fieldwork was done with Clare Cooper Marcus, whose various insights I much appreciate. See also Cooper Marcus *et al.* (1987).

3 There are also differences between Australian and Californian samples, and regional differences in each. Models are generally larger in California, more focused on the top end of the market and they are more likely to be double storey. Australian models were more likely to separate adult and child zones within the house. Beyond these differences, similarities in meaning are consistent; my concern here is with global aspects of the discourse and I shall mostly ignore the regional differences.

4 Key sources include Blakely and Snyder (1997); Flusty (1997); Judd (1995); McKenzie (1994); Caldeira (1999); Glasze *et al.* (2002, 2006); Atkinson and Blandy (2005).

5 While there may be little public planning there are increasing levels of internal conflict and litigation over what were once government functions and funds. Housing Owners Associations are also entering public policy debates in conflict with public community groups. See: McKenzie (2005).

Chapter 11: A Sign for the 21st Century: Euralille

1 Key sources here are Doutriaux (1992); OMA *et al.* (1995); Koolhaas (1994, 1996); Slessor (1991); Buchanan (1995).

2 *Passport for Euralille: Rendezvous with the 21st Century* (1995), Euralille Publicity Brochure, p. 1.

3 Koolhaas is the figurehead of OMA which is a highly collaborative practice. My attribution of the work to Koolhaas is not intended to deny other major contributors. Another key agent of the project was the Mayor of Lille, and former French Prime Minister, Pierre Mauroy.

4 A detailed account of the design process appears in Doutriaux (1992).

5 The observations in this critique are based on site visits from 18–22 July 1998 and 2–4 June 2007. The Congrexpo building is treated in the literature as part of Euralille yet it is separated by a major expressway and a walk of nearly a kilometre. Therefore it will not be considered here.

6 'Passport for Euralille', p. 5.

7 'Passport for Euralille', p. 13.

8 'Passport for Euralille', p. 13.

Chapter 12: Rust and Irony: Rottnest Island

1 Historical material is from Ferguson (1986); Government of Western Australia (1995a, 1995b, 1995c); Seddon (1972, 1983).

2 For a good critique of these and all pre-1970 developments see Seddon (1983).

3 The architect is Ferguson, also one of the island's key historians (Ferguson 1986).

4 Government of Western Australia (1995b).

Chapter 13: Liberty and Complicity

1 This account is based on a brief evaluation of the centre in 1997, including interviews with Anangu elders Barbara Tjikati and Tony Tjamiwa (translated by Karina Lester). Jane Jacobs and Mathilde Lochert shared this field trip and their insights may be apparent here. See also: Dovey (2000).

2 See: Dovey (1996); Jacobs *et al.* (1998)

3 See: Till (1998); Nancy (1991); Rose (1997).

4 See: Till (2005); Miessen and Basar (2006); Hill (1998, 2003); Blundell-Jones *et al.* (2005).

References

Aasen, C. (1998) *Architecture of Siam*, Oxford: Oxford University Press.

Ackerman, J. (1990) *The Villa*, Cambridge, MA: Harvard University Press.

Adams, J. (1984) 'The Meaning of Housing in America', *Annals, Association of American Geographers* 74, 4: 515–526.

Adorno, T. (1974) *Minima Moralia*, London: New Left Books.

—— (1991) 'Fascist Theory and the Pattern of Fascist Propaganda', in J. Bernstein (ed.) *The Culture Industry*, London: Routledge.

Adorno, T. and Horkheimer, M. (1993) 'The Culture Industry', in S. During (ed.) *The Cultural Studies Reader*, London: Routledge.

Airaksinen, T. (1992) 'The Rhetoric of Domination', in T. Wartenberg (ed.) *Rethinking Power*, Albany, NY: SUNY Press.

Alagappa, M. (1995) 'An Anatomy of Legitimation', in M. Alagappa (ed.) *Political Legitimation in Southeast Asia*, Stanford: Stanford University Press, pp. 11–30.

Alexander, C. (1964) *Notes on the Synthesis of Form*, Cambridge, MA: Harvard University Press.

—— (1965) 'A City is not a Tree', *Architectural Forum*, April: 58–62 and May: 58–61.

Alexander, C., Ishikawa, S. and Silverstein, M. (1977) *A Pattern Language*, New York: Oxford University Press.

Altman, I. (1975) *The Environment and Social Behavior*, Monterey, CA: Brooks Cole.

Altman, I. and Chemers, M. (1980) *Culture and Environment*, Monterey, CA: Brooks Cole.

Altman, I. and Werner, C. (eds) (1985) *Home Environments*, New York: Plenum.

Anderson, B. (1983) *Imagined Communities*, London: Verso.

—— (1998) *The Spectre of Comparisons*, London: Verso.

Anderson, M. (1990) *Hidden Power*, New York: Prometheus.

Anjira Assavananda (1999) 'Martyr's Memorial Takes Shape', *Bangkok Post*, 15 October.

Appadurai, A. (1996) *Modernity at Large*, Minneapolis, MN: Minnesota University Press.

Appleton, J. (1975) *The Experience of Landscape*, London: Wiley.

Arato, A. (1987) 'Esthetic Theory and Culture Criticism', in A. Arato and E. Gebhardt (eds) *The Essential Frankfurt School Reader*, New York: Continuum.

Arendt, H. (1958) *The Human Condition*, Chicago, IL: University of Chicago Press.

—— (1986) 'Communicative Power', in S. Lukes (ed.) *Power*, Oxford: Blackwell.

Arun Witchsuwan (ed.) (1998) *Photographs from the Historical Incidents of 14 October 1973 and 6 October 1976*, Bangkok: Arun Withaya Publishing (in Thai).

Askew, M. (1994) *Interpreting Bangkok*, Bangkok: Chulalongkorn University Press.

Atkinson, R. and Blandy, S. (eds) (2005) 'Gated Communities', *Housing Studies* 20, 2, Theme issue.

Augé, M. (1996) *Non-Places*, trans. J. Howe, London: Verso.

Bachelard, G. (1964) *The Psycho/analysis of Fire*, Boston, MA: Beacon.

—— (1969) *The Poetics of Space*, trans. M. Jolas, Boston, MA: Beacon.

Bakhtin, M. (1984) *Rabelais and his World*, London: Midland.

Balfour, A. (1990) *Berlin*, New York: Rizzoli.

Ball, T. (1992) 'New Faces of Power', in T. Wartenberg (ed.) *Rethinking Power*, Albany, NY: SUNY Press.

Ballantyne, A. (2005) *Architecture Theory*, London: Continuum.

Barker, R. (1968) *Ecological Psychology*, Palo Alto: Stanford University Press.

Barna, J. (1992) *The See-Through Years*, Houston, TX: Rice University Press.

Barnes, B. (1988) *The Nature of Power*, Oxford: Polity.

Barthes, R. (1967) *Elements of Semiology*, London: Jonathan Cape.

—— (1973) *Mythologies*, trans. A. Lavers, London: Paladin.

—— (1974) *SIZ*, New York: Hill & Wang.

—— (1976) *The Pleasure of the Text*, trans. R. Miller, New York: Hill & Wang.

—— (1979) *The Eiffel Tower and Other Mythologies*, New York: Hill & Wang.

—— (1988) *The Semiotic Challenge*, Oxford: Blackwell.

Bataille, G. (2005) 'The Obelisk', in A. Ballantyne (ed.) *Architecture Theory*, London: Continuum, pp. 17–25.

Bateson, G. (1972) *Steps to an Ecology of Mind*, New York: Ballantyne.

Baudrillard, J. (1975) *Mirror of Production*, trans. C. Levin, St. Louis, MO: Telos.

—— (1981) *For a Critique of the Political Economy of the Sign*, trans. C. Levin, St. Louis, MO: Telos.

Bauman, Z. (2001) *Community*, Cambridge: Polity.

Benhabib, S. (1992) 'Models of Public Space', in C. Calhoun (ed.) *Habermas and the Public Sphere*, Cambridge, MA: MIT Press.

Benjamin, W. (1974) *Charles Baudelaire*, London: Verso.

—— (1978) *Reflections*, trans. E. Jephcott, New York: Schocken.

—— (1992) *Illuminations*, trans. H. Zohn, London: Fontana.

—— (1999) *The Arcades Project*, Cambridge, MA: Harvard University Press.

Bentley, I., Alcock, A., Murrain, P., McGlynn, S. and Smith, G. (1985) *Responsive Environments*, London: Architectural Press.

Berger, J. (1992) *Keeping a Rendezvous*, Harmondsworth: Penguin.

Berger, R. (1985) *Versailles*, London: Penn State University Press.

Blakely, E. and Snyder, M. (1997) *Fortress America: Gated Communities in the United States*, Washington: Brookings Institute Press, 2nd edition.

Blomeyer, G. (1979) 'Architecture as a Political Sign System', *International Architect* 1, 1: 54–60.

Blum, A. (2005) 'The Mall Goes Undercover', *Slate Magazine*, www.slate.com/id/2116246/.

Blundell-Jones, P., Petrescu, D. and Till, J. (eds) (2005) *Architecture and Participation*, London: Spon.

Borden, I. (2001) *Skateboarding, Space and the City*, Oxford: Berg.

Bourdieu, P. (1973) 'The Berber House', in M. Douglas (ed.) *Rules and Meanings*, Harmondsworth: Penguin.

—— (1977) *Outline of a Theory of Practice*, London: Cambridge University Press.

—— (1984) *Distinction*, London: Routledge.

—— (1990a) *The Logic of Practice*, Cambridge: Polity.

—— (1990b) *In Other Words*, Cambridge: Polity.

—— (1993) *The Field of Cultural Production*, New York: Columbia University Press.

—— (2000) *Pascalian Meditations*, Cambridge: Polity Press.

Boyer, M. C. (1996) *The City of Collective Memory*, Cambridge, MA: MIT Press.

Brook, T. (1992) *Quelling the People*, New York: Oxford University Press.

Buchanan, P. (1995) 'Crossroads of Europe', *Architecture: The AIA Journal*, January: 66–69.

Buck-Morss, S. (1989) *The Dialectics of Seeing: Walter Benjamin and the Arcades Project*, Cambridge, MA: MIT Press.

Buttimer, A. (1980) 'Home, Reach and the Sense of Place', in A. Buttimer and D. Seamon (eds) *The Human Experience of Space and Place*, London: Croom Helm.

Buttimer, A. and Seamon, D. (eds) (1980) *The Human Experience of Space and Place*, London: Croom Helm.

Caldeira, T. (1999) *City of Walls*, Berkeley, CA: University of California Press.

Calhoun, C. (ed.) (1992) *Habermas and the Public Sphere*, Cambridge, MA: MIT Press.

Callahan, W. (1998) *Imagining Democracy*, Singapore: Institute of Southeast Asian Studies.

Calvino, I. (1979) *Invisible Cities*, London: Picador.

Canetti, E. (1962) *Crowds and Power*, London: Phoenix.

—— (1979) *The Conscience of Words*, New York: Continuum.

Casey, E. (1997) *The Fate of Place*, Berkeley, CA: University of California Press.

Cassell, P. (ed.) (1993) *The Giddens Reader*, London: Macmillan.

Chaiwat Surawichai (1998) *14 October 1973 Memorial*, Bangkok: Saitharn Publishing (in Thai).

Charnwit Kasetsiri and Thamsong Petch-lert-anan (eds) (1999) *From 14th to 6th October*, Bangkok: Thammasat University Press (in Thai).

Cheater, A. (1991) 'Death Ritual as Political Trickster in the People's Republic of China', *Australian Journal of Chinese Affairs* 26, July: 67–97.

Chung, H. (1989) *Shouting from China*, Melbourne: Penguin.

Clarke, P. (1989) 'The Economic Currency of Architectural Aesthetics', in M. Diami and C. Ingraham (eds) *Restructuring Architectural Theory*, Evanston, IL: Northwestern University Press.

Coaldrake, W. (1995) *Architecture and Authority in Japan*, London: Routledge.

Colebrook, C. (2002) *Understanding Deleuze*, Sydney: Allen & Unwin.

Colomina, B. (1992) 'The Split Wall', in B. Colomina (ed.) *Sexuality and Space*, Princeton, NJ: Princeton Architectural Press.

Cooper Marcus, C. (1995) *House as a Mirror of Self*, Berkeley, CA: Conari.

Cooper Marcus, C., Francis, C. and Meunier, C. (1987) 'Mixed Messages in Suburbia', *Places* 4, 1: 24–37.

Cox, A., Furlong, P. and Page, E. (1985) *Power in Capitalist Societies*, Brighton: Harvester.

Crawford, M. (1992) 'The World in a Shopping Mall', in M. Sorkin (ed.) *Variations on a Theme Park*, New York: Hill & Wang.

Cresswell, T. (2004) *Place: a Short Introduction*, Oxford: Blackwell.

Crysler, G. (2003) *Writing Spaces*, London: Routledge.

Dal Co, F. (1981) 'The Stones of the Void', *Oppositions* 24: 99–116.

Dandeker, C. (1990) *Surveillance, Power and Modernity*, Cambridge: Polity.

Davis, M. (1991) *City of Quartz*, New York: Verso.

Dear, M. (2000) *The Postmodern Urban Condition*, Oxford: Blackwell.

Debord, G. (1994) *The Society of the Spectacle*, New York: Zone Books.

de Certeau, M. (1984) *The Practice of Everyday Life*, trans. S. Rendall, Berkeley, CA: University of California Press.

—— (1985) 'Practices of Space', in M. Blonsky (ed.) *On Signs*, Baltimore, MD: Johns Hopkins University Press.

Deleuze, G. (1993) *The Fold*, Minneapolis, MI: University of Minnesota Press.

—— (1994) *What is Philosophy?* New York: Columbia University Press.

Deleuze, G. and Guattari, F. (1988) *A Thousand Plateaus*, London: Athlone.

Derrida, J. (1974) *Of Grammatology*, trans. G. Spivak, Baltimore, MD: Johns Hopkins University Press.

Derrida, J. and Eisenman, P. (1997) *Chora L Works*, eds J. Kipnis and T. Leeser, New York: Monacelli Press.

Despres, C. (1991) 'The Meaning of Home', *Journal of Architectural and Planning* Research 8, 2: 96–115.

Deutsche, R. (1996) *Evictions: Art and Spatial Politics*, Cambridge, MA: MIT Press.

Dhiravegin, L. (1992) *Demi Democracy*, Singapore: Times Academic Press.

Doel, M. (1996) 'A Hundred Thousand Lines of Flight', *Environment and Planning D* 14: 421–439.

Donley-Reid, L. (1990) 'A Structuring Structure', in S. Kent (ed.) *Domestic Architecture and the Use of Space*, Cambridge: Cambridge University Press.

Douglas, M. (1966) *Purity and Danger*, London: Routledge and Kegan Paul.

—— (1973) *Natural Symbols*, Harmondsworth: Penguin.

Doutriaux, E. (ed.) (1992) 'Euralille', *l'Architecture d'Aujour d'Hui*, April: 93–169.

Dovey, K. (1985a) 'The Quest for Authenticity and the Replication of Environmental Meaning', in D. Seamon and R. Mugerauer (eds) *Dwelling, Place and Environment*, The Hague: Martinus Nijhof.

—— (1985b) 'Home and Homelessness', in I. Altman and C. Werner (eds) *Home Environments*, New York: Plenum.

—— (1990) 'The Pattern Language and its Enemies', *Design Studies* 11, 1: 3–9.

—— (1993) 'Dwelling, Archetype and Ideology', *Center* 8: 9–21.

—— (1994) 'Dreams on Display', in S. Ferber, C. Healy and C. McAuliffe (eds) *Beasts of Suburbia*, Melbourne: Melbourne University Press.

—— (1996) 'Architecture about Aborigines', *Architecture Australia*, July/August: 98–103.

—— (2000) 'Seeing Uluru', *Thresholds* 21: 60–65.

—— (2002) 'Dialectics of Place: Authenticity, Identity, Difference', in S. Akkach (ed.) *De-Placing Difference*, Conference Proceedings, University of Adelaide, pp. 45–52.

—— (2005a) 'The Silent Complicity of Architecture', in J. Hillier and E. Rooksby (eds) *Habitus: A Sense of Place*, 2nd edition, London: Ashgate, pp. 283–296.

—— (2005b) *Fluid City: Transforming Melbourne's Urban Waterfront*, Oxon: Routledge.

—— (2005c) 'Home as Paradox', in G. Rowles and H. Chuadhury (eds) *Home and Identity in Late Life*, New York: Springer, pp. 361–370.

Dovey, K. and Dickson, S. (2002) 'Architecture and Freedom: Programmatic Innovation in the Work of Rem Koolhaas', *Journal of Architectural Education*, 55, 4: 268–277.

Dovey, K., Woodcock, I. and Wood, S. (2006) 'Contradictory Characters', in K. Anderson *et al.* (eds) *After Sprawl*, Conference Proceedings, Centre for Cultural Research, University of Western Sydney. www.uws.edu.au/research/researchcentres/ccr/publications#5.

Dovey, K., Woodcock, I. and Wood, S. (2007a) 'Senses of Urban Character', in F. Vanclay, J. Malpas and M. Higgins (eds) *Making Sense of 'Place'*, Canberra: National Museum of Australia (forthcoming).

Dreyfus, H. and Rabinow, P. (1982) *Michel Foucault: Beyond Structuralism and Hermeneutics*, Chicago, IL: Chicago University Press.

Eagleton, T. (1990) *The Ideology of the Aesthetic*, Oxford: Blackwell.

Egan, T. (2000) 'Retail Darwinism Puts Old Malls in Jeopardy', *New York Times*, 1 January.

Eisenman, P. (2004) 'Liberal Views Have Never Built Anything of Value', Interview by Robert Locke, July 27. www.archinect.com/features/article.php?id=4618_0_23_0_M. Accessed 7 October 2004 and 11 March 2006.

Etlin, R. (1991) *Modernism in Italian Architecture*, Cambridge, MA: MIT Press.

Evans, R. (1982) *The Fabrication of Virtue*, London: Cambridge University Press.

Ewen, S. (1988) *All Consuming Images*, New York: Basic Books.

Fairclough, N. (1995) *Critical Discourse Analysis*, London: Longmans.

Featherstone, M. (1991) *Consumer Culture and Postmodernism*, London: Sage.

—— (1993) 'Global and Local Cultures', in J. Bird, B. Curtis, T. Putnam and L. Tickner (eds) *Mapping the Futures*, London: Routledge.

Featherstone, M., Lash, S. and Robertson, R. (eds) (2001) *Global Modernities*, London: Sage.

Ferguson, G. (1986) *Rottnest Island*, Perth: University of Western Australia Press.

Ferguson, H. (1992) 'Watching the World Go Round', in R. Shields (ed.) *Lifestyle Shopping*, London: Routledge.

Findley, L. (2005) *Building Change*, Oxon: Routledge.

Fiske, J. (1989) *Understanding Popular Culture*, London: Routledge.

Florida, R. (2005) *Cities and the Creative Class*, New York: Routledge.

Flusty, S. (1997) 'Building Paranoia', in N. Ellin (ed.) *Architecture of Fear*, New York: Princeton Architectural Press, pp. 48–59.

Forester, J. (ed.) (1985) *Critical Theory and Public Life*, Cambridge, MA: MIT Press.

Forty, A. (2000) *Words and Buildings*, London: Thames & Hudson.

Forty, A. and Moss, H. (1980) 'A Housing Style for Troubled Consumers', *Architectural Review* 167, 996: 72–78.

Foucault, M. (1979) *Discipline and Punish*, trans. A. Sheridan, New York: Vintage.

—— (1980) *Power/Knowledge*, ed. C. Gordon, New York: Pantheon.

—— (1988) 'On Power', in L. Kritzman (ed.) *Michel Foucault*, New York: Routledge.

—— (1997) 'Space, Power and Knowledge', in N. Leach (ed.) *Rethinking Architecture*, London: Routledge.

Frampton, K. (1983) 'Towards a Critical Regionalism', in H. Foster (ed.) *The Anti-Aesthetic*, Port Townsend, WA: Bay Press.

Franck, K. (1997) 'The Suburban Sanctuary', in M. Gray (ed.) *Evolving Environmental Ideals*, Stockholm: International Association for People–Environment Studies (IAPS), 14 Proceedings.

Franck, K. and Schneekloth, L. (eds) (1994) *Ordering Space*, New York: Van Nostrand Reinhold.

Fraser, N. (1989) *Unruly Practices*, Minneapolis: University of Minnesota Press.

Frichot, H. (2005) 'Stealing into Gilles Deleuze's Baroque House', in I. Buchanan and G. Lambert (eds) *Deleuze and Space*, Edinburgh: Edinburgh University Press, pp. 61–79.

Garreau, J. (1991) *Edge City*, New York: Doubleday.

Geertz, C. (1985) 'Centers, Kings and Charisma', in S. Wilentz (ed.) *Rites of Power*, Philadelphia, PA: Pennsylvania University Press.

Ghirardo, D. (1994) 'Eisenman's Bogus Avant-Garde', *Progressive Architecture* November: 70–73.

Giddens, A. (1979) *Central Problems in Social Theory*, London: Macmillan.

—— (1981) *A Contemporary Critique of Historical Materialism: Vol. 1 Power, Property and the State*, Berkeley, CA: University of California Press.

—— (1984) *The Constitution of Society*, Cambridge: Polity.

—— (1990) *The Consequences of Modernity*, Stanford, CA: Stanford University Press.

—— (1991) *Modernity and Self Identity*, Cambridge: Polity.

Gilloch, G. (1996) *Myth and Metropolis*, Cambridge: Polity.

Girouard, M. (1978) *Life in the English Country House*, Harmondsworth: Penguin.

Glasze, G., Frantz, K. and Webster, C. (2002) (eds) 'The Global Spread of Gated Communities', *Environment and Planning B* 29, 3 (whole issue).

Glasze, G, Webster, C. and Frantz, K (ed.) (2006) *Private Cities: Global and Local Perspectives*, Oxon: Routledge.

Goffman, E. (1959) *The Presentation of Self in Everyday Life*, New York: Doubleday.

Goodsell, C. (1988) *The Social Meaning of Civic Space*, Lawrence: Kansas University Press.

Gorz, A. (1989) *Critique of Economic Reason*, trans. G. Handiside and C. Turner, London: Verso.

Gottdiener, M. (1985) *The Social Production of Urban Space*, Austin, TX: University of Texas Press.

—— (1995) *Postmodern Semiotics*, Oxford: Blackwell.

Government of Western Australia (1995a) *Rottnest Island Review*, Perth: Advance Press.

—— (1995b) *Rottnest Island Draft Management Plan*, Perth: Advance Press.

—— (1995c) *Chronological History of Rottnest Island*, Perth: Advance Press.

Graham, S. and Marvin, S. (2001) *Splintering Urbanism*, Oxford: Blackwell.

Green, N. and Moon, S. (1997) *Far from Home*, Dictionary of Western Australians, Volume 10, University of Western Australia Press.

Greenwald, A. (1980) 'The Totalitarian Ego', *American Psychologist* 35, 7: 603–618.

Gregory, D. (1994) *Geographical Imaginations*, Oxford: Blackwell.

Habermas, J. (1971) *Toward a Rational Society*, London: Heinemann.

—— (1975) *Legitimation Crisis*, Boston, MA: Beacon.

—— (1984) *The Theory of Communicative Action: Volume 1*, trans. T. McCarthy, Cambridge: Polity.

—— (1989) *The Structural Transformation of the Public Sphere*, trans. T. Burger and F. Lawrence, Cambridge: Polity.

Hall, E. T. (1966) *The Hidden Dimension*, New York: Doubleday.

Hannerz, U. (1996) *Transnational Connections*, London: Routledge.

Hardwick, M. J. (2004) *Mall Maker*, Philadelphia, PA: University of Pennsylvania Press.

Harries, P., Lipman, A. and Purden, S. (1982) 'The Marketing of Meaning', *Environment and Planning B* 9: 457–466.

Harris, H. and Lipman, A. (1986) 'A Culture of Despair', *Sociological Review* 34, 41: 837–854.

—— (1989) 'Form and Content in Contemporary Architecture', *Design Studies* 10, 1: 67–72.

Harris, S. and Burke, D. (eds) (1997) *Architecture of the Everyday*, Princeton, NJ: Princeton Architecture Press.

Harvey, D. (1985) *The Urbanization of Capital*, Baltimore, MD: Johns Hopkins University Press.

—— (1989) *The Condition of Postmodernity*, Oxford: Blackwell.

—— (1993) 'From Space to Place and Back Again', in J. Bird, B. Curtis, T. Putnam and L. Tickner (eds) *Mapping the Futures*, London: Routledge, pp. 3–29.

—— (1996) *Justice, Nature and the Geography of Difference*, Oxford: Blackwell.

—— (2000) *Spaces of Hope*, Edinburgh: University of Edinburgh Press.

—— (2001) *Spaces of Capital*, London: Routledge.

—— (2006) *Spaces of Global Capitalism*, London: Verso.

Hayden, D. (2004) *A Field Guide to Sprawl*, New York: W.W. Norton.

Heidegger, M. (1962) *Being and Time*, trans. J. Macquarie and E. Robinson, Evanston, IL: Northwestern University Press.

—— (1971) *Poetry, Language, Thought*, New York: Harper & Row.

Helmer, S. (1985) *Hitler's Berlin*, Ann Arbor, MI: UMI Research Press.

Hewison, K. (1997) 'The Monarchy and Democratization', in K. Hewison (ed.) *Political Change in Thailand*, London: Routledge.

Heynen, H. (1999) *Architecture and Modernity*, Cambridge, MA: MIT Press.

Hill, J. (1998) (ed.) *Occupying Architecture*, London: Routledge.

—— (2003) *Actions of Architecture*, London: Routledge.

Hillier, B. (1988) 'Against Enclosure', in N. Teymur, T. Markus and T. Wooley (eds) *Rehumanising Housing*, London: Butterworths.

—— (1996a) *Space is the Machine*, Cambridge: Cambridge University Press.

—— (1996b) 'Cities as Movement Economies', *Urban Design International* 1, 1: 47–60.

Hillier, B. and Hanson, J. (1984) *The Social Logic of Space*, New York: Cambridge University Press.

Hillier, B., Penn, A., Hanson, J., Grajewski, T. and Xu, J. (1993) 'Natural Movement', *Environment and Planning B* 20: 29–66.

Hindley, D. (1976) 'Thailand: The Politics of Passivity', in C. Neher (ed.) *Modern Thai Politics*, Cambridge, MA: Schenkman.

Hochman, E. (1989) *Architects of Fortune*, New York: Weidenfeld & Nicolson.

Hollier, D. (1989) *Against Architecture*, trans. B. Wing, Cambridge, MA: MIT Press.

Holyoak, J. (1996) 'Rational Theories for Contradictory Reality', *The Architects' Journal*, 24 October: 43.

Hughes, R. (1991) *The Shock of the New*, London: Thames & Hudson.

—— (1994) *Culture of Complaint*, London: HarperCollins.

Huxtable, A. (1984) *The Tall Building Artistically Reconsidered: The Search for a Skyscraper Style*, New York: Pantheon.

Isaac, J. (1992) 'Beyond the Three Faces of Power', in T. Wartenberg (ed.) *Rethinking Power*, Albany, NY: SUNY Press.

Jackson, P. (1991) 'Thai-Buddhist Identity', in C. Reynolds (ed.) *National Identity and its Defenders*, Melbourne: Monash Papers on Southeast Asia, No 25.

Jacobs, J. (1965) *The Death and Life of Great American Cities*, Harmondsworth: Penguin.

Jacobs, J., Dovey, K. and Lochert, M. (1998) 'Authorizing Aboriginality in Architecture', in L. Lokko (ed.) *White Papers, Black Marks*, London: Wiley.

Jameson, F. (1984) 'Postmodernism, or The Cultural Logic of Late Capitalism', *New Left Review* 146: 53–92.

—— (1988) 'Cognitive Mapping', in C. Nelson and L. Grossberg (eds) *Marxism and the Interpretation of Culture*, Chicago, IL: University of Illinois.

Jarman, T. (1956) *The Rise and Fall of Nazi Germany*, New York: New York University Press.

Jaskot, P. (2000) *The Architecture of Oppression*, London: Routledge.

Jay, M. (1973) *The Dialectical Imagination*, Boston, MA: Little, Brown.

Jencks, C. (1988) 'Deconstruction: The Pleasures of Absence', *Architectural Design* 58, 3/4: 17–31.

Jenkins, R. (1992) *Pierre Bourdieu*, London: Routledge.

Jhally, S. (1977) *The Codes of Advertising*, London: Frances Pinter.

Judd, D. (1995) 'The Rise of the New Walled Cities', in H. Ligget and D. Perry (eds) *Spatial Practices*, London: Sage.

Jung, C. (1972) *Mandala Symbolism*, Princeton, NJ: Princeton University Press.

Kahn-Ackermann, M. (1980) *China: Behind the Outer Gate*, London: Marco Polo.

Kant, I. (1974) *Critique of Judgement*, trans. J. Bernard, New York: Hafner.

—— (1979) 'A Theory of Esthetic Experience', in M. Rader (ed.) *A Modern Book of Esthetics*, New York: Holt, Rinehart and Winston.

Karasov, D. and Martin, J. (1993) 'The Mall of America', *Design Quarterly*, spring: 18–27.

Kasian Tejapira (1996) 'Signification of Democracy', *Thammasat Review* 1, 1: 5–13.

Kertzer, D. (1988) *Ritual, Politics and Power*, New Haven, CT: Yale University Press.

King, A. D. (1976) *Colonial Urban Development*, London: Routledge.

—— (2004) *Spaces of Global Cultures*, London: Routledge.

King, R. (1996) *Emancipating Space*, New York: Guilford.

Knox, P. (1982) 'Symbolism, Styles and Settings', *Architecture and Behaviour* 2, 2: 107–122.

Koolhaas, R. (1995) 'Generic City' in OMA, R. Koolhaas and B. Mau, *Small, Medium, Large, Extra-Large*, ed. J. Sigler, New York: Monacelli Press.

—— (1996) 'No Grounds Against a Non-Place', in *Euralille*, Basel: Birkhauser, pp. 51–71.

Korff, R. (1993) 'Bangkok as a Symbol?' in P. Nas (ed.) *Urban Symbolism*, Leiden: Brill, pp. 229–250.

Kostof, S. (1991) *The City Shaped*, London: Thames & Hudson.

Kowinski, W. (1985) *The Malling of America*, New York: Morrow.

Krier, L. (1981) 'Vorwarts, Kameraden, Wir Mussen Zuruck', *Oppositions* 24: 27–37.

—— (1985a) 'An Architecture of Desire', in L. Krier (ed.) *Albert Speer*, Brussels: Aux Archives d'Architecture Moderne.

—— (ed.) (1985b) *Albert Speer*, Brussels: Aux Archives d'Architecture Moderne.

Kusno, A. (2000) *Behind the Postcolonial*, London: Routledge.

Kwanjai Eamjai (1998) 'The People's Path', *Sarakhadee Feature Magazine*, Bangkok, pp. 81–155.

Ladd, B. (1997) *The Ghosts of Berlin*, Chicago, IL: University of Chicago Press.

Lane, B. (1968) *Architecture and Politics in Germany, 1918–1945*, Cambridge, MA: Harvard University Press.

Langman, L. (1992) 'Neon Cages', in R. Shields (ed.) *Lifestyle Shopping*, London: Routledge.

Lao Tzu (1963) *Tao Te Ching*, Harmondsworth: Penguin.

Lawrence, R. (1991) 'The Meaning and Use of Home', *Journal of Architectural and Planning Research* 8, 2: 91–95.

Lefebvre, H. (1971) *Everyday Life in the Modern World*, trans. S. Rabinovitch, Harmondsworth: Penguin.

—— (1991) *The Production of Space*, trans. D. Nicholson-Smith, Oxford: Blackwell.

—— (1996) 'Writings on Cities', trans. and ed. E. Kofman and E. Lebas, Oxford: Blackwell.

Leisch H (2002) 'Gated communities in Indonesia', *Cities* 19: 341–350.

Li, Z. (1994) *The Private Life of Chairman Mao*, New York: Random House.

Lipman, A. and Harries, P. (1984) 'Working Hard at Looking Good', *Spazio e Societa*, March: 104–110.

Lipman, A. and Parkes, P. (1986) 'The Engineering of Meaning', *Design Studies* 7, 1: 31–39.

Lipman, A. and Surma, P. (1986) 'Aldo Rossi, architect, scientist – a storm of silence . . . an architecture of alienation', *Design Studies* 7, 2: 58–66.

Lobell, J. (1979) *Between Silence and Light*, Boulder, CO: Shambhala.

Lukes, S. (1974) *Power: A Radical View*, London: Macmillan.

—— (ed.) (1986) *Power*, Oxford: Blackwell.

Lynch, K. (1969) *The Image of the City*, Cambridge, Mass: MIT Press.

—— (1981) *A Theory of Good City Form*, Cambridge, Mass: MIT Press.

Lyotard, J-F. (1984) *The Postmodern Condition*, trans. G. Bennington and B. Massumi, Manchester: Manchester University Press.

McKenzie, E. (1994) *Privatopia*, New Haven, CT: Yale University Press.

—— (2005) 'Constructing The Pomerium in Las Vegas', *Housing Studies* 20, 2: 187–203.

Malpas, J. (1999) *Place and Experience*, Cambridge: Cambridge University Press.

Markus, T. (1987) 'Buildings as Classifying Devices', *Environment and Planning D* 14: 467–484.

—— (1988) 'Down to Earth', *Building Design*, 15 July: 16–17.

—— (1993) *Buildings and Power*, London: Routledge.

Markus, T. and Cameron, D. (2002) *The Words Between the Spaces*, London: Routledge.

Martins, M. (1982) 'The Theory of Social Space in the Work of Henri Lefebvre', in R. Forrest, J. Henderson and P. Williams (eds) *Urban Political Economy and Social Theory*, Aldershot: Gower.

Maser, W. (ed.) (1973) *Hitler's Letters and Notes*, London: Heinemann.

Massey, D. (1992) 'A Place Called Home?' *New Formations* 17, 3–15.

—— (1993) 'Power-geometry and a Progressive Sense of Place', in J. Bird, B. Curtis, T. Putnam and L. Tickner (eds) *Mapping the Futures*, London: Routledge, pp. 59–69.

—— (1995) *Space, Place and Gender*, London: Polity.

—— (2005) *For Space*, London: Sage.

Massumi, B. (1992) *A User's Guide to Capitalism and Schizophrenia*, Cambridge, MA: MIT Press.

Mayo, J. (1985) 'Political Avoidance in Architecture', *Journal of Architectural Education* 38, 2: 18–25.

Merleau-Ponty, M. (1962) *Phenomenology of Perception*, trans. C. Smith, London: Routledge.

Meyer, J. (1991) *The Dragons of Tiananmen*, Columbia, SC: South Carolina University Press.

Miessen, M. and Basar, S. (eds) (2006) *Did Someone Say Participate?* Cambridge, MA: MIT Press.

Miles, M. (2004) *Urban Avant-Gardes*, London: Routledge.

Miller, J. (1993) *The Passion of Michel Foucault*, London: HarperCollins.

Milne, D. (1981) 'Architecture, Politics and the Public Realm', *Canadian Journal of Political and Social Theory* 5, 1–2: 131–146.

Mitchell, W. (2000) *E-topia*, Cambridge, MA: MIT Press.

Moholy-Nagy, S. (1969) *Moholy-Nagy: Experiment in Totality*, Cambridge, MA: MIT Press.

Morell, D. and. Chai-anan, S. (1981) *Political Conflict in Thailand*, Cambridge, MA: Oelgeschlager, Gunn & Hain.

Moulaert, F., Salin, E. and Werquin, T. (2001) 'Euralille: Large-Scale Urban Development and Social Polarization', *European Urban and Regional Studies* 8, 2: 145–160.

Mugerauer, R. (1994) *Interpretations on Behalf of Place*, Albany, NY: SUNY Press.

—— (1995) *Interpreting Environments*, Austin, TX: University of Texas Press.

Nancy, J. (1991) *The Inoperative Community*, Minneapolis, MN: Minnesota University Press.

Newman, P. and Thornley, A. (1997) *Urban Planning in Europe*, London: Routledge.

Ng, S. (1980) *The Social Psychology of Power*, London: Academic Press.

Nietzsche, F. (1968) *The Will to Power*, New York: Vintage.

Norberg-Schulz, C. (1980) *Genius Loci*, New York: Rizzoli.

—— (1985) *The Concept of Dwelling*, New York: Rizzoli.

Ockman, J. (1981) 'The Most Interesting Form of Lie', *Oppositions* 24: 38–47.

O'Connor, R. (1990) 'Place, Power and Discourse in the Thai Image of Bangkok', *Journal of the Siam Society* 78, 2.

O'Donnell, J. (1979) *The Berlin Bunker*, London: Dent.

Olsen, M. (1993) 'Forms and Levels of Power Exertion', in M. Olsen and M. Marger (eds) *Power in Modern Societies*, Boulder, CO: Westview.

Olsen, M. and Marger, M. (eds) (1993) *Power in Modern Societies*, Boulder, CO: Westview.

OMA, Koolhaas, R. and Mau, B. (1995) *Small, Medium, Large, Extra-Large*, ed. J. Sigler, New York: Monacelli Press.

Orwell, G. (1954) *Nineteen Eighty-Four*, Harmondsworth: Penguin.

Panofsky, E. (1967) *Architecture Gothique et Pensée Scholastique*, trans. P. Bourdieu, Paris: Minuit.

Patton, P. (2000) *Deleuze and the Political*, Routledge, London.

Pecora, V. (1991) 'Towers of Babel', in D. Ghirardo (ed.) *Out of Site*, Seattle, WA: Bay Press.

Perez-Gomez, A. (1983) *Architecture and the Crisis of Modern Science*, Cambridge, MA: MIT Press.

Perouse de Montclos, J. (1991) *Versailles*, New York: Abbeville.

Petrescu, D. (2005) 'Losing Control, Keeping Desire', in P. Blundell-Jones, D. Petrescu and J. Till (eds) *Architecture and Participation*, London: Spon, pp. 43–61.

Pile, S. (1997) 'Introduction', in S. Pile and M. Keith (eds) *Geographies of Resistance*, London: Routledge, pp. 1–32.

Piromruen, S. (2005) 'Sanam Luang', Proceeding, Asian Planning Schools Assn., Penang. www.apsa2005.net/FullPapers/AuthorList.htm

Pongsudhirak, T. (1997) 'Thailand's Media', in K. Hewison (ed.) *Political Change in Thailand*, London: Routledge.

Portes, A. (1998) 'Social Capital', *Annual Review of Sociology* 24: 1–24.

Pred, A. (1981) 'Power, Everyday Practice and the Discipline of Human Geography', *Geographiska Annaler* 63: 30–55.

—— (1990) *Making Histories and Constructing Human Geographies*, Boulder, CO: Westview Press.

Prizzia, R. (1985) *Thailand in Transition*, Honolulu: University of Hawaii Press.

Putnam, R. (1995) 'Bowling Alone: America's Declining Social Capital', *Journal of Democracy* 6: 65–78.

Rajchman, J. (1998) *Constructions*, Cambridge, MA: MIT Press.

—— (2000) *The Deleuze Connections*, Cambridge, MA: MIT Press.

Rapoport, A. (1982) *The Meaning of the Built Environment*, Beverly Hills, CA: Sage.

Reich, R. (1992) *The Work of Nations*, New York: Vintage.

Relph, E. (1976) *Place and Placelessness*, London: Pion.

—— (1981) *Rational Landscapes and Humanistic Geography*, New York: Barnes and Noble.

—— (1987) *The Modern Urban Landscape*, Baltimore, MD: Johns Hopkins University Press.

Rendell, J. (2002) *The Pursuit of Pleasure*, London: Athlone.

Reynolds, C. (1991) 'Introduction', in C. Reynolds (ed.) *National Identity and its Defenders*, Melbourne: Monash Papers on Southeast Asia, No. 25.

—— (1992) 'The Plot of Thai History', in G. Wijeyewardene and E. Chapman (eds) *Patterns and Illusions*, Singapore: Institute of Southeast Asian Studies, pp. 313–332.

—— (1998) 'Globalization and Cultural Nationalism in Modern Thailand', in J. Kahn (ed.) *Southeast Asian Identities*, Singapore: Institute of Southeast Asian Studies.

Rheingold, H. (1993) *The Virtual Community*, New York: Harper Collins.

Ricoeur, P. (1965) *History and Truth*, Evanston, IL: Northwestern University Press.

Robbins, D. (1991) *The Work of Pierre Bourdieu*, Milton Keynes: Open University Press.

Robinson, J. (1994) 'Messages from Space', in R. Feldman, G. Hardie and D. Saile (eds) *Power by Design*, Oklahoma: Environmental Design Research Association (EDRA) 24 Proceedings.

Rorty, A. (1992) 'Power and Powers', in T. Wartenberg (ed.) *Rethinking Power*, Albany, NY: SUNY Press.

Rose, G. (1997) 'Performing Inoperative Community', in S. Pile and M. Keith (eds) *Geographies of Resistance*, London: Routledge, pp. 184–202.

—— (2001) *Visual Methodologies*, London: Sage.

Rosenbaum, A. (1986) *Coercion and Autonomy*, New York: Greenwood.

Rossi, A. (1982) *The Architecture of the City*, Cambridge, MA: MIT Press.

Rüedi, K. (1998) 'Curriculum Vitae: The Architect's Cultural Capital', in J. Hill (ed.) *Occupying Architecture*, London: Routledge, pp. 23–38.

Rybczynski, W. (1993) 'The New Downtowns', *Atlantic Monthly*, May: 98–106.

Salisbury, H. (1989) *Tiananmen Diary*, Boston, MA: Little, Brown.

Sandercock, L. (1998) *Cosmopolis*, Chichester: Wiley.

Sarfatti Larson, M. (1993) *Behind the Postmodern Facade*, Berkeley: University of California Press.

Sassen, S. (2006) *Cities in a World Economy*, 3rd edition, Thousand Oaks, CA: Pine Forge Press.

Saul, J. (1997) *The Unconscious Civilization*, Harmondsworth: Penguin.

Saunders, P. and Williams, P. (1988) 'The Constitution of the Home', *Housing Studies* 3, 2: 81–93.

Savage, M. (1995) 'Walter Benjamin's Urban Thought', *Environment and Planning D* 13: 201–216.

Seamon, D. (1979) *A Geography of the Lifeworld*, London: Croom Helm.

Seamon, D. and Mugerauer, R. (eds) (1985) *Dwelling, Place and Environment*, The Hague: Martinus Nijhof.

Seddon, G. (1972) *Sense of Place*, Perth: University of Western Australia Press.

—— (1983) 'The Rottnest Experience', *Journal of the Royal Society of Western Australia* 66: 34–40.

Sennett, R. (1973) *The Uses of Disorder*, Harmondsworth: Penguin.

—— (1974) *The Fall of Public Man*, Cambridge: Cambridge University Press.

—— (1994) *Flesh and Stone*, London: Faber & Faber.

Sereny, G. (1995) *Albert Speer*, London: Macmillan.

Shields, R. (1989) 'Social Spatialization and the Built Environment', *Environment and Planning D* 7: 147–164.

—— (1992) 'Spaces for the Subject of Consumption', in R. Shields (ed.) *Lifestyle Shopping*, London: Routledge.

Shirer, W. (1960) *The Rise and Fall of the Third Reich*, New York: Simon & Schuster.

Slessor, C. (1991) 'Lille Revival', *The Architect's Journal*, 18 September: 72–75.

Soja, E. (1989) *Postmodern Geographies*, New York: Verso.

—— (1991) 'Henri Lefebvre 1901–1991', *Environment and Planning D* 9: 257–259.

—— (2000) 'Thirdspace' in A. Read (ed.) *Architecturally Speaking*, London: Routledge, pp. 13–30.

Solâ-Morales I. (1997) 'Terrain Vague', in C. Davidson (ed.) *Anyplace*, Cambridge, MA: MIT Press, 119–123.

Sorkin, M. (1992) *Variations on a Theme Park*, New York: Hill & Wang.

Speer, A. (1970) *Inside the Third Reich*, New York: Weidenfeld & Nicolson.

Spence, J. (1990) *The Search for Modern China*, New York: Norton.

Starobinski, J. (1966) 'The Idea of Nostalgia', *Diogenes* 54: 81–103.

Steinhardt, S. (1990) *Chinese Imperial City Planning*, Honolulu: University of Hawaii Press.

Stevens, G. (1998) *The Favoured Circle*, Cambridge, MA: MIT Press.

Storper, M. (2004) 'Buzz', *Journal of Economic Geography* 4 (4): 351–370.

Sudjic, D. (1993) *The 100 Mile City*, London: Flamingo.

Sukatipan, S. (1995) 'Thailand: The Evolution of Legitimacy', in M. Alagappa (ed.) *Political Legitimacy in Southeast Asia*, Stanford, CA: Stanford University Press.

Swartz, D. (1997) *Culture and Power: The Sociology of Pierre Bourdieu*, Chicago, IL: University of Chicago Press.

Tafuri, M. (1979) 'The Disenchanted Mountain', in G. Ciucci, F. Dal Co, M. Manieri-Elia and M. Tafuri (eds) *The American City*, Cambridge, MA: MIT Press.

Tambiah, S. (1973) 'Classification of Animals in Thailand', in M. Douglas (ed.) *Rules and Meanings*, Harmondsworth: Penguin, pp. 127–166.

—— (1976) *World Conqueror and World Renouncer*, Cambridge: Cambridge University Press.

Tawa, M. (1996) 'Uluru-Kata Tjuta Cultural Centre', *Architecture Australia* 85, 6: 60–61.

Taylor, R. (1974) *The Word in Stone*, Berkeley, CA: University of California Press.

Terzani, T. (1986) *Behind the Forbidden Door*, London: Unwin.

Thies, J. (1983) 'Nazi Architecture', in D. Welch (ed.) *Nazi Propaganda*, London: Croom Helm.

Thongchai Winichakul (1994) *Siam Mapped*, Honolulu: Hawaii University Press.

—— (1999) 'Thai Democracy in Public Memory', Paper presented at 7th International Conference on Thai Studies, Amsterdam.

Thrift, N. (1997) 'The Still Point', in S. Pile and M. Keith (eds) *Geographies of Resistance*, London: Routledge, pp. 124–151.

—— (1999) 'Steps to an Ecology of Place', in D. Massey, J. Allen and P. Sarre, *Human Geography Today*, Cambridge: Polity, pp. 295–322.

Till, J. (1998) 'Architecture of the Impure Community', in J. Hill (ed.) *Occupying Architecture*, London: Routledge, pp. 61–76.

—— (2005) 'The Negotiation of Hope', in P. Blundell-Jones, D. Petrescu and J. Till (eds) *Architecture and Participation*, London: Spon, pp. 23–41.

Tschumi, B. (1987) *Cinegram Folie*, New York: Princeton Architectural Press.

—— (1988) 'Parc de la Villette, Paris', *Architectural Design* 58, 3/4: 33–39.

Tuan, Y. (1977) *Space and Place*, Minneapolis, MA: Minnesota University Press.

Turton, A. (1978) 'Architectural and Political Space in Thailand', in G. Milner (ed.) *Natural Symbols in South East Asia*, London: University of London, School of Oriental and African Studies.

Uluru-Kata Tjuta Cultural Centre (1997) *Architecture and Urbanism* May, 320: 87–101.

Underwood, D. (1996) 'Snake Charmer', *Architectural Review* 200, 1197: 46–51.

Vale, L. (1992) *Architecture, Power and National Identity*, New Haven, CT: Yale University Press.

Vasana Chinvarakorn (1999) 'A Monument to Change', *Bangkok Post*, 24 June.

Virilio, P. (1986) 'The Overexposed City', *Zone*, 1/2: 15–31.

Wark, M. (1993) 'Vectors of Memory . . . Seeds of Fire', in E. Carter, J. Donald and J. Squires (eds) *Space and Place*, London: Lawrence & Wishart.

—— (1994) *Virtual Geography*, Bloomington, IN: Indiana University Press.

Wartenberg, T. (ed.) (1992) *Rethinking Power*, Albany, NY: SUNY Press.

Watson, E. (1998) *Rottnest: Its Tragedy and its Glory*, Perth: Rottnest Island Authority.

Webster, C. (2002) 'Property Rights and the Public Realm', *Environment and Planning B: Planning and Design* 29, 3: 397–412.

Weinstein, M. (1972) 'Coercion, Space and the Modes of Human Domination', in J. Pennock and J. Chapman (eds) *Coercion*, New York: Aldine.

Weirick, J. (1989) 'Don't You Believe it', *Transition*, summer/autumn: 7–66.

Weng, W. (1982) *The Palace Museum*, New York: Abrams.

Werckmeister, O. (1991) *Citadel Culture*, Chicago, IL: University of Chicago Press.

Wernick, A. (1983) 'Advertising and Ideology', *Theory Culture and Society* 2, 1: 16–33.

Wigley, M. and Johnson, P. (1988) *Deconstructivist Architecture*, New York: Museum of Modern Art.

Williams, R. (1980) *Problems in Materialism and Culture*, London: Verso.

Williamson, J. (1978) *Decoding Advertisements*, London: Marion Boyars.

Wilson, D. (1962) *Politics in Thailand*, Ithaca, NY: Cornell University Press.

Wilson, E. (1991) *The Sphinx in the City*, London: Virago.

Wittgenstein, L. (1967) *Philosophical Investigations*, Oxford: Blackwell.

Wiwat Panthawatthiyenan *et al.* (eds) (1998) *Wandee Feature Magazine*, Bangkok (in Thai).

Wong, K. (2006) *Vision of a Nation*, Bangkok: White Lotus.

Wrong, D. (1979) *Power*, New York: Harper & Row.

Wu, H. (1991) 'Tienanmen Square', *Representations* 35: 84–118.

—— (2005) *Remaking Beijing: Tiananmen Square and the Creation of a Political Space*, London: Reaktion.

Yu, Z. (1984) *Palaces of the Forbidden City*, New York: Viking.

Zhou, S. (1984) *Beijing Old and New*, Beijing: New World Press.

Zhu, J. (1994) 'A Celestial Battlefield', *AA [Architectural Association] Files* 28: 48–60.

—— (2005) *Chinese Spatial Strategies: Imperial Beijing 1420–1911*, London: Routledge.

Zukin, S. (1991) *Landscapes of Power*, Berkeley: University of California Press.

—— (1995) *The Cultures of Cities*, Oxford: Blackwell.

Index